Why Aren't We There Yet?

College Student Educators International (ACPA) Books and Media Contact Information

Why Aren't We There Yet?

Taking Personal Responsibility for Creating an Inclusive Campus

Edited by

JAN ARMINIO, VASTI TORRES,
and RAECHELE L. POPE

STERLING, VIRGINIA

Published by Stylus Publishing, LLC
22883 Quicksilver Drive
Sterling, Virginia 20166-2102

Library of Congress Cataloging-in-Publication Data
Why aren't we there yet? : taking personal responsibility for
creating an inclusive campus / edited by Jan Arminio, Vasti
Torres, and Raechele L. Pope.—1st ed.
   p.   cm.
Includes bibliographical references and index.
ISBN 978-1-57922-465-3 (cloth : alk. paper)
ISBN 978-1-57922-466-0 (pbk. : alk. paper)
ISBN 978-1-57922-748-7 (library networkable e-edition)
ISBN 978-1-57922-749-4 (consumer e-edition)
1. Discrimination in higher education—United States.
2. Educational equalization—United States.
3. Multicultural education—United States.   4. College
environment—United States.   I. Arminio, Jan L.
II. Torres, Vasti, 1960–   III. Pope, Raechele L., 1958–
LC212.42.W47   2012
370.1170973—dc23   2011030193

13-digit ISBN: 978-1-57922-465-3 (cloth)
13-digit ISBN: 978-1-57922-466-0 (paper)
13-digit ISBN: 978-1-57922-748-7 (library networkable
e-edition)
13-digit ISBN: 978-1-57922-749-4 (consumer e-edition)

Printed in the United States of America

All first editions printed on acid-free paper
that meets the American National Standards Institute
Z39-48 Standard.

Bulk Purchases

Quantity discounts are available for use in workshops
and for staff development.
Call 1-800-232-0223

First Edition, 2012

10 9 8 7 6 5 4 3 2 1

The editors and authors dedicate this book to all those who enter into difficult dialogues with the genuine intent of increased understanding.

Contents

Acknowledgments

THE EDITORS AND AUTHORS would like to thank Denise Collins, Jon Dooley, Stephanie Bondi, Rebecca Eby, Timothy Ecklund, Jennifer Forbes, Cynthia Hernandez, Marcus Langford, Jacob Sneva, and Nurredina Workman for assistance in the preparation of the manuscript.

Introduction

Are We There Yet?

Vasti Torres, Jan Arminio, and Raechele L. Pope

A RE WE THERE YET? That question probably evokes memories of traveling by car to some distant location. It signals the anxiety and the desire for the journey to end, to have reached the destination. Those committed to creating welcoming and engaging campus environments for all students recognize that we are not there yet, and that there is much more work to be done. Some ask, "Why aren't we there yet? We have been addressing these issues for decades now; when will we be done?" One of the possible answers is that these issues were framed in an overly simple manner that focused on assimilation so all people could be seen as similar, which has not been effective. Dealing with difference has always been more complex and more difficult than one could imagine. Too often the creation of welcoming campus environments has been oversimplified. In this book the conversation about inclusion is broadened to explore that complexity and difficulty.

MAPPING OUT THE COMPLEXITY
OF DIVERSITY

Historically, administrators of diversifying campuses focused on increasing access to those previously denied admittance. Some would argue that our campuses have evolved from being exclusionary and intolerant to tolerant environments that attempt to include everyone. Now the assumption is that institutions strive to be welcoming, accepting, affirming, and engaging. Some members of the campus community believe their institutions have achieved that goal. This belief has lulled educators into thinking that no

1

further work is necessary. However, admissions, retention, and graduation data tell another story.

The contributors to this book believe that without recognizing the influences of privilege and inequality, educators cannot offer truly welcoming environments. One of the inherent problems in doing more to create inclusive campuses is that many in the United States think American society has entered a color-blind (postracial) era where equality exists for all. The postracial emphasis on individual effort denies the historical and current inequalities based on income and other social identities (Conley, 1999). Professionals working with college students must recognize the tension that arises between the beliefs of a color-blind era versus the current realities of inequalities. How can educators prepare students for dealing with today's realities in an age of privilege, ever-changing oppressions, and fear of the uncontrollable? In this book the contributors seek to offer new insights to improve student affairs practice, emphasizing action that recognizes this is a complex, multifaceted yet not impossible process.

The contributors believe Americans enjoy holding on to broad, desirable ideals, yet arguably our institutions and our country have not always lived up to their ideals. There are numerous examples of actions not being consistent with the value of equality for all—examples such as Takaki's (2000) poignant book illustrating the desire for a double victory in World War II. This book exposed the contradiction between President Franklin D. Roosevelt's war for four freedoms (freedom of speech and expression, freedom of every person to worship God in his or her own way, freedom from want, and freedom from fear) and the reality of many Americans' lives. Service members of color fought in a segregated Jim Crow army to rid Europe of fascism and returned home without those four freedoms. Takaki pointed out that for many Americans, "The war for freedom had to be fought in their country's own backyard" (p. 24).

A current example of U.S. society's not living up to its ideals was provided by Ladson-Billings (2006) in her analysis of unequal school funding in the same U.S. city. This same incongruence can be found on college campuses and can be illustrated through the decline of government funding for public education and the resource disparities between predominantly White and minority-serving schools. Like these societal examples, inequality in higher education has not always been recognized or acknowledged by those who participate in higher education. Hence, as professionals who work in higher education, it is not enough to simply espouse multicultural and equity values. Instead, we must demonstrate our commitment through our actions.

In addition to more accurately describing the complexity of inclusion, this book focuses on how educators can take action. Previously, multicultural training often focused on the *other* or on where to place blame. That approach has not been effective in making values congruent with actions. The contributors want to illustrate and add to the literature that knowledge about difference is not sufficient to achieve multicultural competence (Pope, Reynolds, & Mueller, 2004) and create inclusive campus environments (Harper & Quaye, 2009; Reynolds & Pope, 1994; Torres, Howard-Hamilton, & Cooper, 2003). We agree with Watt (2007) that welcoming campus environments are created through difficult dialogues. Every educator should be asking, "In what ways have I initiated a dialogue that promoted human dignity, equality, and community that serves to move institutions to become truly inclusive?" Through engaging in fruitful dialogues regarding differing social identities including race, ethnicity, religion, gender, and sexual orientation, readers of this book are led through a process that advocates for justice. This advocacy begins by recognizing that *I* am part of the problem—and responsible for contributing to the solution. This *I* includes everyone, regardless of social identity. We all live in this environment, and it is important that we all take responsibility for improving and reshaping it. We believe that through dialogue necessary action can be framed and taken. This book integrates concepts highlighted throughout the higher education multicultural literature creating elements of a process that not only advocate for change but also create and manage change.

In this introduction we initiate the exploration of the complex elements that must be understood to create inclusive campuses through difficult conversations. Though subsequent chapters will more thoroughly address elements of the required process that lay the foundation for action, at the outset, a guiding principle campus members must acknowledge is that all of us are never finished learning about ourselves and others—we don't know it all.

Self-knowledge is the first necessary element (Chapter 1). Only after educators are honest and knowledgeable about their own cultures, beliefs, values, privileges, and biases can they begin to interact with others authentically in their daily contexts. The second element is knowledge of and experiences with others (Chapter 2). This element is often falsely assumed to be needed only by majority White people. Yet, in today's world we believe everyone has something to work on, and there are a plethora of others whom we need to know. Once educators begin to genuinely interact with others, we can move into the next element: understanding historical and institutional contexts (Chapters 3 and 4). We believe these contexts inevitably perpetuate the status quo. Understanding how educators need to change the status quo allows us to move into action, the final element. Action is not merely incorporating newly found awareness and knowledge into practice; it also encourages transformation of our institutions and society. During action, difficult conversations are commonplace, and the need for change is acknowledged (Chapter 5). A truly welcoming and inclusive environment is one where difficult conversations are the norm, and individuals are empowered to notice, question, and stop inequality (Chapter 6).

We framed this book around the five elements of the process of engaging in difficult conversations that not only advocate for change but also create change. It is our goal that by threading these elements together educators, student affairs professionals, and faculty will be better able to deal with the complexities of difference and take action to create campus environments where students can learn, grow, and thrive.

CONTENTS OF THIS BOOK

This book focuses on guiding individuals and groups through learning how to have difficult conversations that lead us to act to create more just campuses. We also provide illustrations of multiple ways to respond to difficult situations. We focused this book on the elements identified by the 2007–2009 Student Affairs Educators International (ACPA) Presidential Task Force, "Engaging the Complexities of Difference: What Does Inclusion Really Look Like," charged with identifying the next steps in achieving inclusion. During task force meetings members agreed on the elements of the process, which are described in the preceding section. The following chapters, written by student affairs professionals, provide an in-depth treatment of each element. To understand the process, we recommend reading the chapters as stand-alone but sequentially successive chapters.

"Awareness of Self," the first chapter, is the first of the process elements to enact change. Anna M. Ortiz and Lori D. Patton offer insight on how interpretations of the self influence this work and how this work is influenced by others' interpretation of us. There is a synergistic relationship between self-awareness and understanding one's own culture and its influence, and how they influence our interactions with the outside world. This means that how we are identified influences how we identify ourselves and others. To be knowledgeable about differences, we must be knowledgeable about the self. The perspective of ourselves influences our attitudes, reactions, and relationships. For example, a sense of confidence in one's ability to make a difference is fundamental to one's willingness to engage in action for the betterment of inclusion.

With a sense of the self, the next process element that Jan Arminio and Vasti Torres focus on in Chapter 2 is the self-in-relation (Ivey, 1995) with the other. By the other we refer to those racially different from us, but simultaneously we include considerations of multiple social identities. While this second chapter focuses on the other, the inclusion of all groups as others is intentional. Therefore, when we write of the other, we refer to African Americans; Latinos; Asian Americans; White people; the poor and working class; lesbian, gay, bisexual, and transgender people; Muslims; Jews; and Christians, to name only a few. Educators must acknowledge the powerful learning potential of self in transactional relationships.

The self cannot be extracted from its historical context. Indeed, "all our knowledge about human nature is historically conditioned" (Levin, 1988, p. 59). The next process element guiding individuals and groups through difficult conversations is to explore how who we *were* influences who we *are*. In Chapter 3, John A. Mueller and Ellen M. Broido discuss the importance of historical context in conversations and present a synopsis of the historical context of higher education in the United States. This chapter provides the setting for exploring how it is that we can honor inclusion and welcome others today in the context of a past where we did not. With the historical context set, Raechele L. Pope and Lucy A. LePeau in Chapter 4 examine the influence of current institutional contexts on attitudes, beliefs, and behaviors. How does the national context influence our institutional cultures? How do our institutional cultures and missions influence how dialogues can occur? Within institutional contexts, how can interventions that positively influence these dialogues occur?

This process begins to frame the action that must take place in Chapter 5. Sherry K. Watt offers tips and cautions about engaging others in dialogue and being intentional advocates. This work conjures uncomfortable and even unsettling emotions, such as guilt, acquiescence, resentment, and fear. It can also elicit liberation and fulfillment. This chapter's author seeks to instill the hope, courage, and confidence that educators can do better by supporting and challenging others as they place themselves in challenging and growth-producing opportunities. Learning is never complete. To facilitate dialogues that encourage action requires making meaning of the knowing/being gaps within ourselves, our students, and our institutions. Komives (2000) asked educators in higher education to address the gap between how we know to behave and how we actually do behave. This chapter offers findings of a more inclusive theory that seeks to narrow this gap.

To illustrate there is no one right way to initiate change, Chapter 6 contains two case studies with responses from a variety of individuals who represent many different social identities and roles in higher education. By including multiple responses, authors Matthew J. Weigand and Lucy A. LePeau illustrate there is no one magical response or no silver bullet; rather, there are essentials that help us think through issues in deciding the best ways to create change in one's context. The cases and corresponding responses embrace the notion that life is a lab—we must all learn to see multiple options in determining how best to respond.

The final chapter summarizes the key points of the preceding chapters and offers suggestions and resources for beginning or continuing the process of examining the internal and external growth necessary to create lasting change. Plenty of other books detail the myriad problems and barriers to inclusion; while we the editors certainly acknowledge the causes and effects of the intolerance that still exists on college campuses, that is not our purpose. Instead, we hope to provide a process that encourages transformation. While complex in many ways, we believe it can be accomplished with this blueprint for change. Returning to the opening paragraph, some individuals are frustrated by the impatience of the question, Are we there yet? However, we hope to conclude through discussion and case examples that the problem is not impatience but rather the question itself. Asking if we are there yet assumes there is a recognizable end point we can all achieve. If we are to truly embrace the complexity of inclusion, it is essential we understand the open-ended nature of multicultural change and the lifelong journey it requires.

REFERENCES

Conley, D. (1999). *Being Black, living in red: Race, wealth, and social policy in America.* Berkeley: University of California Press.

Harper, S. R., & Quaye, S. J. (Eds.). (2009). *Student engagement in higher education.* New York, NY: Routledge.

Ivey, A. E. (1995). Psychotherapy as liberation: Toward specific skills and strategies in multicultural counseling and therapy. In J. G. Ponterotto, J. M. Casas, L. A. Suzuki, & C. M. Alexander (Eds.), *Handbook of multicultural counseling* (pp. 53–72). Thousand Oaks, CA: Sage.

Komives, S. (2000, November). Inhabit the gap. *About Campus, 5*(5), 31.

Ladson-Billings, G. (2006). From the achievement gap to the educational debt: Understanding achievement in U.S. schools. *Educational Researcher, 35*(7), 3–12.

Levin, M. D. (1988). The opening of vision: Seeing through the veil of tears. In K. Hoeller (Ed.), *Heidegger & psychology* (pp. 113–141). Seattle, WA: Review of Psychology and Psychiatry.

Pope, R. L., Reynolds, A. L., & Mueller, J. A. (2004). *Multicultural competence in student affairs.* San Francisco, CA: Jossey-Bass.

Reynolds, A. L., & Pope, R. L. (1994). Perspective on creating multicultural campuses: An introduction. *Journal of American College Health, 42,* 229–233.

Takaki, R. (2000). *Double victory: A multicultural history of America in World War II.* New York, NY: Basic Books.

Torres, V., Howard-Hamilton, M., & Cooper, D. L. (2003). Identity development of diverse populations: Implications for teaching and practice. *ASHE-ERIC Higher Education Report, 29*(6).

Watt, S. K. (2007). Difficult dialogues, privilege and social justice: Uses of the privileged identity exploration (PIE) model in student affairs practice. *College Student Affairs Journal, 26,* 114–126.

1

Awareness of Self

Anna M. Ortiz and Lori D. Patton

Metro University has become increasingly ethnically diverse over the past decade or so. The career development staff have prided themselves on the high level of service provided to students and alumni. However, they have noticed their usage numbers have decreased in recent years, and they conducted a study the previous semester to gain a better sense of who is using the career development center and its services. The center director included a number of demographic questions on a short survey all users completed while they were either waiting for their appointments or using the resource library. The findings of the usage study suggested that students of color and those from other underrepresented groups used the center services in numbers far below their proportion in the general student population. In subsequent staff meetings, the director helped staff explore possible explanations for this finding. Because staff members take such pride in their work with students, there was resistance to the director's request that everyone take a critical look at his or her own work with students, the philosophy of the center, and general services provided. To help make this process of exploration more concrete, the director formed small work teams assigned with a variety of tasks. One team conducted a literature review to learn about current research on the career development of students of color; lesbian, gay, bisexual, and transgender students; and international students. A second team conducted a benchmark study of like institutions to examine best practices elsewhere. A third group reached out to student organizations to obtain direct feedback from the groups that used the center less frequently than expected. After an additional semester of assessment, the director and her

staff had learned about best practices, current research, and student needs.
They considered adding a few additional programs to their workshop sched-
ule, but other than that, the staff believed their practices were consistent
with what they learned in their research. The following semester, changes
in the workshop schedule were implemented, and a second usage survey was
conducted that unfortunately showed no increase in the use of the center by
the groups previously identified as less likely to use the center. The director,
discouraged, realized that the model employed the year before relied on staff
making changes based on their assumptions. This may not have been the
best approach.

THE DIRECTOR IN OUR fictional career development center was trying to practice inclusion as well as using strategies that many view
as exemplary. She looked to the published research, consulted her
colleagues, and talked directly to the students she wanted to serve. After a
year of discovery, she was disappointed that small changes made only a little
difference in addressing the initial lack of involvement among students of
color and from other underrepresented populations. In this case, the director
ends with a hunch that the staff needed a different approach. Our fictional
director is wise. When student affairs staff look to practice inclusion, it is
not only a rational process where objective data direct program development
and change. These objective data points do not always uncover the values,
biases, and assumptions staff use when working with students, which may
leave educators believing they have little responsibility in creating more welcoming and effective environments. To practice inclusion, individual professionals need to conduct a profound exploration of their personal values and
beliefs as well as understand how they enter into their work with students
and institutions. This level of self-awareness, of self-discovery, is paramount
to enacting real change on college campuses. Without self-exploration, structural diversity (the proportion of students and faculty from non-White
ethnic or racial groups) may only represent the revolving door of underrepresented students attending and leaving higher education institutions and not
necessarily contribute to the creation of inclusive campuses.

The increasing structural diversity of our campuses forces educators to
examine practices in inclusivity. In Tanaka's (2003) study of an intercultural
campus he argued that diverse campuses

> will force white students to examine for the first time how they will form
> connections with people from different racial or ethnic backgrounds, and this

in turn forces them to confront who they are (what makes for *their* own social and cultural identities). (p. 115)

In this chapter we argue that student affairs professionals need to lead, not through helping students examine their connection to diverse others and personal identities, but through beginning the examination with themselves. Thus, we discuss the role of self-awareness; the tensions involved with examining our beliefs, attitudes, values, and behavior; and ultimately how engagement with diverse others brings about a synergy that leads to overcoming barriers to personal change that brings about inclusion. This synergy and the sense of competence it creates have the potential to generate the perseverance and enthusiasm necessary to foster genuine inclusive communities in higher education.

The role of self in multicultural competence and education is well established. Pope and Reynolds (1997) described 11 characteristics of multicultural awareness; among them, the following five are relevant for this discussion:

- ♦ a willingness to take risks *and* see risk taking as necessary for self-awareness;
- ♦ a belief that understanding one's own cultural heritage and worldview is the starting place for understanding others;
- ♦ a willingness to self-examine values and assumptions, and to make changes according to that examination;
- ♦ a belief that change is necessary and positive; and
- ♦ an awareness of how one's attitudes and behaviors affect others.

These characteristics are fundamental for leaders who seek to build more inclusive campuses and promote inclusivity in their practices and those of their staff and units. Embedded within these characteristics is the absolute necessity of developing self-awareness—balancing confidence so we can carry out difficult work that may challenge our core sense of self with the humility of knowing there is always more to learn and there are more ways to improve. Sleeter and Grant (2008) referred to this kind of self-education in their human relations approach to multicultural education. With this approach, the focus is on how attitudes such as prejudice develop and the role of self-awareness in interrupting that process. How individuals perceive themselves and their respective space and place in the world leads to a self-concept that shows readiness to engage in inclusion and multicultural education. In Allport's (1979) foundational work on prejudice, the concept of readiness is pivotal to the actual recognition that the lack of inclusion and multiculturalism is a societal problem. His explanation of the strength of durable categories that enable the efficiency of prejudice and its correlate of least effort shows that when we take the easier road we do not interrogate cognitive structures and beliefs that make exclusion a reality in higher education. This may play out in student affairs when professionals enter into prejudice reduction or multicultural education with a belief that their good intentions take them far in their own journey to undo the durable categories that have developed through living in a racist society. Stopping short of transformation allows the principle of least effort to invade inclusion work. The alternative road takes considerable cognitive effort and is filled with emotional and affective sand traps that sometimes lead to sustaining the status quo instead of creating change in ourselves and in our institutions. Therefore, an examination of self in relation to social identities, interpersonal communication, and multicultural competence is absolutely a prerequisite to building inclusive campuses.

INTERPRETATIONS OF SELF/SELF-AWARENESS

A number of characteristics factor into having an awareness of self and understanding how individuals interpret themselves individually and in relation to others. We argue that self-awareness requires confidence in oneself as a person and a cultural being. As simple as this may appear, self-awareness is quite a complex process and requires individuals to engage in metathinking regarding how they see themselves as well as how they are perceived by others. In most models or theories of multicultural competence, self-awareness is as important as knowledge and skills (Pope, Reynolds, & Mueller, 2004; Sleeter & Grant, 2008). The ability to engage in difficult dialogues and situate oneself in a way that values inclusion requires the ability to respond to such central questions as, Who am I? What are my identities? How do my identities intersect? and How do I see myself in relation to others? These critical questions are key toward facilitating reflection on, What does it mean to be me? Embedded in the responses to these questions are qualities that are necessary to position ourselves to be leaders in building inclusive campus communities.

An important quality of self-awareness is acceptance of the notion that coming to understand oneself intrapersonally and in relation to others is an ongoing process; it cannot happen overnight and does not produce a finite set of answers that remain unchanged over time. Self-awareness is a cumulative process, one that ensures and expects that learning about oneself is a daily task. It is important to note that one of the major challenges with regard to self-awareness, particularly in relation to identity, is the misconception that identities are fixed, concrete, and stable rather than fluid, contextual, and ever changing (Jones & McEwen, 2000). Anzaldúa (as cited in Keating, 2000) accurately noted:

> An identity is sort of like a river. It's one and it's flowing and it's a process. By giving different names to different parts of a single mountain range or different parts of a river, we're doing that entity a disservice. We're fragmenting it. I'm struggling with how to name without cutting it up. (p. 132)

Thus, an established sense of self-awareness is rooted in the notion that the self is continually evolving and grounded in how individuals understand their respective identities in relation to one another. Of particular importance is recognition of intersectionality. A host of scholars (Abes, Jones, & McEwen, 2007; Crenshaw, 1989; Dill & Zambrana, 2009; Hill Collins, 1986; Jones, 2009; Keating, 2000) have written extensively about intersectionality. Key to this research is understanding that an individual's various identities mutually shape one another. For example, in discussing indigenous two-spirit people, Wilson (1996) argued,

> Despite the relationship between sexual and racial identity development presented in European American models, for Indigenous American lesbian, gay, or bisexual people, the effects of racism and homophobia cannot be separated from each other or from the rest of their experiences. (p. 316)

Thus, we the authors believe identities do not exist as single components that are manifested independently. Instead, they are interrelational and coexist in ways that culminate one's overall sense of identity and awareness. In an interview with Hammond (1981), Lorde explained,

> There's always someone asking you to underline one piece of yourself—
> whether it's *Black, woman, mother, dyke, teacher,* etc.—because that's the piece
> that they need to key in to. They want to dismiss everything else. But once
> you do that, then you've lost because then you become acquired or bought
> by that particular essence of yourself, and you've denied yourself all of the
> energy that it takes to keep all those others in jail. (p. 15)

To be sure, the salience of identities will be different for each person based
upon individual constructions and the influence of larger societal constructions. However, it is important to fully comprehend that despite the level of
salience attributed to a particular identity, how one understands salient identity is contextualized by other present identities. For example, as an African
American woman, I (Lori) recognize that while race has strong salience in my
life, how I understand myself, especially how I perform my racial identity, is
affected by my identity as a woman. Moreover, other social identities, such
as being heterosexual, middle class, and educated, play a major role (whether
I recognize it or not) in how my self-awareness is shaped. Williams (1991),
a legal scholar, has a similar perspective:

> While being black has been the powerful social attribution in my life, it is
> only one of a number of governing narratives or presiding fictions by which I
> am constantly reconfiguring myself in the world. Gender is another, along
> with ecology, pacifism, my peculiar brand of colloquial English, and Roxbury,
> Massachusetts. (pp. 256–257)

Along with acknowledging the intersectionality of identities, self-awareness
is fostered through recognizing that how individuals understand themselves
does not occur in isolation. Thus, self-awareness is not simply about the self,
but more accurately speaking, it is about the self in relation to others. Ackelsberg (1996) argued the importance of "seeing individuals and communities
as engaged in a dynamic relationship" (p. 88). She referred to the work of a
host of women of color scholars whose scholarship is grounded in the notion
that it is impossible to understand what it means to be a woman without
accounting for her racial, spiritual, socioeconomic, sexual, and so on selves.
Much of how individuals come to know themselves is facilitated through
their experiences with diverse others. So in many ways, identity and one's
awareness of identity is learned through social interactions that not only
identify who you *are,* but also, who you *are not.*

These perspectives are important to the goal of inclusion because they demonstrate the complexity of individual identities and underscore that simple treatment of an examination of self is insufficient. We have presented examples of intersectionality among identities that are commonly believed to be oppressed identities. However, they serve as models for how others may perform similar exercises. For example, it is critical that a White heterosexual male not only examine the identity of a White person as he prepares to practice inclusion, but also consider how being straight intersects with this goal and how being a man intersects with this goal. Likewise, a gay man doesn't necessarily get a pass on self-examination because he is a member of an oppressed group; he must also contend with what it means to be male in environments where privilege is conferred based on that status. Without careful consideration of multiple social identities and how they affect worldviews, it is difficult to consistently perform inclusion behaviors.

A strong sense of self-awareness is evident in individuals who are capable of integrating thoughts with behaviors. Stated differently, one's actions are reflective of one's thoughts and words. To fully engage in the work of promoting inclusivity is not about making verbal statements or presenting oneself in a manner that is politically correct. It involves asking critical questions of oneself, some of which may not result in answers we wish to readily accept. For example, Leonardo (2004) referred to a "double bind" at work for White people who on one hand believe in racial justice, while on the other hand must make sacrifices for racial justice to be realized. He stated, "Although it is crucial that whites 'buy into' racial justice, . . . they also have the most to give up in terms of material resources. Consequently, convincing them to appropriate racial analysis for their own lives runs into difficulties" (p. 143). While Leonardo deals specifically with the notion of whiteness and White supremacy, issues such as sexism, homophobia, and ableism can also manifest themselves in the midst of reflecting on one's thoughts and words as well as how these aspects stem from one's identity and awareness. Coming to terms with the seemingly uncomfortable aspects of identity is absolutely necessary to gain greater awareness of self and engage in efforts to promote inclusion. Coming to terms with the uncomfortable aspects of self-awareness should spur salient questions that involve serious self-examination and introspection. These questions revolve around values and assumptions instilled during our upbringing. They include historical understandings of issues of difference, experiences with diverse others, where we fit into society's hierarchy, and whether a balance exists between who we *think* we are and who we *really* are. Zetzer (2004) shared her own struggles with acknowledging this balance while coming to terms with racism and privilege as a White person. She reflected on a personal history of growing up in a White world where no one in her immediate surroundings openly acknowledged racism. It was never the topic of discussion but existed in the subtexts of conversations. She soon recognized a clear disconnect:

> The psychological discordance between the text and the subtext was very confusing. How could I be free of prejudice and filled with prejudicial thoughts? How could I be color-blind and react so viscerally to cultural differences? How could my Black friends and White friends be so similar and yet so different? (p. 3)

Gauging this balance between who we are and who we think we are and coming to terms with the possibility of incongruence requires that individuals alter their epistemological approach to their thinking about difference. It involves a willingness to engage in a paradigmatic shift that challenges conventional ways of knowing and being. It requires a move toward a worldview in which individuals see the importance of different perspectives and toward a willingness to explore how they situate themselves in relation to those whom they perceive to possess divergent viewpoints and identities. Moreover, this change in worldview entails establishing an identity that is realized when grounded in relationships with others. Balance between thought and action—between who we think we are and who we actually are—does not come without critical interrogation of the self and where one fits in regimes of oppression and difference. This balance must be negotiated within a process of consciousness raising in which individuals "recognize, broaden, and challenge individual, cultural, and institutional beliefs and behaviors that perpetuate estranged and oppressive relations between groups" (Zuniga, Naagda, & Sevig, 2002, p. 9). Nor does self-awareness exist without establishing a sense of agency to delve into difficult questions about oneself and the belief systems that guide how individuals respond to those whom they view as different from themselves. Engaging in critical interrogation of self and self in relation to others allows space for moving beyond the rhetoric of difference toward asking deeper questions about how difference is constructed, who is constructed as different, and whether one's participation in the discourse of difference is merely circumstantial or rooted in efforts to promote social justice and social change. Thus, the process of addressing difference and challenging the status quo not only is about individual self-awareness but also requires acknowledgment of a large societal system that dictates the social construction of difference (Johnson, 2006). Social change has to be rooted in individual awareness and congruence that prompts individuals to act in ways that disrupt how difference is socially constructed.

If challenging systems that promote the exclusion of minoritized groups in society were easy, perhaps all humans would be in a much different place. However, the reality is that inclusivity for all is a lofty goal, yet one worth fighting for. Herein lies the point where agency becomes crucial to self-awareness. Possessing a sense of agency translates into having a sense of ownership over one's thoughts and behaviors and initiating a constant process of balancing these entities in a way that acknowledges the self as consciously, intricately, and actively involved in bringing about social justice.

THE INFLUENCE OF OTHERS ON THE INTERPRETATIONS OF SELF

Psychosocial theories of identity development have long held the tenet that the self is socially constructed and developed in concert with context, which can be translated into interactions in our environments: home, school, work, and so forth. Erikson's (1968) classic example of peers acting as a mirror to the adolescent—casting others' perceptions back to the adolescent, thereby allowing others to define the adolescent self—demonstrates the strength of others in developing identity and self. That influence, which may be strongest in adolescence, is present throughout life if we accept the argument that identity and self are ever evolving. When Ting-Toomey (2005) applied this to cultural identity negotiation, we saw the utility of transferring Erikson's concept to the discussion of self and interactions with others in preparing to carry out the work of inclusion. Ting-Toomey noted that "identity is viewed as reflective self-images constructed, experienced, and communicated by the individuals within a culture and a particular interaction situation," and, further, that identity negotiation is a process where "individuals in an intercultural situation attempt to assert, define, modify, challenge, and/or support their own and others' desired self-images" (p. 217). Thus, in a multicultural context, part of the dynamic that occurs between people engaging in discussion regarding difference is one where individuals manage how they view themselves as competent actors in the exchange with how the other person or people view them. How self and competence is projected and how they are interpreted and responded to constructs a feedback loop that puts the self at risk through the gateway made available for evaluation by others. Therefore, family, friends, coworkers, and even those we do not necessarily know, such as leaders, authors, and activists, are influential in everyone's development of a disposition for inclusion that relies on accurate interpretations of self.

Families of origin provide the primary context that influences how we come to understand ourselves as members of societal communities, and, depending on the family's inclination toward multicultural communities, they launch our disposition toward inclusion. Our families distribute rules of our cultures, such as gender role socialization and communicative and relational patterns among children, parents, extended family members, and authority figures. Families also provide the location of our first understandings of and responses to difference. Often, prejudicial attitudes stem directly from messages heard when growing up. Children have little control over the information they take in from adults, especially those from whom they want to earn and maintain love and attention. This is precisely why, as adults, challenging the lessons learned in childhood can be a trying and time-consuming process. Understanding this influence on self is an important step in unlearning racism, understanding our specific responses to those different from ourselves, and ultimately clearing the ground for the confidence and integrity necessary to *believe* that through changing the way we think about, view, and interact with diverse others we do not put ourselves at risk for loss. By advocating for equity, educators risk loss of respect and esteem from others when we make missteps along the way (Ortiz & Rhoads, 2000; Torres, 2009).

Peers also exert influence on the self. It could be said that everyone has peers. Some are considered coethnics, meaning they share a common ethnic background. This concept can be extended to a shared cultural background if that is more appropriate for a specific context. Coethnics' perceptions of an individual yield influence by setting the parameters for interaction with other ethnic groups, indicating whether and when such interaction is appropriate. Coethnics monitor criteria for membership within a group that have an effect on interpretations of the self. Specifically, if coethnic judgment is particularly acute or in conflict with how an individual views the self, confidence and integrity necessary for an inclusive disposition may erode (Ortiz & Santos, 2009). Peers from other ethnic groups also influence the sense of self in a variety of ways. If prejudicial attitudes are communicated, then individuals may be made to feel inferior or rejected from the peer group. Because of the cumulative effects of racial microaggressions, subtle expressions of prejudice have been shown to do harm to students' efficacy and sense of self as valued members of the community (Steele, 1997; Yosso, Smith, Ceja, & Solorzano, 2009). Peers also have the capacity for exerting a positive influence on one's disposition for inclusion. Therefore, just as in other areas of life, peer influence sets parameters for acceptable behavior for continued membership and distributes group-held values and beliefs with that membership.

The concept of in- and out-group members discussed by Allport (1979) in *The Nature of Prejudice* gives credence to the effect that family and friends have on the development of prejudice. In groups, rules of behavior, criteria for membership, and benefits of membership that engender loyalty are structured and relayed to members either informally or formally. The benefits of membership are extensive. A sampling of these includes a sense of belonging, protection by group members, and love and affection. Being a member of one's in-group is so critical that the values and beliefs of the group become guiding principles for the individual. This enables the group to be protected against possible threats. Such threats might include more macro-oriented ones including group resources or group prestige, or on the microlevel threats that are directed at family members and friends. The power of in-group membership is also evident in Bogardus's (1928) concept of social distance, where in-group members are more likely to occupy social roles closest to us, such as partners. In the past this theory has been used as an explanation for residential segregation and in-group marriage. Social distance is perpetuated through the socialization that occurs within families, communities, and institutions such as religious organizations and schools. Agents of these institutions make clear, in overt and covert ways, acceptable relationships, friendships, residences, and memberships. In essence this tendency to associate with people most like us is the opposite of inclusion and is the force to be contended with in building inclusive communities.

The interpersonal effects of how we interpret the self in relationship to diverse others coincides with cognitive processes by which racial attitudes and prejudice are developed. Through the process of categorization, assimilation calls for sorting information into categories established by social forces and in-group influences (Allport, 1979). Only when information cannot be sorted into existing categories does the individual make accommodations by creating new categories and understanding. Cognitive development theorists such as Piaget (1973) and Perry (1970) described the process of assimilation and accommodation as being routine ways individuals make sense of information. When considering racial attitudes and prejudice, this process is important because existing categories are more likely influenced by in-group values and beliefs developed to protect and reproduce the group. By passing values and beliefs on to new members, stereotypes are developed and sustained. One way to judge the merit of this claim is to observe how quickly newly immigrated Americans begin to subscribe to society's stereotypes. Stereotypes have an important element of efficiency in that they allow individuals to believe information, express feelings, and generate conclusions without careful consideration. Problems arise when these information-processing strategies are applied to others and their characteristics, such as gender, ethnicity, race, socioeconomic class, occupation, and so on. Thus, the values, beliefs, and attitudes learned from family and close friends have the potential to significantly shape how students, faculty, and staff perceive and think about diverse others in their campus communities.

TENSIONS BETWEEN SELF AND OTHERS

A host of tensions may arise when self-awareness and understanding conflicts with external interpretations of ourselves. Zetzer (2004) contended, "There are no breaks from the work of living in a multicultural community. Oppression is real and seeking social justice for oneself and others is a difficult job" (p. 4). Practicing inclusion in theory may be easy, but in practice it is neither easy nor pleasurable because it typically involves sacrifice. Feelings of anxiety, fear, discomfort, and shame are common among those who consider themselves to be open to different viewpoints and perspectives. Tensions arise quickly when individuals realize that how they perceive themselves is vastly different from how others perceive them. For example, tensions consistently emerge for some White individuals who confidently attest to their ability to discuss issues pertaining to race and racism and deny any role in racism. However, when classic lines such as "I don't see color; I see people" and "I am not a racist" emerge and are challenged, White people are instantaneously moved beyond their comfort zone because tension materializes. They feel ashamed and guilty for not having thought deeper about racism, White privilege, power relations, the complexities of whiteness, and the ways they have more often than not perpetuated the racism they vehemently claimed to want to eradicate. The tension grows even more intense as they begin to question whether their out-group peers now perceive them as racist, a label they were never aware of having. hooks (1990) wrote:

> Race is always an issue of Otherness that is not white; it is black, brown, yellow, red, purple even. Yet only a persistent, rigorous, and informed critique of whiteness could really determine what forces of denial, fear, and competition are responsible for the gaps between professed political commitment to eradicating racism and the participation in the construction of a discourse on race that perpetuates racial domination. Many scholars . . . preface their work by stating they are white, as though mere acknowledgement of this fact were sufficient, as though it conveyed all we need to know of standpoint, motivation, and direction. (p. 54)

These tensions are uncomfortable, and they are absolutely necessary. Moreover, Giroux (1997) described these tensions as trauma. He noted:

> While white students may well feel traumatized in putting their racial identities on trial, trauma . . . can become a useful pedagogical tool in helping them locate themselves within and against the discourse and practice of racism. . . . Trauma represents that pedagogical moment when identities become unsettled, provoking both anxiety and the opportunity to rethink the political nature and moral content of one's own racial identity, and the roles it plays in shaping one's relationship to those who are constituted as racially "other." (p. 293)

It is extremely difficult to come to terms with what Swiencicki (2006) referred to as "the turning of a gap in consciousness" (p. 337). It is the notion that our self-awareness conflicts with how others perceive us. However, these tensions allow us to make important choices about whom we wish to become. Making the choice depends upon responding to the question of whether the tension gives rise to an issue we have not yet addressed, or does the tension remind us of why we engage in promoting inclusion and motivate us to continue? What becomes most important is how we move forward. The reality is that we cannot go backward, rerun the tape, and start from the beginning, but we must grapple with who we are (Swiencicki). Do we allow the tensions to stifle or immobilize us? Giroux reminded us that

> all students need to feel that they have a personal stake in their racial identity (however fluid, unstable, and transitory), an identity that will allow them to assert a view of political agency in which they can join with diverse groups around a notion of democratic public life that affirms racial differences. (p. 297)

Educators must as well.

Rather than allow tensions to immobilize us, we can learn from them in a way that helps us to "gain greater clarification of underlying sources of tension and to engage in new behaviors that communicate increased self-awareness, sensitivity to experiences of others, and relational ways of being with each other" (Zuniga et al., 2002, p. 9). Maher and Thompson Tetreault (1997) provide an excellent example of how they used tensions as teachable moments to move forward. In their book, *The Feminist Classroom* (2001), they firmly represented themselves in a way they believed was a reflection of solidarity with women of color in an effort to disrupt patriarchy within the academy. They later realized that the book was a representation of their failure to question, scrutinize, and disrupt their own whiteness. Upon gaining this realization, they revisited their work to interrogate assumptions about whiteness in the classroom and its role in shaping knowledge production in classroom settings (Maher & Thompson Tetreault, 1997).

Coming to terms with the tensions that reside within and are manifested externally also involves recognizing the politics of identity. "That is, how can we acknowledge differences among ourselves—and the fluid nature of our identities—while still making space not only for connections among people but for productive alliances between them?" (Ackelsberg, 1996, p. 90). Responding to this question would require individuals to engage in perspective taking, which allows for critical reflection and critical questioning regarding who we are and how who we are affects those with whom we interact. In addition to perspective taking and turning difficult situations into learning moments, grappling with tensions should involve a willingness to make sacrifices and engage in actions. One action may be admitting lack of knowledge and information while committing to increase one's self-knowledge and knowledge of others. Alleviating tensions could also be fostered through having difficult conversations rather than avoiding them. In these conversations it can be helpful to remember basic, good communication skills such as the use of "I" statements and a readiness to admit to misunderstandings rather than waiting for the others involved to do so. Finally, it may mean acknowledging that when tensions arise, the change has to begin with the self before it can begin with others.

SYNERGY IN WORKING WITH OTHERS

Although tension is often present in many first steps during working with others to enhance multicultural competence and ultimately practice inclusion, it is only through working with others that the most progress is made. Reaching a level of self-awareness where prior lessons are understood and unlearned, and where a new identity as change agent comes to fruition, materializes when feedback from others corrects and ultimately confirms multiculturally competent skills, knowledge, and awareness. When the feedback loop displays that perceptions are correct, that empathy is achieved, and that the work is valued, individuals gain confidence to engage in more challenging conversations, activities, and strategies. Repeated success or even attempts with successful corrections help individuals trust that taking risks is likely to result in positive outcomes. The synergistic relationship that develops through these encounters and lessons has the most potential to sustain the ego strength necessary for leaders to take risks and face vulnerability in creating inclusive campuses.

An example of when the synergy of working together outlasts the effectiveness of more singular approaches comes from Tanaka's (2003) study of an intercultural campus. He found that the most successful strategy in intercultural training for staff members took place in two workshops, one that focused on teaching cultural awareness and issues such as power and privilege

and a second one in which staff members exchanged stories of their families'
histories in the United States. This worked best when staff members were
divided into groups that were diverse in multiple ways: ethnicity, position
level, areas of responsibility, and so on. This synergy (the space and relationships that were created because of the dialogue) was critical in moving staff
members to the process of examining their practice in becoming an intercultural university. This is in contrast to the pedagogy workshops conducted
for faculty that were primarily lecture based, which addressed "faculty only
on an intellectual register and, as a result, did not lead participants to investigate their own feelings, perspectives or assumptions about diversity" (Tanaka,
p. 140). Ramsey (1996) said that through comparative processes, like those
the staff in the opening scenario participated in, people learn about and
recognize cultural difference and in turn learn about themselves—as cultural
beings and as members of intercultural interactions. He also noted that these
kinds of interactions allow for the development of empathy that "involves
doing one's best to imagine another person's situation without projecting
self into it. We try to enter into the others' experience more purely from
their point of view. . . . Thus, do unto others as they would have you do unto
them" (p. 11). The importance of knowing others' histories and context in
creating empathy through relationships is discussed in Chapters 2 and 3 of
this book.

The caveat of not projecting one's self into the situation is an important
one; it requires that the experience of the other stand alone, without interpretation or application to another's circumstance. This calls for a sense of
confidence and integrity in knowing that the self will withstand the shift of
focus onto another.

Ting-Toomey (2005) determined that this mindfulness derived from
empathetic intercultural interaction is a component in identity negotiation.
It is the first step in "raising our awareness of our own systems of thinking
and judging" (p. 225). Through mindfulness we are continually aware of
scripts we own that tell us what we know about others. It is the continual
revisiting of these scripts that can help us challenge them—an important
step in developing a disposition toward inclusion. With mindfulness we can
anticipate others' needs for expression and inclusion, in essence increasing
our ability to take the perspective of another. Perspective taking enables us
to work to shift our behavior to create more welcoming and, ultimately,
transformative environments where meaningful multicultural interactions,

policies, and practice can prevail. Through what becomes a mutual construction of reality, we are affirmed for taking risks, and others are encouraged to trust that we can be allies in creating inclusive environments on our campuses.

While synergy with others is optimal, there is the risk that overly challenging situations or programs may stall development. Gudykunst (1993) warned that there is an equilibrium to be maintained when individuals engage in intercultural communication, meaning that if the challenge is too great, if the difference is too great, then the individuals are unable to manage the uncertainty and anxiety the difference creates. Ting-Toomey (2005) confirmed this when she wrote, "Individuals in all cultures or ethnic groups have the basic motivation needs for identity security, inclusion, predictability, connection and consistency on both group-based and person-based identity levels," but "too much insecurity (or vulnerability) will lead to fear of out groups or strangers" (p. 218). Those successful in practicing inclusion continually escalate their optimal range through risk taking and holding others accountable for being part of the effort. The work almost becomes, as Ting-Toomey phrased it, "effortlessly mindful," leading to a "state of shifting among multiple cultural mindscapes and multiple cultural/ethnic identity issues," characteristic of "dynamic cultural transformers" (p. 225).

KEY STEPS TO DEVELOPING
AN INCLUSIVE DISPOSITION

We recommend a number of key steps to take in preparation for building inclusive campus communities. It is clear that growth in self-awareness is a process. Furthermore, it comprises triumphs and challenges. The following recommendations can be realistically implemented to positively promote greater awareness of self.

Set an Agenda for Self-Exploration

All too often the quest to gain multicultural or intercultural competence begins with external discoveries. However, a disposition for inclusion cannot take place without a significant dose of self-exploration. Following the multicultural competence model of awareness, knowledge, and skills (Pope et al.,

2004; Sleeter & Grant, 2008), the first step needs to involve an honest evaluation of current attitudes and beliefs regarding difference. It can be helpful to examine true feelings and thoughts about social issues and reflect on where these beliefs originated; this level of self-reflection can reveal deep-seated values regarding difference. Some examples of social issues might be illegal immigration, gay marriage and parenting, cross-racial adoption, causes of poverty, the public's responsibility for social welfare programs, or others. Once an honest account is established, the origin of those values (family or friends) needs to be explored so that one can carefully think about how they can be deconstructed to the point where more inclusive points of view can be considered. If the values come from hurtful personal experiences, it may be helpful to engage in dialogue or other educational efforts so that their continued expression does not prevent authentic interactions with diverse others.

Gaining knowledge about social issues or about the history and contemporary situation of ethnic or racial, sexual orientation, or socioeconomic status groups is helpful not only in reversing noninclusive values but in building a knowledge base necessary for multicultural competence. Texts in history, sociology, ethnic studies, or queer studies are good places to begin. However, it is important to remember that many accounts of history or explanations for social problems carry with them the biases of their authors. Therefore, it can be helpful to read with a partner or as a part of a group and critically interrogate the readings, taking the perspective of the different interest groups involved. For example, the history of the Battle of the Alamo is different depending on the perspective of the United States or Mexico. It's also important to consider reading a wide range of literature, including fiction from diverse perspectives, to more fully understand individual experiences in these groups. Not only does enhanced knowledge communicate caring enough about becoming inclusive to extend one's effort and time, but also the security acquired knowledge conveys goes a long way to building confidence for intercultural interactions and relationships.

It can be difficult to imagine skill building in isolation, but there are activities that can be done individually to enhance inclusiveness. Written dialogue is an effective exercise to prepare to engage in difficult conversations. Stevens and Cooper (2009) recommended dialogues where the writer is in dialogue with an entity—self, another, a conflict, emotions, and so on. Through this activity a person can practice what to say and experience what it might feel like to be a part of the conversation. It enhances a sense of empathy by considering how the other in the conversation might react. It can also be a productive way to debrief situations that called for a response different from what was given. A case of "I wish I said that!" is better remembered when scripted out with reflective notes. Reading and responding to cases is also a skill that can be practiced individually. In a particularly trying situation in walking the talk, writing about a case can often illuminate strategies that have been missed or elements of a solution that need to be revised.

Establish a Safe Space for Yourself and Others

In the journey of self-awareness, individuals are bound to have missteps that appear to be setbacks. Withdrawal is also a possibility when those on the journey experience challenges that seem insurmountable. On the other hand, exploring awareness of self can help individuals discover things about themselves that they had not previously considered. Regardless of what emerges on the journey, it is important to establish a *homeplace*. A homeplace according to hooks (1990) is

> the construction of a safe place where black people could affirm one another and by so doing heal many of the wounds inflicted by racist domination. We could not learn to love or respect ourselves in the culture of white supremacy, on the outside; it was there on the inside, in that "homeplace," most often created and kept by black women, that we had an opportunity to grow and develop, to nurture our spirits. (p. 42)

Although hooks referred specifically to Black people, her idea of a homeplace raises important points for examining one's sense of self. It is vital to have a space where judgments are suspended, and trusted friends and allies are there not only to listen but also to encourage individuals to express their feelings and thought processes. These homeplaces are ideal for inviting feedback on the self-exploration activities discussed in the previous section. Leaders who practice inclusivity know the value their confidants play in their ability to persist in their work. A homeplace provides the opportunity to reflect, process, learn, and become rejuvenated while taking advantage of the synergy created by being in the company of trusted allies. With time, the trust established can enable the homeplace to serve as a starting point. Further exploration makes conversations formerly considered difficult a natural extension of the work needed to continue inclusive agendas.

Courageously Engage in Risk Taking

It is difficult to develop a strong sense of self without having engaged in opportunities for taking risks. It is impossible to know every single outcome, but the willingness and ability to explore the possibilities can make a significant difference in learning about oneself. Risk taking might involve initiating a friendship with someone who is viewed as different. Remaining in this friendship despite missteps takes the risk even further. It also provides the platform to learn the value of offering an apology, asking for forgiveness, and engaging in honest conversations to offset future missteps. Placing yourself in high-risk situations, such as culturally different spaces, long-term workshops or courses, and work task forces, has the potential for personal and professional growth. It is also risky to participate in a class or workplace discussion because how you make sense of your identity is shared. Similarly, risk taking could also involve admitting one's mistakes and pursuing corrective actions. This display of vulnerability serves as a model for others who may be embarking on their own journeys, making it easier for them to take risks. Voicing an unpopular opinion that promotes a socially just perspective also represents a risk-taking behavior. This is particularly important because aptitude in this area is a must in creating inclusive campus environments. The experiences that grow out of risk taking can reveal much about who a person is and where this person stands. Martin Luther King Jr. (as cited in Carson, 1998) eloquently captured this sentiment when he stated, "The ultimate measure of a man is not where he stands in moments of comfort and convenience, but where he stands at times of challenge and controversy" (p. 342).

STRIVE FOR CONSISTENCY
AND COHERENCE OF IDENTITY

An identity or disposition for inclusion depends on consistent behavior from a place of coherence. This means two things: Educators practice and learn to enact their inclusion beliefs in the many worlds they inhabit, and they work to infuse inclusive values in the many elements of their identity. We as educators do not reserve these behaviors or values only for the workplace, but we work to integrate them throughout life. We seek to balance this identity while we develop our multiple social identities, such as gender, ability, sexual orientation, ethnicity, and so forth. This is a challenge that calls for much of what we have discussed in this chapter. Families, friends, and colleagues may need to be challenged on their noninclusive values whenever they arise, not just when they are egregious or when it is convenient. Likewise, personal values and beliefs need to be confronted no matter the target. Risks need to be taken to advocate for students or community members. We use the power and expertise we gain throughout our careers to clear the way and correct injustices so that inclusive equitable environments are established. Overcoming fear and the need to play it safe is absolutely necessary for developing an inclusive disposition, and the self-work to do both is essential before any other actions can be authentically taken.

In conclusion, through contemplating interpretations of self and the influence of others on that interpretation, then negotiating tensions between self and the other to work synergistically, the staff of the career development center in our opening scenario will be more likely to address substantial causes for the lack of a diverse student clientele. This moves the campus closer to becoming truly inclusive. But, who is the other we are to work with synergistically? In continuing the themes of this chapter, the authors of Chapter 2 consider the next element in the process toward inclusion—learning about others through relationships.

REFERENCES

Abes, E. S., Jones, S. R., & McEwen, M. K. (2007). Reconceptualizing the model of multiple dimensions of identity: The role of meaning-making capacity in the construction of multiple identities. *Journal of College Student Development, 48*(1), 1–22.

Ackelsberg, M. A. (1996). Identity politics, political identities: Thoughts toward a multicultural politics. *Frontier: A Journal of Women Studies, 16*(1), 87–100.

Allport, G. W. (1979). *The nature of prejudice.* Reading, MA: Addison-Wesley.

Bogardus, E. S. (1928). *Immigration and race attitudes.* Boston, MA: D. C. Heath.

Carson, C. (Ed.). (1998). *The autobiography of Martin Luther King, Jr.* New York, NY: Warner Books.

Crenshaw, K. (1989). Demarginalizing the intersection of race and sex: A Black feminist critique of antidiscrimination doctrine, feminist theory and antiracist politics. *University of Chicago Legal Forum, 1,* 139–167.

Dill, B. T., & Zambrana, R. E. (2009). *Emerging intersections: Race, class, and gender in theory, policy, and practice.* New Brunswick, NJ: Rutgers University Press.

Erikson, E. H. (1968). *Identity: Youth and crisis.* New York, NY: Norton.

Giroux, H. (1997). Rewriting the discourse of racial identity: Towards a pedagogy and politics of whiteness. *Harvard Educational Review, 67*(2), 285–320.

Gudykunst, W. (1993). Toward a theory of effective interpersonal and intergroup communication: An anxiety/uncertainty management (AUM) perspective. In R. Wiseman & J. Koester (Eds.), *Intercultural communication competence* (pp. 33–71). Newbury Park, CA: Sage.

Hammond, C. M. (1981). Audre Lorde: Interview. *Denver Quarterly, 16*(1), 10–27.

Hill Collins, P. (1986). Learning from the outsider within: The sociological significance of Black feminist thought. *Social Problems, 33*(6), 745–773.

hooks, b. (1990). *Yearning: Race, gender, and cultural politics.* Boston, MA: South End Press.

Johnson, A. G. (2006). *Privilege, power, and difference* (2nd ed.). New York, NY: McGraw-Hill.

Jones, S. R. (2009). Constructing identities at the intersections: An autoethnographic exploration of multiple dimensions of identity. *Journal of College Student Development, 50,* 287–304.

Jones, S. R., & McEwen, M. K. (2000). A conceptual model of multiple dimensions of identity. *Journal of College Student Development, 41*(3), 405–413.

Keating, A. (Ed.). (2000). *Gloria E. Anzaldúa: Interview/entrevistas.* New York, NY: Routledge.

Leonardo, Z. (2004). The color of supremacy: Beyond the discourse of White privilege. *Educational Philosophy and Theory, 36*(2), 137–152.

Maher, F. A., & Thompson Tetreault, M. K. (1997). Learning in the dark: How assumptions of whiteness shape classroom knowledge. *Harvard Educational Review, 67*(2), 321–349.

Maher, F. A., & Thompson Tetreault, M. K. (2001). *The feminist classroom.* Lanham, MD: Rowman & Littlefield.

Ortiz, A. M., & Rhoads, R. A. (2000). Deconstructing whiteness as a part of a multicultural education framework: From theory to practice. *Journal of College Student Development, 41*(1), 81–93.

Ortiz, A. M., & Santos, S. J. (2009). *Ethnicity in college: Improving diversity practices on campus and advancing theory.* Sterling, VA: Stylus.

Perry, W. G., Jr. (1970). *Forms of intellectual and ethical development in the college years: A scheme.* New York, NY: Holt, Rinehart & Winston.

Piaget, J. (1973). *The child and reality: Problems of genetic psychology.* New York, NY: Grossman.

Pope, R. L., & Reynolds, A. L. (1997). Student affairs core competencies: Integrating multicultural awareness, knowledge, and skills. *Journal of College Student Development, 38*(3), 266–277.

Pope, R. L., Reynolds, A. L., & Mueller, J. A. (2004). *Multicultural competence in student affairs.* San Francisco, CA: Jossey-Bass.

Ramsey, M. (1996). Diversity identity development training: Theory informs practice. *Journal of Multicultural Counseling and Development, 24*(4), 229–240.

Sleeter, C. E., & Grant, C. A. (2008). *Making choices for multicultural education: Five approaches to race, class and gender* (6th ed.). San Francisco, CA: Jossey-Bass.

Steele, C. M. (1997). A threat in the air: How stereotypes shape intellectual identity and performance. *American Psychologist, 52*(6), 613–629.

Stevens, D. D., & Cooper, J. E. (2009). *Journal keeping: How to use reflective writing for learning, teaching, professional insight and positive change.* Sterling, VA: Stylus.

Swiencicki, J. (2006). The rhetoric of awareness narratives. *College English, 68*(4), 337–355.

Tanaka, G. (2003). *The intercultural campus: Transcending culture and power in American higher education.* New York, NY: Peter Lang.

Ting-Toomey, S. (2005). Identity negotiation theory: Crossing cultural boundaries. In W. B. Gudykunst (Ed.), *Theorizing about intercultural communication* (pp. 211–233). Thousand Oaks, CA: Sage.

Torres, V. (2009). The developmental dimensions of racist thoughts. *Journal of College Student Development, 50*(5), 504–520.

Williams, P. (1991). *Alchemy of race and rights.* Cambridge, MA: Harvard University Press.

Wilson, A. (1996). How we find ourselves: Identity development and two-spirit people. *Harvard Educational Review, 66*(2), 303–317.

Yosso, T. J., Smith, W. A., Ceja, M., & Solorzano, D. G. (2009). Critical race theory, racial microaggressions, and campus racial climate for Latina/o undergraduates. *Harvard Educational Review, 79*(4), 658–690.

Zetzer, H. A. (2004). White out: Privilege and its problems. In S. K. Anderson & V. A. Middleton (Eds.), *Explorations of privilege, oppression, and diversity* (pp. 3–16). Florence, KY: Cengage.

Zuniga, X., Naagda, B. A., & Sevig, T. D. (2002). Intergroup dialogues: An educational model for cultivating engagement across differences. *Equity & Excellence in Education, 35*(1), 7–17.

2

Learning Through Relationships With Others

Jan Arminio and Vasti Torres

TWO SEPARATE INVITATIONS TO LUNCH, and the comments guests made, resulted in poignant learning, which highlights how people learn about others through their experiences of relationships.

Dining with a colleague: Upon entering the restaurant, the colleague said, "Thanks for inviting me out to lunch, but can we change tables? I never sit at a restaurant with my back to the door." This statement required that I (Jan) learn that others do not have the same sense of safety I had always taken for granted as a White person.

Dining with a student: After having asked a student to lunch to discuss research interests, he said to me (Jan), "Thanks for inviting me out to lunch, but can we eat at a buffet? Growing up, we always ate at buffets. My parents feared that waitstaff would spit in our food." This request exemplified the microaggressions I was unaware of that Black people had experienced.

These comments are examples of poignant learning garnered through everyday interactions in the context of relationships and the critical role relationships play in creating inclusive campuses. As discussed in Chapter 1, it is impossible to gain self-awareness without contemplating relationships. According to Kroger (2004), people formulate identities by balancing the beliefs and wants of the self with those of others. Identities are a balance between how we see ourselves and how others see us. They are intrinsically influenced by our relationships. We share Baxter Magolda's (2009) call for educators to focus on "intersections rather than separate constructs" (p. 621) of development. This chapter focuses on intersections and relationships and the broadest nature of otherness. To begin, we explore the notion of self-in-relation (Ivey, 1995) and briefly review the student development literature on interpersonal growth. Pope and Reynolds (1997) identified characteristics of multiculturally competent student affairs professionals in three domains: awareness, knowledge, and skills. Because the previous chapter explored awareness, and Chapter 5 focuses on skills in using difficult dialogues to frame action, this chapter highlights knowledge necessary in establishing cross-cultural relationships.

SELF-IN-RELATION TO OTHERS

Our world necessitates that people establish relationships beyond our friends and families. As Ortiz and Patton discussed in Chapter 1, empathy allows people to initiate relationships that lead to greater insight about the self and others. However, historically, people have more often responded to others from socially constructed cultural beliefs, assumptions, and projections. The beliefs that are created through social construction can lead to stereotypes, negative images, and oppressive societal policies. These culturally con-structed beliefs determine social distance between groups that are a part of every society and are illustrated through interracial, gender, religious, and class interactions that include the compositions of neighborhoods and what are deemed as appropriate partnerships (Quintana, 2007).

  According to Ivey (1995), self-in-relation appropriately alters the empha-sis on the autonomous individual self. Self-in-relation adopts Freire's (1970/ 2000) notion that the goal of education is to liberate people through under-standing themselves in a social context. Feminist theory and Freire's work as well as that of other social justice advocates emphasize how sharing power people "work together to find new meaning and new ways of being, . . . helping individuals and groups become intentionally conscious of themselves and conscious of consciousness" (Ivey, p. 57). This imposes "more complex cognitions and behaviors as one comes to see oneself in context" (p. 58). In addition to empathy (as mentioned in Chapter 1), Ivey believed this coming together with others requires passive acceptance to hear others' experience. Rice (K. L. Rice, personal communication, 1998) called this acceptance "soft belly" in contrast to "hard belly," which embodies defensiveness and deflects new insight. This literal soft belly aims to "increase our attention to the direct experience of the individual through immediate sensimotor reality and [help us to] consider how that reality is affected by systematic contextual/cultural issues" (Ivey, p. 65). The following from Raybon's (1996) moving personal account of self-acceptance and forgiveness is an example of soft belly:

> We sit there, indeed, facing each other with different tapes playing in each of our heads. And amazingly, we often understand each other. It is not always pretty or perfect; cultural dissonance can be loud—and it is demanding. It asks me to teach. (p. 209)

Hard bellies impede learning by deflecting empathy and blocking the ability to hear others' experiences.

As individuals we may not maintain conscious attention of how our assumptions are embedded in societal systems of power and oppression. The discourse we hope to encourage illuminates how the self-in-relation may not be fully acknowledged in daily interactions. How can educators encourage connections that do acknowledge self-in-relation? Furthermore, how can these connections further the goal of inclusive campuses?

RELATIONSHIPS AND DEVELOPMENT

Numerous developmental theorists have written and researched the critical role relationships play in development. For example, Gilligan (1982) noted the balance necessary in relationships—not losing the self to relationships with others but considering the needs of others in relationships. Josselson's (1991) research on women demonstrated that a crisis in relationships leads to development of the individual. Among the college student literature, Chickering and Reisser (1993) found that establishing mature relationships was one of the vectors that contribute to identity construction. Yet, more specifically, what types of relationships are useful in establishing inclusive campuses?

Kegan (1994) described the type of relationships that we believe are crucial to the intent of this book. People making the transition from Kegan's second to third order of consciousness begin to pay attention to the feelings and needs of others. These are relationships in which individuals stop seeing

others as being made up of their own experiences and begin to see others as
more than their own experiences. This requires what Kegan referred to as
fourth-order consciousness, one's "capacity to *relate to* one's *inter*personal
relationships [with others] and *intra*personal relationships [sense of self]
rather than *be made by them*" (p. 176, emphasis in original). Of course, what
is a mature and balanced relationship is influenced by cultural context. Torres (2003) noted how her Latino familial relationships differed from those
of her Anglo classmates. "Definitions of autonomy, independence, and
interdependence differ from the definitions accepted within the majority
white culture" (p. 6). Navigating these differences occurs on many levels for
students, staff, and faculty on every campus. Inclusive campuses acknowledge and act on the culturally influenced nature of relationships while
upholding community members' human rights.

According to Baxter Magolda (2001), most if not all traditionally aged
college students arrived on campus with

> relationships constructed before the internal voice emerged sometimes
> required reshaping after its arrival. Relationships constructed from an
> externally-defined identity emphasized what the other wanted whereas rela-
> tionships constructed from internally-defined identity brought what the self
> wanted into the forefront to be negotiated. (p. 15)

The construction of an internal voice can take on different dimensions for
nonmajority members of the campus community. In their longitudinal
study of Latino/Latina students, Torres and Hernandez (2007) examined
the influence of ethnic identity on establishing internal foundations of self
and discovered that the recognition of racism was a necessary developmental task. They emphasized that educators too must recognize the role
of racism in the development process. Institutional practices influence relationships formed on campus and help determine whether Latinos/Latinas
grow or retreat. The recognition of racism requires that majority members
on college campuses be familiar with the microaggressions that are seen as
racist for nonmajority members. It also requires that nonmajority members
of the community recognize the many intersecting identities among the
diversity of individuals that are labeled nonmajority. No one knows everything there is to know about every other group, and everyone has some
assumptions that must be examined.

Identity development theories promote the power of encounters with others. It is through relationships with others that people are forced to question the idea that difference is insignificant (Torres, Howard-Hamilton, & Cooper, 2003). Moreover, it is also through encounters with others that people recognize discriminatory attitudes and behaviors in themselves, their communities, and their families. Through the process of making meaning of the encounter situation, people understand the self in context with others. These encounters can be hurtful, and so it is critical that student affairs educators be sensitive to conflictual moments.

Research confirms the important learning outcomes in diverse educational environments, particularly for White students (Blimling, 2001). To bring life to these data, there are a number of poignant memoirs explicating the importance of cross-cultural encounters in relationships and learning. The following is one example of the learning potential of relationships across differences. In describing an incident in which two doctoral students had a conflict over the deletion of material on homophobia for a conference presentation, Mobley and Pearson (2005) wrote,

> The look of horror on the face of this person who had become more than a peer—a friend—hit me so hard I thought I would faint or throw up right there in the computer lab. That feeling of queasiness is still present as I write this piece now, not only because I was outed as an oppressor, but also because I had hurt my friend. (pp. 89–102)

The difficult and necessary task that must occur is to maintain the relationship while deep, personal learning is taking place. Creating a space to share feelings and walk in each other's shoes is an example of Kegan's (1994) fourth order of consciousness. Mobley (Mobley & Pearson) stated,

> I now recognize the importance of maintaining my power in self-identifying but also affording a safe space for another to respond genuinely while remaining open that a conflict, cultural impasse, may result. . . . Today I am very proud of the depth of our relationship. (pp. 93–94)

Pearson (Mobley & Pearson) wrote, "Over the years I have continued to explore what parts of my cultural and religious identities are salient and which parts no longer fit" (p. 93). Significantly, Mobley and Pearson provided an example of poignant learning through everyday interactions in the context of relationships.

As Ortiz and Patton wrote in Chapter 1, self-awareness gives people confidence that encourages them to take risks in initiating relationships outside their established social circle. Yet, it is through relationships that greater self-awareness is achieved. In any case, knowledge of others helps *begin* the process of creating that safe space where deeper learning can take place.

KNOWLEDGE COMPETENCIES THAT ENCOURAGE RELATIONSHIPS ACROSS DIFFERENCES

Baxter Magolda (1999) wrote that "adult life requires the capacity for self-authorship," which is "simultaneously a cognitive (how one makes meaning of knowledge), interpersonal (how one views oneself in relationship to others), and intrapersonal (how one perceives one's sense of identity) matter" (p. 10). In 1994 Kegan wrote that when self-authored, "The expectation [is] that we be self-initiating, self-correcting, and self-evaluating rather than depend on others to frame the problems, initiate the adjustments, or determine whether things are going acceptably well" (p. 168). Baxter Magolda advocated for educators to use strategies that encouraged self-authorship, linking the intertwined dimensions of cognitive, interpersonal, and intrapersonal development. The most complex way of knowing that she discovered in college students is what she called *contextual knowing*, which "involved constructing one's perspective in the context of one's experience, available information, and the experience of others" (p. 51). The reader can certainly see the connections among experience, available information (knowledge), and relationships. Consequently, what basic knowledge is required of educators to create growth-producing relationships? If exchanging views, being open to others' views, and focusing on one's own thinking are essential to interpersonal development, what knowledge promotes it?

Pope and Reynolds (1997) identified dimensions of knowledge necessary to be multiculturally competent. These include knowledge of diverse cultures, how change occurs within individuals, the impact of social identities on the perception of experience, cultural differences in communication, information about the nature of institutional oppression and power, identity development models, within-group differences, internalized oppression, institutional barriers that limit access, and systems change theories. The following examples of more specific knowledge pertinent to maintaining relationships are highlighted here but are only a starting point. Lack of knowledge communicates a lack of interest and demonstrates incompetence. Though some people are willing to be others' teachers, each individual must ultimately be responsible for knowing information crucial to establishing, navigating, and maintaining relationships. In the following we offer a sample of the requisite knowledge in Pope and Reynolds's dimensions that is useful in establishing, maintaining, and navigating relationships with others. Note that *other* is defined and described broadly. While reading, it is imperative to consider the circumstances of the information. In what ways is this knowledge familiar or new? How might having or not having this knowledge influence relationships?

Diverse cultures. Numerous cultures are found on campuses, some of which have been welcomed and expected, whereas others have been excluded. For example, according to Rankin's 2005 study of 14 college campuses, 36% of lesbian, gay, bisexual, and transgender (LGBT) undergraduate students experienced harassment. Challenges facing LGBT students "can prevent them from achieving their academic potential or participating fully in campus communities" (Rankin, 2005, p. 17). In communities, legislative policies and laws limit the rights granted to LGBT citizens. The National Coalition of Anti-violence Programs (2010) reported 2,181 incidents of violence committed against lesbian, gay, bisexual, transgender, and questioning (LGBTQ) people in 2009, which is a decrease from 2008. Also, 22 anti-LGBTQ murders reported in 2009—which thankfully represents a 30% decline from the peak year, 2008—is the second-highest annual total of such incidents reported in the United States over a 10-year period. Yet, according to the report, violence against this community is not lessening, but rather the ability of community organizations to report violence has decreased because of budget restraints.

Groups that may not be considered a culture include those labeled conservative and liberal, often heard on college campuses. These labels are associated with the socially influenced context that tends to promote common thinking among all those involved in a particular formal or informal organization (Wald, Owen, & Hill, 1988). It is difficult to define an idea as solely conservative or liberal because its historical context changes with the community's belief system (Bensko, Canetto, Sugar, & Viney, 1995). The values of these groups can vary over history (Bensko et al.), yet the two labels tend to illustrate opposite ends of a spectrum of beliefs. Conservatism is assumed to favor the maintenance of traditional values and positions, yet as community belief systems change so does anything defined as traditional. Liberals are often associated with wanting to change traditional values or positions. Results of a study of young adults illustrated that neither liberals nor conservatives could recognize past conservative positions or failed liberal positions (Bensko et al.). The reason is that although at one point in history a position may be liberal (e.g., supporting Social Security) eventually it may become part of the widely held community belief system and cease to be a liberal ideal. Concerns have been raised about liberal bias in higher education; however, these concerns seem more connected to politics than philosophy (Wilson, 2006). In any case, understanding the contextual aspects of what is liberal and what is conservative may assist in conversations about how to understand differing ideals.

Numerous examples of religious bias in higher education are discussed in more detail in Chapter 3. Whether it is anti-Semitic graffiti, quotas of Jewish students, or taunting of Muslim students, nonmajority religions have historically been discriminated against. According to Kaplin and Lee (2006),

> Under the establishment clause of the First Amendment, public institutions must maintain a neutral stance regarding religious beliefs and activities. . . . In other words they cannot favor or support one religion over another, and they cannot favor or support religion over nonreligion. (p. 57)

Kaplin and Lee also explain that this does not mean public institutions are to prohibit religious activity. Rather, individuals or organizations with religious purposes have the right to freedom of speech and expression. How to maintain this neutral stance while allowing freedom of speech and expression has been a difficult balance. For example, several legal cases concern the ability of public institutions to limit the recognition of student religious groups that deny membership or leadership roles because of gender, religion, or sexual orientation. Though the U.S. Supreme Court ruled that institutional policies requiring recognized student groups to accept all comers is constitutional, the decision did not address the question of the legality of student groups that mandate membership or leadership requirements (Schmidt, 2010). Regardless of the establishment clause, a number of scholars have urged educators to truly consider the development of the whole student including spiritual development (Chickering, Dalton, & Stamm, 2006; Jablonski, 2001; King, 2009; Love & Talbot, 1999). These scholars have also deemed it important to differentiate religion and spirituality. Many authors view religion as a formal organization of people that offers doctrine about the quest for the divine (Love, 2002; Stamm, 2006), whereas spirituality is more an individual and informal search for wholeness, purpose, and meaning, which was found to contribute to cognitive development (Love).

Although only a few cultural groups are discussed here, they provide examples of basic knowledge about the experiences of these groups that help inform relationship building.

How change occurs within individuals. The reader will most likely be familiar with the notion of challenge and support (Sanford, 1966). Putting this concept in a more current context, Chavez, Guido-DiBrito, and Mallory (2003) noted that in the higher education community, members "value both connection and autonomy and seek growth when encouraged independently and collectively to reflect on their thinking, feeling, and behavior towards those they think of as other" (p. 456). They identified understanding individual needs and motivations as important to establishing relationships. This includes validating others as well as validating the "otherness within ourselves" (p. 457). To move from knowing something to applying this knowledge requires questioning and self-exploration, risk taking, exploration of others, and a commitment of integrity where thoughts, values, and behaviors are congruent. Their framework emphasized the importance of cross-cultural interactions, which must include structured and unstructured opportunities (Tatum, 1997). Ortiz and Rhoads (2000) identified a similar process of encouraging change but emphasized the influence of culture. They wrote that people must first understand the nature of culture, learn about others' cultures, learn about one's own culture, and commit to social action to achieve true equality.

These are two of many models that emphasize knowing the self and others as well as interacting with others to foster change. When educators provide opportunities for interaction across groups, they encourage growth and create relationships in the process.

Cultural differences in communication. Many factors influence how people communicate—culture is one. Individual preference, family upbringing, and geography are others. However, educators cannot ignore the nuances of cross-cultural communication in establishing, navigating, and maintaining relationships. For example, generally, African Americans and those of Arab descent value expressiveness more so than Asian Americans, Native Americans value nonverbal behaviors, and White Americans tend to value emotional restraint and communication that reflects the individual rather than the group (Nassar-McMillan, Gonzalez, & Mohamed, 2010; Sue, Ivey, & Pedersen, 1996). Some Asian cultures (Inman & Alverez, 2010) and Latino/Chicano cultures (Sue et al., 1996) emphasize *saving face*, the notion of protecting and honoring family, particularly authorities. Because the eyes are often seen as the pathway to the spirit, looking directly at a Native American's eyes may be seen as a sign of aggression (Garrett, 2010). Though Native Americans appreciate silence upon meeting someone new (Garrett), many White Americans do not. Touching and what it signifies is also influenced by culture. Hugging, kissing cheeks, and handshakes are all greetings influenced by culture. In the Middle East holding hands by adults of the same gender is common and may not reflect a romantic relationship, but rather friendship. Anger is often misperceived across cultures. For example, people from cultures that value emotional restraint may misperceive emotional displays from people whose cultures value expressiveness or directness. Consequently, in learning through relationships, extra effort is often necessary to ensure the intent of the communication is accurately perceived.

Information about the nature of institutional oppression and power. Because of the history of legalized slavery and discrimination in the United States, race continues to be a socially constructed difference that greatly affects society. Cross-racial relationships, particularly between White and Black people, remain a source of great tension. The oppression of African Americans in U.S. history creates a historical context that influences multiple nonmajority groups today in how individuals relate to others within and outside their social groups, as well as how they internalize their identity (Wing & Rifkin, 2001). This historical context continues to permeate higher education, affecting who works at the institution and in what roles, who is admitted, and who graduates.

In his second edition of *Privilege, Power, and Difference*, Johnson (2006) noted his omission of disability in the first edition:

> The main reason is that I, as a nondisabled person, was blinded by my own privilege to the reality of how disability status affects people. . . . I had to

educate people and listen to those who knew more about this than I did. In short, I had to come to terms with what I didn't know about privilege and what I thought I *did* know. . . . Unlike race, gender, and sexual orientation, disability status can change during a person's lifetime. In fact as the saying goes, everyone will experience some form of disability during their lives unless they die first. People with disabilities, then, are a constant reminder of the full reality of the human experience—how vulnerable we are and how much there is in life that we cannot control. For many nondisabled people, this is a frightening thing to contemplate. (p. viii)

Kaplin and Lee (2006) quoted federal law as defining disability as a "physical or mental impairment that substantially limits one or more major life activities" (p. 1381). According to statistics from the U.S. Department of Education, 10.8% of all undergraduates in 2007–2008 reported a disability: 19.2% had an attention-deficit disorder, 15.4% had an orthopedic disability, 13.3% suffered from depression, and 10.8% reported a mental illness other than depression (Roberts, 2009). Students with disabilities experience college life as being misunderstood and at times demeaned, but often on the margins of dominant culture. The experience of otherness includes students with learning disabilities being suspected of inventing their conditions to secure advantages over others, and faculty and staff members refusing to provide students with reasonable accommodations (McCune, 2001). Faculty can humiliate students by discussing individual accommodations publicly and claiming that other students feel too uncomfortable with them in the classroom (McCune). These behaviors mirror attitudes that require students with disabilities to advocate for themselves. Advocating means that students learn policies that govern the institution, use their voices to articulate what it is they need to succeed, and at times adopt new expectations (McCarthy, 2007).

Identity development models. While there is no one way to be a member of any group, racial identity theories illustrate there is a process in which a person moves away from an identity prescribed by the dominant culture to one that is more focused on authentic group membership (Torres et al., 2003). Cross (1971; Cross & Vandiver, 2001) and Helms (1990) theorized how a person can move from experiencing race with little salience toward experiencing race (African American) with a more integrated sense of self, which includes positive views of the African American race as well as other races. Also, American Indians have experienced forced assimilation for many generations, and yet they have maintained their tribal affiliations and cultural values. Critical to understanding American Indians is the acceptance of sovereignty of the tribal nations (Torres & Bitsói, 2011). The attempts to destroy Native culture are the basis for LaFromboise, Trimble, and Mohatt's (1990) five categories of Indianness. In these categories, the level of acculturation to U.S. mainstream culture is contrasted with the maintenance of the ethnic identity exhibited by the individual. Though many American Indians have adapted to U.S. culture, this should not be taken as assimilation or rejection of Native values and beliefs.

For many multiracial individuals, the pressure to choose between racial identities can cause conflict, thus prompting multiracial people to confront issues of racial identity earlier in their lives than monoracial people (Renn, 2008; Root, 2003). Individuals can attain a sense of self within multiple races and have a more complex understanding of race that is inclusive of multiple racial perspectives. One of the issues higher education must consider is the classifications used in applications and student demographic forms. This way of categorizing humans must be updated to represent the interracial children who are prevalent today.

Helms (1990) described relationship dyads based on racial identity development theory. In regressive relationships the authority (faculty member, administrator, or counselor) understands race less complexly than those with less power (students, clerical, or support staff). In parallel relationships, authorities and nonauthorities have similar understandings of racial dynamics. The relationship with the most learning potential, according to Helms, is a progressive one in which those with the most power in the relationship have the most complex understanding of race and social justice. Obviously, taking action to ensure progressive relationships is tantamount to creating inclusive campuses. Understanding the nature of development allows educators to better understand their own attitudes and behaviors, as well as those of students, and what happens when they interact. Educators should use developmental theory to guide educational practices, particularly how development promotes learning through relationships.

Within-group differences. *Asian American* is a panethnic label that incorporates many countries and cultures that have differing languages, foods, and cultural traditions. Though Asian Americans are seen as highly successful in higher education, the variance within the group is great and should be considered. A fourth-generation Japanese American should not be compared with an immigrant from Laos; their experiences and acculturation to societal norms are very different. Kim (2001) created a theory that focuses on Asian American development of a positive sense of self. The theory's stages are strongly influenced by family and the racial composition of the community around the individual. Kodama, McEwen, Liang, and Lee (2002) offered insight into the development of Asian American college students by placing familial and cultural expectations as the core of the Asian American identity. This model illustrates the importance of family and cultural beliefs over other areas of development. It is important to recognize that some Asian Americans may not see some individualistic values as attractive or desirable, thus placing them at odds with some majority, or mainstream, beliefs about autonomy.

Like Asian American, *Latino* is a panethnic term that encompasses people from Spanish-speaking countries in the Caribbean and Central and South America (Torres & Delgado-Romero, 2008). Though Latinos do tend to share a common language, the various countries of origin provide great variety in food, music, and cultural values. Two factors can influence the experiences of Latinos: immigration status and level of acculturation. Immigration status tends to revolve around political and economic issues, with groups immigrating under the political category tending to have higher levels of education and possibilities for social mobility. Those who immigrate for economic reasons are more likely to come for higher-paying jobs in the United States, which are often in trades or service fields with less opportunities for social mobility (Torres, 2004a). Generation in the United States also influences the level of acculturation and the maintenance of cultural behaviors. More acculturated families are more likely to reflect the U.S. culture (Torres, 2004b). Depending on the level of acculturation, Latinos may respond differently to societal beliefs and may choose to integrate or maintain separate cultural enclaves and cultural orientation (Torres, 1999).

White immigrants to the United States have been able to assimilate into mainstream society in ways that people of color could not. Some authors have noted how Irish and Jewish immigrants became White (Brodkin, 1998; Ignatiev, 1995). However, the Irish, especially because they were Catholic, were often deemed less valuable than slaves (Ignatiev). Many White people today lament the loss of their cultural heritage and engage in festivals, genealogy, and other means to recapture it.

Educators should use caution in making broad generalizations about cultural groups. Rather, they should become informed about the within-group differences, several examples of which are identified here.

Internalized oppression. Tatum (1997) noted that oppression is like pollution in the air. All people breathe it, take it in, and are influenced by it often to the point of believing the inferior messages not only about others but ourselves as well. Sometimes these inferior notions about ourselves are subconscious and need to be brought to our attention by others (Vasquez, 2010). In lamenting internalized oppression in the Black community, Madhubuti (1990) declared,

> who in the Black community has not heard,
> if you're white you're alright
> yellow you're mellow,
> brown stick around, but if you're Black step back. (p. 264)

Creating inclusive campuses means exposing the ways people and groups oppress themselves by believing negative messages about themselves. One concrete example of how internalized oppression harms students is in their career choices (Pope, 2010). Messages about who is and who is not smart and who is appropriate for which careers permeate U.S. culture. Self-in-relation through authentic relationships can expose, change, and replace the negative messages people believe about themselves.

Institutional barriers that limit access. The social construction of gender is such that those other than men (i.e., "real men") have been deemed subordinate. Clarke's 1873 text, *Sex in Education: Or a Fair Chance for the Girls,* offered women's smaller brains as evidence that they were inadequate for the educational rigors of men. This text also concluded that intense brain activity would harm a woman's reproductive system. Unfortunately, the vestiges of such beliefs continue today. Examples include the salary discrepancy between men and women (Armas, 2005), the decrease in income of female college students (Sax, 2007), the common episodes of violence against women around the world (Rosenthal, 2006), and self-reported higher levels of stress and lower levels of physical and emotional health of college women (Sax). Feminists have been the ones who have combated discrimination and violence against women. hooks (2000) wrote that "feminism is a movement to end sexism, sexist exploitation, and oppression" (p. 1). The reluctance of 21st-century populations to embrace feminism is another indication of the continuance of 19th-century beliefs.

Considerable progress has been made in the education of women, particularly middle-class women, since Clarke (1873) wrote of the inability of women to be successful in rigorous educational environments. In fact, there has been much in the mainstream press about the fact that over half of college students are indeed women. In criticizing admissions policies of institutions that allow less qualified males to be admitted over more qualified females to ensure more of a gender balance, Whitmire (2007) wrote that almost 57% of college students today are female. Sax and Arms (2008) confirmed that "indeed numerous survey items point to a stronger academic orientation among women" (p. 31). However, despite this orientation, numerous studies also point to the continued lower confidence levels of young women (Dugan, 2006; Sax, 2007). Sax and Arms encouraged educators to realize that women's "outward image may not be the best reflection of their actual talents" (p. 33). Their research indicated that though women continue to pursue careers in traditional fields such as teaching and nursing more than men, and men continue to pursue careers in engineering, business, and computer science more than women, there has been a dramatic narrowing of the gender gap in medicine and law.

According to census data from 2005, 12.6% of the U.S. population lives below the poverty line. Among families headed by women, 31% live below the poverty line. Newitz and Wray (1997) without apology stated that "Americans love to hate the poor" (p. 1). Gardner (1993) wrote that social "class is more than an abstract category" (p. 50); it is a culture that influences our behaviors, attitudes, and interests. Criteria that determine class status include a combination of the class one is born into, wealth, education, and occupation. However, determinants are fluid. For example, a factory worker on an assembly line may earn a higher salary than a schoolteacher but can be less educated. Though class status is somewhat nebulous, its influences on daily life are significant. Mantsios (2000) wrote of the myths and realities of class. Myths include that the United States is fundamentally a classless society or a middle-class society, Americans are all becoming wealthier, and everyone has an equal chance to succeed. However, Mantsios indicated that in reality there are "enormous differences in the economic status of American citizens" (p. 171), the economic inequality is becoming larger, the middle class is shrinking, class influences health and life expectancy, class "has a significant impact on our chances for survival" (p. 177), "dramatic advances in class standing are relatively few" (p. 178), and unfortunately Americans do not have similar chances of succeeding. Gardner identified middle-class values as doing and thinking, reflecting, being independent and self-reliant, demonstrating cognitive agility, respecting authorities, viewing discussion as important to learning, competing, respecting standard English, and accumulating material objects as they indicate moral attributes. Working-class values include doing (especially physical work), honoring group affiliation, believing that success happens through hard physical labor, being physically tough, being practical, distrusting authorities, not caring about standard English, and believing that arguing is rude (Gardner). As the current economic recession reminds us, many income earners new to the middle class are one paycheck away from financial ruin. However, as Conley's (2000) research exposes, wealth passed on from generation to generation enables people to stay in the middle and upper classes regardless of the economy. In essence, the ability of middle-class, upper-middle-class, and wealthy people to make choices differentiates them from the poor and working class (Langston, 1993).

Though rarely discussed, college students across a range of social classes articulated the importance of cultural rules and class symbols as definers of social class in the campus environment (Schwartz, Donovan, & Guido-DiBrito, 2009), including how one talked and what one wore in particular circumstances. There is evidence that as tuition costs increase fewer low-income college students graduate, whereas there is little connection between cost and graduate rates of wealthier students (Carey, 2009). Increased attention paid to first-generation college students indicates that many of them are low income and have a more difficult transition into college life than students whose parents attended college (Howard, 2001; Pascarella, Wolniak, Pierson, & Terenzini, 2004; Vander Putten, 2001). Though these students demonstrate academic deficiencies when compared with classmates of college-educated parents, they also demonstrate resilience and substantial academic gains over two years (Pascarella et al.). To establish rapport with first-generation and poor students, substantial training of staff and faculty that focuses on particular academic and social challenges poor students face while attending college is imperative (Howard, 2001). As tuition continually increases and government support for higher education decreases, structured barriers to a college education remain. This decreases the diversity of campuses and the potential of learning through cross-group relationships.

USING KNOWLEDGE TO CREATE
SPACE FOR RELATIONSHIPS

It is important to understand that knowledge is not enough to create inclusive campuses. One may know information from a cognitive perspective but not actually know how to apply that knowledge to behaviors that can promote meaningful dialogue. Educators often write about the importance of *safe space*—a place where people are heard and can be themselves. As the quotes at the beginning of the chapter illustrate, however, what is deemed safe is related to the social identities we hold and those identities that people perceive us to hold. For example, people with more privilege have more access to safe places. Self-in-relation requires safe space and space of vulnerability. Read again the words of Mobley (Mobley & Pearson, 2005): "I now recognize the importance of maintaining my power in self-identifying but also affording a safe space for another to respond genuinely while remaining open that a conflict, cultural impasse, may result" (p. 93).

This statement exemplifies the juxtaposition of self-in-relation. It is the nature of Kegan's (1994) fourth order of consciousness that self-in-relation requires a safe space and a space to defend one's identity. It requires that people take risks and are vulnerable to others but trust that they are heard. Sometimes people are not heard and a "cultural impasse" results. Mobley and Pearson (2005) defined *cultural impasse* as "dynamics that adversely affect the optimal functioning of cross-cultural interactions" (p. 89). Students often ask for a safe space to study and experience multicultural issues. But a safe space cannot be guaranteed. To engage in education is to take risks. To be self-in-relation means to take acceptable risks. Inclusive campuses provide both—opportunities and power to offer self-identification and opportunities to listen with an understanding that conflict is natural and can be navigated.

In summary, when lives intersect we experience knowledge of otherness. Reading about others while being "intentionally conscious of consciousness"

(Ivey, 1995, p. 57) places knowledge in a social context. Hopefully, this knowledge imposes "more complex cognitions and behaviors as one comes to see oneself in context" (p. 58). This chapter, as well as Chapter 1, illustrated how we are all other in some way—while we may not have minority status, we may hold an ideal that is contrary to others, thus making us the outsider. The fluidity of what makes someone an other is critical to understanding our own role in the social construction of the values that are considered mainstream. Being self-aware is understanding how interactions with others may be affected by social identities. While information about other groups is important, this information must be considered in the context of self, self-in-relation, and people's historical context.

REFERENCES

Armas, G. C. (2005, March 28). Census bureau finds disparities in women's pay. *Patriot News*, A5.

Baxter Magolda, M. (1999). *Creating contexts for learning and self-authorship: Constructive-developmental pedagogy.* Nashville, TN: Vanderbilt University Press.

Baxter Magolda, M. B. (2001). *Making their own way.* Sterling, VA: Stylus.

Baxter Magolda, M. B. (2009). The activity of meaning making: A holistic perspective on college student development. *Journal of College Student Development, 50*(6), 621–639.

Bensko, N. L., Canetto, S. S., Sugar, J. A., & Viney, W. (1995). Liberal or conservative? Gender, identity, and perceptions of historical religious positions. *Journal of Psychology, 129*(6), 629–641.

Blimling, G. S. (2001). Diversity makes you smarter. *Journal of College Student Development, 42*(6), 517–519.

Brodkin, K. (1998). *How Jews became White folks and what that says about race in America.* New Brunswick, NJ: Rutgers University Press.

Carey, K. (2009, September 17). Wasting financial aid on rich people [Web log post]. *The Chronicle of Higher Education.* Retrieved from http://chronicle.com/blogPost/Wasting-Financial-Aid-on-Ri/8087/

Chavez, A. F., Guido-DiBrito, F., & Mallory, S. L. (2003). Learning to value the "other": A framework of individual diversity development. *Journal of College Student Development, 44*(5), 453–460.

Chickering, A. W., Dalton, J. C., & Stamm, L. (2006). *Encouraging authenticity and spirituality in higher education.* San Francisco, CA: Jossey-Bass.

Chickering, A. W., & Reisser, L. (1993). *Education and identity* (2nd ed.). San Francisco, CA: Jossey Bass.

Clarke, E. H. (1873). *Sex in education: Or a fair chance for the girls.* Boston, MA: J. R. Osgood.

Conley, D. (2000). *Honky.* New York, NY: Vintage Books.

Cross, W. E. (1971). The Negro-to-Black conversion experience. *Black World, 20,* 13–27.

Cross, W. E., & Vandiver, B. J. (2001). Nigrescence theory and measurement introducing the Cross Racial Identity Scale (CRIS). In J. G. Ponterotto, J. M. Casas, L. A. Suzuki, & C. M. Alexander (Eds.), *Handbook of multicultural counseling* (2nd ed., pp. 371–393). Thousand Oaks, CA: Sage.

Dugan, J. P. (2006). Involvement and leadership: A descriptive analysis of socially responsible leadership. *Journal of College Student Development, 47*(3), 335–343.

Freire, P. (2000). *Pedagogy of the oppressed* (M. B. Ramos, Trans.). New York, NY: Continuum. (Original work published 1970)

Gardner, S. (1993). "What's a nice working-class girl like you doing in a place like this?" In M. M. Tokarcyzyk & E. A. Fay (Eds.), *Working-class women in the academy: Laborers in the knowledge factory* (pp. 49–59). Amherst: University of Massachusetts Press.

Garrett, M. T. (2010). Native Americans. In D. G. Hays & B. T. Erford (Eds.), *Developing multicultural counseling competence: A systems approach* (pp. 301–332). Boston, MA: Pearson.

Gilligan, C. (1982). *In a different voice.* Cambridge, MA: Harvard University Press.

Helms, J. E. (1990). *Black and White racial identity: Theory, research and practice.* Westport, CT: Greenwood Press.

hooks, b. (2000). *Feminism is for everybody: Passionate politics.* Cambridge, MA: South End Press.

Howard, A. (2001, November–December). Students from poverty: Helping them make it through college. *About Campus, 6*(5), 5–12.

Ignatiev, N. (1995). *How the Irish became White.* New York, NY: Routledge.

Inman, A., & Alvarez, A. (2010). Individuals and families of Latin descent. In D. G. Hays & B. T. Erford (Eds.), *Developing multicultural counseling competence: A systems approach* (pp. 246–276). Boston, MA: Pearson.

Ivey, A. E. (1995). Psychotherapy as liberation: Toward specific skills and strategies in multicultural counseling and therapy. In J. G. Ponterotto, J. M. Casas, L. A. Suzuki, & C. M. Alexander (Eds.), *Handbook of multicultural counseling* (pp. 53–71). Thousand Oaks, CA: Sage.

Jablonski, M. A. (Ed.). (2001). *The implications of student spirituality for student affairs.* New Directions for Student Services (95). San Francisco, CA: Jossey-Bass.

Johnson, A. G. (2006). *Privilege, power, and difference* (2nd ed.). Boston, MA: McGraw-Hill.

Josselson, R. (1991). *Finding herself: Pathways to identity development in women.* San Francisco, CA: Jossey-Bass.

Kaplin, W. A., & Lee, B. A. (2006). *The law of higher education* (4th ed.). San Francisco, CA: Jossey-Bass.

Kegan, R. (1994). *In over our heads: The mental demands of modern life.* Cambridge, MA: Harvard University Press.

Kim, J. (2001). Asian American identity development theory. In C. L. Wijeye-singhe & B. W. Jackson, III (Eds.), *New perspectives on racial identity development: A theoretical and practical anthology* (pp. 67–90). New York: New York University Press.

King, P. (2009). Principles of development and developmental change underlying theories of cognitive and moral development. *Journal of College Student Development, 50*(6), 597–627.

Kodama, C. M., McEwen, M. K., Liang, C. T. H., & Lee, S. (2002). An Asian American perspective on psychosocial student development theory. In M. K. McEwen, C. M. Kodama, A. N. Alvarez, S. Lee, & C. T. H. Liang (Eds), *Working with Asian American college students* (New Directions for Student Services No. 97, pp. 45–60. San Francisco, CA: Jossey-Bass.

Kroger, J. (2004). *Identity in adolescence: The balance between self and other* (3rd ed.). London, UK: Routledge.

LaFromboise, T. D., Trimble, J. E., & Mohatt, G. V. (1990). Counseling intervention and American Indian tradition: An integrative approach. *Counseling Psychologist, 18*(4), 628–654.

Langston, D. (1993). Who am I now? The politics of class identity. In M. M. Tokarczyk & E. A. Fay (Eds.), *Working-class women in the academy: Laborers in the knowledge factory* (pp. 60–72). Amherst: University of Massachusetts Press.

Love, P. G. (2002). Comparing spiritual development and cognitive development. *Journal of College Student Development, 43*(3), 357–373.

Love, P. G., & Talbot, D. (1999). Defining spiritual development: A missing consideration for student affairs. *NASPA Journal, 37*(1), 376–385.

Madhubuti, H. R. (1990). *Black men, obsolete, single, dangerous? The Afrikan American family in transition.* Chicago, IL: Third World Press.

Mantsios, G. (2000). Class in America: Myths and realities. In P. S. Rothenberg (Ed.), *Race class, and gender in the United States* (pp. 168–182). New York, NY: Worth Publishers.

McCarthy, D. (2007, November–December). Teaching self-advocacy to students with disabilities. *About Campus, 12*(5), 10–16.

McCune, P. (2001, May–June). What do disabilities have to do with diversity? *About Campus, 6*(2), 5–12.

Mobley, M., & Pearson, S. M. (2005). Blessed be the ties that bind. In J. M. Croteau, J. S. Lark, M. A. Lidderdale, & Y. B. Chung (Eds.), *Deconstructing heterosexism in the counseling professions: A narrative approach* (pp. 89–102). Thousand Oaks, CA: Sage.

Nassar-McMillan, S. C., Gonzalez, L. M., & Mohamed, R. H. (2010). Individuals and families of Arab descent. In D. G. Hays & B. T. Erford (Eds.), *Developing multicultural counseling competence: A systems approach* (pp. 216–245). Boston, MA: Pearson.

National Coalition of Anti-violence Programs. (2010). *Hate violence against the lesbian, gay, bisexual, transgender and queer communities in the United States in 2009.* Retrieved from http://www.avp.org/documents/NCAVP2009HateViolenceRe portforWeb_000.pdf

Newitz, A., & Wray, M. (1997). Introduction. In M. Wray & A. Newitz (Eds.), *White trash* (pp. 1–12). New York, NY: Routledge.

Ortiz, A. M., & Rhoads, R. A. (2000). Deconstructing whiteness as part of a multicultural educational framework: From theory to practice. *Journal of College Student Development, 41*(1), 81–93.

Pascarella, E. T., Wolniak, G. C., Pierson, C. T., & Terenzini, P. T. (2004). Experiences and outcomes of first-generation students in community colleges. *Journal of College Student Development, 44*(3), 420–429.

Pope, M. (2010). Career counseling with diverse adults. In J. G. Ponterotto, J. M. Casas, L. A. Suzuki, & C. M. Alexander (Eds.), *Handbook of multicultural counseling* (3rd ed., pp. 731–743). Los Angeles, CA: Sage.

Pope, R. L., & Reynolds, A. L. (1997). Student affairs core competencies: Integrating multicultural awareness, knowledge, and skills. *Journal of College Student Development, 38*(3), 266–277.

Quintana, S. (2007). Racial and ethnic identity: Developmental perspectives and research. *Journal of Counseling Psychology, 54*(3), 259–270.

Rankin, S. R. (2005). Campus climates for sexual minorities. In R. L. Sanlo (Ed.), *Gender identity and sexual orientation: Research, policy, and personal perspectives* (pp. 17–24). San Francisco, CA: Jossey-Bass.

Raybon, P. (1996). *My first White friend: Confessions on race, love, and forgiveness.* New York, NY: Penguin Books.

Renn, K. A. (2008). Research on biracial and multiracial identity development: Overview and synthesis. *New Directions for Student Services* (123), 13–21.

Roberts, L. (2009, October 11). Have wheelchair, will travel: Disabled students study abroad, too. *The Chronicle of Higher Education.* Retrieved from http://chronicle.com/article/Students-With-Disability-St/48740/

Root, M. P. P. (2003). Racial identity development and persons of mixed race heritage. In M. P. P. Root & M. Kelley (Eds.), *Multiracial child resource book: Living complex identities* (pp. 34–41). Seattle, WA: Mavin Foundation.

Rosenthal, E. (2006, October 8). Violence against women "common" worldwide. *Patriot News*, A20.

Sanford, N. (1966). *Self and society.* New York, NY: Atherton Press.

Sax, L. J. (2007, September 28). College women still face many obstacles in reaching their full potential. *The Chronicle of Higher Education, 54*(4), B46.

Sax, L., & Arms, A. (2008). Gender differences over the span of college. *Journal About Women in Higher Education, 1,* 23–48.

Schmidt, P. (2010, July 11). Supreme Court upholds campus anti-bias policy, but questions linger. *The Chronicle of Higher Education.* Retrieved from http://chronicle.com/article/Supreme-Courts-Ruling-in/66217/

Schwartz, J. L., Donovan, J., & Guido-DiBrito, F. (2009). Stories of social class: Self-identified Mexican male college students crack the silence. *Journal of College Student Development, 50*(1), 50–66.

Stamm, L. (2006). The dynamics of spirituality and the religious experience. In A. E. Chickering, J. C. Dalton, & L. Stamm (Eds.), *Encouraging authenticity and spirituality in higher education* (pp. 37–65). San Francisco, CA: Jossey Bass.

Sue, D. W., Ivey, A. E., & Pedersen, P. B. (1996). *A theory of multicultural counseling and therapy.* Pacific Grove, CA: Brooks/Cole.

Tatum, B. D. (1997). *"Why are all the Black kids sitting together in the cafeteria?" And other conversations about race.* New York, NY: Basic Books.

Torres, V. (1999). Validation of a bicultural orientation model for Hispanic college students. *Journal of College Student Development, 40*(3), 285–299.

Torres, V. (2003, May–June). *Mi casa* is not exactly like your house. *About Campus, 8*(2), 2–7.

Torres, V. (2004a). The diversity among us: Puerto Ricans, Cubans, Caribbean, Central and South Americans. In A. M. Ortiz (Eds.), *Addressing unique needs of Latino Students.* (New Directions for Student Services No. 105, pp. 5–16). San Francisco, CA: Jossey-Bass.

Torres, V., & Bitsói, L. (2011). American Indians in college. In M. Cuyjet, M. F. Howard-Hamilton, & D. L. Cooper (Eds.), *Multiculturalism on campus* (pp. 169–190). Sterling, VA: Stylus.

Torres, V., & Delgado-Romero, E. (2008). Defining Latino/a identity through late adolescent development. In K. L. Kraus (Ed.), *Lifespan development theories in action: A case study approach for counseling professionals* (pp. 363–388). Boston, MA: Lahaska Press.

Torres, V., & Hernandez, E. (2007). The influence of ethnic identity on self-authorship: A longitudinal study of Latino/a college students. *Journal of College Student Development, 48*(5), 558–573.

Torres, V., Howard-Hamilton, M., & Cooper, D. L. (2003). Identity development of diverse populations: Implications for teaching and practice. *ASHE/ERIC Higher Education Report, 29*(6).

Vander Putten, J. (2001, November–December). Bringing social class to the diversity challenge. *About Campus, 6*(5), 14–19.

Vasquez, M. J. T. (2010). Ethics in multicultural counseling practice. In J. G. Ponterotto, J. M. Casas, L. A. Suzuki, & C. M. Alexander (Eds.), *Handbook of multicultural counseling* (3rd ed., pp. 127–146). Los Angeles, CA: Sage.

Wald, K. D., Owen, D. E., & Hill, S. S. (1988). Churches as political communities. *American Political Science Review, 82*, 531–548.

Whitmire, R. (2007, July 7). The latest way to discriminate against women. *The Chronicle of Higher Education, 53*(46), B16. Retrieved from http://chronicle.com/article/The-Latest-Way-to-Discrimin/34773/%20Volume%2053,%20Issue%2046,%20Page%20B16

Wilson, R. (2006, November 3). Report assails professors' liberalism. *The Chronicle of Higher Education.* Retrieved from http://chronicle.com/article/Report-Assails-Professors-/7697/

Wing, L., & Rifkin, J. (2001). Racial identity development and the mediation of conflicts. In C. L. Wijeyesinghe & B. W. Jackson, III (Eds.), *New perspectives on racial identity development: A theoretical and practical anthology* (pp. 182–208). New York: New York University Press.

3

Historical Context

Who We Were Is Part of Who We Are

John A. Mueller and Ellen M. Broido

MEMBERS OF THE College Student Educators International (ACPA) convention planning team developed a marketing campaign for an upcoming convention that unwittingly connected the logo "What's brewing?" with the host city, Boston. Further connecting the logo to the host city was the conference theme that featured the word *revolutionary*. Almost immediately, members of the association brought their concerns about the theme and the related marketing to the attention of the convention planners, arguing that linking the words *Boston*, *brewing*, and *revolution* suggested the Boston Tea Party, whether or not it was intended. Members and allies of the Native American community in ACPA found the theme offensive. The reason? The theme and the marketing raised concerns about the historical misrepresentation of Native Americans because the colonists had dressed up as members of the Mohawk Nation in a direct attempt to blame Native people for dumping shiploads of tea into Boston Harbor. This issue with the conference, though eventually resolved, serves as a reminder of the importance of knowing and appreciating the depth and breadth of our nation's history and the power it has to inform and shape our perceptions (or misperceptions) and our understanding (or lack thereof) of today's decisions, values, and assumptions.

Often, when issues or events are discussed in student affairs literature, a historical context is provided. While these historical contexts are comprehensive, detailed, and quite informative, it sometimes appears that each is provided as a perfunctory preface to the discussion at hand. At other times, the historical context seems to suggest that the cause of what educators see today (the effect) is clearer once it is traced to its roots (the cause). But discussions of diversity, access, inclusion, and multiculturalism are not easily (or appropriately) framed as cause and effect. These issues are simply too complex with many variables, layers, and dimensions. A historical context can honor this complexity by focusing on events, individuals, and prevailing perspectives that surround the topic of discussion. Context helps us understand the importance of an issue, its structure, and its contours (Belanger, 2006).

Crucial to presenting a historical context, particularly on diversity and inclusion in higher education, is conceding to the cautionary note from Bowen, Kurzweil, and Tobin (2005) to be mindful of the assumption that our history portrays the continuous progression of increasing opportunity and equity. These scholars contend that examining each succeeding decade in our history "is more like observing someone taking a step forward and step backward than it is like watching a steady sequence of forward moving giant steps" (p. 14). Therefore, while on the surface this history may appear even and linear in its presentation, it is actually multilayered with progress and setbacks that cannot be fully explored within the boundaries of this chapter. Still, much is revealed about our society and our profession as we examine the evolution of—as well as the lessons learned with respect to—diversity and inclusion in high education.

In this chapter we place the concepts of diversity, access, and inclusion in higher education in their historical context. First, we examine the advances and challenges of inclusion of an array of historically marginalized constituency groups based on gender, race, sexual orientation, religion, and class, tracing their participation in higher education from its earliest days through later decades. This overview lays the foundation for considering the evolving definition of diversity over the history of higher education. Finally, we integrate the history of inclusion and the evolution of diversity in higher education and address what we have learned from this historical context, noting that this integration is central to approaching open and challenging dialogues about diversity and inclusion.

HISTORICAL CONTEXT

Beginning with the founding of Harvard in 1636, higher education in what would become the United States was designed to educate the leaders of an emerging nation. Although the primary focus was on training clergy, from the beginning universities also trained future lawyers, teachers, doctors, and government leaders (Newcomer, 1959; Thelin, 2004). The founders of the nine colonial colleges still in operation in 1959 "would probably have scoffed if anyone had predicted that by mid-twentieth century eight of the nine . . . would be admitting women to some or all of their courses of instruction" (Newcomer, p. 6). One can only imagine their shock had they known that by the mid-1980s all their colleges would enroll roughly equal numbers of women and men in their undergraduate programs, or that people of color, immigrants, gay men and lesbians, and non-Protestants would make up significant percentages of their student bodies. In this section of the chapter, we present a concise overview of the history of groups who were far from the colonial college founders' conception of who should be educated. While trying to be as inclusive as possible, space constraints and significant gaps in the historical record keep this from being complete. However, we do our best to trace the social conditions and activism that led to the expansion of access to education, the extent and consequences of accommodation for different groups, and the limited inroads to full inclusion that have occurred.

Women

While they may have been lone voices in the wilderness, calls for the education of women date to the colonial years of the United States. White women in the New England colonies were required to learn to read, and some were taught to write, especially as merchant trade developed and families began to run small businesses from home (Newcomer, 1959; Solomon, 1985). Still, before the Revolutionary War, education for White women was informal, usually based in the home or in "dame schools," and there was no consideration of formal higher education for women, even those who showed exceptional achievement in the sciences and languages. Circumstances began to change with the founding of a nation in which all property-owning White men were potential voters. Literacy for all Whites became a national interest; men benefitted directly from formal education, and formally educated women were needed to further the education of their sons (Solomon).

In the late 1700s and into the 1800s affluent White women often were educated either at home or in private academies and seminaries. It was not unusual for these women to receive greater education in science, history, and modern languages than did their male counterparts, who were being educated in more classical curricula (Newcomer, 1959). Women first enrolled in a U.S. college in 1837 at Oberlin (Newcomer), and over the next 20 years a small number of public and private universities began to admit women, albeit in very small numbers. Sometimes women enrolled and took classes with men, and sometimes freestanding women's colleges with an affiliation to a men's college or women's divisions of universities were established. College-level institutions for women developed quickly, primarily in the South and in New England, and "by 1860, there were approximately 100 women's colleges in existence, about half of which offered a collegiate level curriculum" (Wolf-Wendel, 2002, p. 62), although Thelin (2004) estimated the number to be only 14.

Profound social changes during and following the Civil War fundamentally altered the educational opportunities available to women. With women having to fill in the positions vacated by men fighting in the war and taking on new roles during the war, women's and some men's beliefs about women's capabilities changed. The great numbers of men killed, and the postwar migration of men to the West, meant that many women had limited marriage prospects and had to find ways to support themselves. Finally, with the rapid postwar expansion of higher education, and fewer young men available, women became a potential source of revenue for colleges (Newcomer, 1959; Nidiffer, 2002; Solomon, 1985; Wolf-Wendel, 2002).

While most women attending college in the 1800s were affluent, a growing need for women elementary school teachers (preferred because they could be paid less than men) meant there was some public subsidy for public secondary education. Thus, more women (Black and White) than before were gaining an education that would enable them to consider college (Newcomer, 1959). Moreover, the rapidly increasing demand for primary and secondary education for men, necessitated by a need for an educated citizenry, heightened the demand for teachers, who increasingly were women.

According to the first comprehensive set of statistics on education in the United States in 1870, roughly 11,000 women were attending college, making up about 25% of enrolled students and earning about 15% of bachelor's degrees (Newcomer, 1959). Ten years later about 20,000 women were in college, making up a third of enrolled students (Wolf-Wendel, 2002). The two Morrill Act bills of 1862 and 1890 (officially named the Agricultural College Act of 1890) established public land-grant universities, all of which were coeducational. While the growth of coeducation exceeded the development of private women's colleges, the 1870s were the height of the development of women's colleges.

Still, this progress for women's higher education must be viewed against a society whose members still believed women's minds were inferior to those of men, and women who did indeed match or surpass their male colleagues could do so only because they had "men's" minds (Newcomer, 1959). In addition to believing women were intellectually inferior to men, other objections to their higher education attendance were common. College was thought to be too physically taxing for women, harming their brains and their future ability to bear children (Nidiffer, 2002). A number of additional arguments against coeducation were raised, although in these cases "most of the opposition was less concerned with whether education was good for women than whether educated women were acceptable to men" (Newcomer, p. 31).

Despite these obstacles, "between 1890 and 1910, enrollment at women's colleges increased by 348 percent [while] female matriculation at coeducational colleges rose 438 percent" (Wolf-Wendel, 2002, p. 63), growth rates that exceeded men's 214% increase. "By the turn of the twentieth century, coeducation had become the norm for women" (p. 63), with more than 70% of women in coeducational institutions by 1910 (Nidiffer, 2002). Women's experiences on coeducational campuses were hardly parallel to those of men; they were segregated in classes, denied scholarship funding, excluded from campus housing and gymnasiums, subjected to ridicule, ignored by faculty, and excluded from most extracurricular activities (Nidiffer; Thelin, 2004). Nonetheless, women were receiving honors and awards at such high rates "it prompted some universities to impose limits on the numbers of honors women were eligible to earn" (Nidiffer, p. 11).

The 1920s marked a high point for women's presence and success in American higher education. During this decade they made up almost half of the undergraduate enrollment (Nidiffer, 2002). "By 1930, almost a third of all college presidents and professors were women" (Lucas, 2006, p. 214). This demographic spike did not tell the whole story, however. Women faculty routinely were paid less than men, tenured less often, and promoted more slowly (Lucas).

Reflecting societal trends that pushed women back to more conventional roles, later decades had less participation by women, with women making up only about 32% of college enrollment in 1950 (Thelin, 2004) and rising only to 35% in 1958 (Newcomer, 1959). While women took far greater advantage of the GI Bill (Servicemen's Readjustment Act of 1944) educational benefits than did their male counterparts, this did not lead to gender parity on campus. About 30% of eligible women used these benefits, compared to about 18% of eligible men. However, because of the far greater pool of eligible men, campuses shifted from close to equal enrollment before World War II (in 1939–1940 women made up 40% of undergraduates) to being overwhelmingly male in the postwar years. This shift in the participation rate was exacerbated in traditionally masculine fields like engineering and business, with large declines in women's enrollment in these majors during the 1950s (Thelin, 2004), whereas earlier they had been closer to equal.

Women in graduate programs had the same patterns. In 1920 women had earned one in six doctorates, but in 1956 the number had declined to less than one in ten. Absolute numbers of women earning the doctorate increased, as did the proportion of women in given age groups attending college, but these increases were dwarfed by the increase in men's enrollment, making women's overall share of degrees much smaller (Newcomer, 1959).

The past 50 years have seen massive growth in women's enrollment at all levels of higher education. In 1991 more women than men in the 25–29 age group had bachelor's degrees. "In 2001, women accounted for 43 percent of all MDs, 47 percent of all law degrees, and 41 percent of master's degrees in business" (Bowen et al., 2005, p. 44).

Three pieces of federal legislation—the Fourteenth Amendment to the Constitution, the 1964 Civil Rights Act, and Title IX of the Educational Amendments of 1972—greatly influenced the experiences of women in higher education. In particular, Title IX prohibited discrimination or exclusion from participation on the basis of sex in any program receiving federal funding. While it passed with little controversy, regulations for its implementation took three years to develop, and higher education institutions often have implemented it with a distinct lack of fervor (Somers, 2002). Title IX was most effective in removing gender as an admission criterion (particularly in military programs), preventing discrimination against pregnant students, providing an avenue to address sexual harassment (for women and men), and pushing institutions to move toward parity of funding for women's athletic programs. These benefits have been hard fought, usually in the courts, but have created campus climates in which at least blatant discrimination against women can be addressed (Somers).

While issues of access for women students seem to have been resolved, campus climates still present challenges for women as students, faculty, and staff (Guido-DiBrito, 2002). Estimates of the prevalence of sexual harassment of undergraduate students range from 50% to 70% (Guido-DiBrito). Perhaps the most explicit account of what women face was presented in Hall and Sandler's 1984 report, *Out of the Classroom: A Chilly Campus Climate for Women.* They identified double standards of appropriate behavior for women and men, expectations that women take on nurturing and support roles rather than formal leadership positions, and women being assessed on their looks and dress rather than their skills.

Opportunities for women in higher education have ebbed and flowed, allowing women entrance when society allows. The concern that too many women are currently enrolled has led to some admissions officers' admitting less qualified men. Whitmire (2007) called this the "latest way to discriminate against women" (p. B16).

Asian Americans

The scholarly literature on Asian Americans in U.S. higher education almost never covers history before the 1970s, and more often begins in the 1980s (with the notable exception of Austin's 2004 research on the experiences of Japanese American collegians in the internment camps of World War II). Asian Americans are not listed in the index of three major histories of U.S. higher education written by Lucas (2006), Rudolph (1990), and Thelin (2004). Bits and pieces of that history can be reconstructed from more global histories of Asians and Asian Americans in the United States. The gap in the history of higher education reflects an issue that continues to face Asian Americans in higher education: the presumption that their experiences are neither fully minority nor majority, making their experiences invisible. Asian

Americans had relatively limited representation in the United States prior to the 1965 Immigration and Naturalization Act, but rapid growth has occurred in the last 30 years.

A number of laws passed in the late 1800s restricted entry into the United States by people from China, followed in 1908 by prohibiting the immigration of Japanese. Further restrictions against Asian immigrants were enacted in 1917 and again in 1924 (Asian Pacific Americans and Immigration Law, 2010). In several of these laws, exemptions were provided for students, but they severely restricted the numbers of Asians who were able to begin their lives in the United States. These restrictions meant that from the 1920s until the late 1960s, Asian Americans (in particular, Chinese and Japanese Americans) were far more likely to be second- or third-generation Americans than immigrants.

Records exist of Chinese students coming to the United States to receive a university education as early as 1854, when the first Chinese student graduated from Yale (Daniels, 1988). According to Alegado, between 1903 and 1910, "more than 200 Filipino students, 8 of whom were women" enrolled at leading U.S. universities (as cited in *Pensionado Women*, n.d.). In the early 1900s, those few Chinese allowed into the United States to attend college often were imprisoned for weeks upon entry (Daniels). Eventually some Chinese and Japanese Americans were allowed to attend U.S. universities. Still, they faced limited vocational opportunities, tending to find jobs only within their own communities, even with graduate and professional degrees (Daniels).

In 1941 about 3,500 Japanese American students were enrolled in higher education in the United States, virtually all of them on the West Coast, and, like other Japanese Americans living on the West Coast, were incarcerated in internment camps (Austin, 2004). Although most of these students were soon thereafter "resettled" at "inland" (Daniels, 1988, p. 243) institutions, many were unable to leave because of their desire to remain with family in the camps, lack of access to funds, inability to obtain travel permits, and a host of other challenges (Austin; Daniels).

Enrollment in higher education for Asian Americans as a group is strong, with Asians making up 8.5% of undergraduate students in the fall of 2010 and 8.3% of domestic doctoral students in 2008–2009 (*The Chronicle of Higher Education*, 2011). However, these figures hide vast disparities in educational access and attainment in the Asian American community, where recent immigrants fare far worse than Asian Americans whose families have lived in the United States for multiple generations (Chang & Kiang, 2002), and far worse than the post-1965 immigrants from China, India, Korea, and the Philippines who were allowed entry if they were professionals in fields with labor shortages in the United States. For example, in 1990 poverty rates among South Asian Americans (Vietnamese Americans, Hmong Americans, Cambodian Americans, and Laotian Americans) and Pacific Island Americans ranged between 17.7% and 63.6% (Park & Teranishi, 2008), versus 9.2% for Whites and 13.1% for the nation as a whole (Chang & Kiang). These immigrants had college degrees at rates (between 5.1% and 13.8%) closer to, and sometimes lower than, African Americans and Latino/Latina Americans to whom they were similar in socioeconomic status (Nakanishi, 2002). To address these economic and educational disparities, institutional efforts dating from the late 1990s continue to obtain the federal designation of Asian American– and Pacific Islander–serving institutions (Park & Teranishi, 2008) and thus to receive the same federal funding provided to designated historically Black colleges and universities (HBCUs) and Hispanic-serving institutions (HSIs).

Perceptions of Asian Americans as the *model minority* (i.e., academically successful, wealthy, compliant, uncomplaining, and problem free) overlook the ways they are still perceived as racial beings (Chang & Kiang, 2002). Chang and Kiang noted, "While many Asian American high school students receive 4.0 grade point averages, graduate as valedictorians, and enroll at Harvard or Stanford, even more barely pass high school, enroll at local community colleges, or never participate in postsecondary institutions" (p. 145). Those who make it to college experience levels of discrimination and harassment far exceeding that of their White peers and similar to those of their Black and Latino classmates (Suarez-Balcazar, Orellana-Damacela, Portillo, Rowan, & Andrews-Guillen, 2003).

Asian Americans have been compared to and placed in competition with Latino/Latina and African American students on several fronts. In particular, Asian Americans are labeled a model minority with the implied (and sometimes explicit) argument that if one racial minority group can obtain educational and economic success, the reason others do not is their own lack of effort, not structural racism. Additionally, Asian Americans have been presumed to oppose Affirmative Action policies, under the assumption that Asian American admissions at elite universities have been restricted to allow for greater numbers of African American and Latino/Latina students (Ng, Lee, & Pak, 2007). At the same time, Asian American students have been portrayed as "foreign and the yellow peril taking over campuses" whose enrollment needed to be restricted "because they did not contribute to diversity because they were all the same" (Ng et al., p. 110).

To gain an accurate perspective of the historical context of Asians and Asian Americans in higher education, one must look across nationalities and generations. Generalized data hide the nuanced experiences of members of this diverse group.

Latinos/Latinas

As with Asian Americans, minimal written history exists about Latinos/Latinas in U.S. higher education. This problem is heightened by a lack of accurate statistical data, given that no consistent definition of Hispanic existed until the late 1970s (MacDonald & Garcia, 2003). Thus, much of the following history is based upon using Spanish family names as a proxy for a Latino/Latina or Hispanic identity.

What is now the southwestern United States (Arizona, Colorado, New Mexico, Texas, and California) became a part of this country in 1848 at the conclusion of the Mexican-American War. Higher education in this area began 20 years later with the founding of the University of California in 1868. No laws restricted Latinos/Latinas from higher education, and two Latino students enrolled in the University of California immediately, apparently the only Hispanics at the University of California until the 1960s (MacDonald & Garcia, 2003). A Mexican American student graduated from the University of Texas in 1894, nine years after the university enrolled its first students, and in 1928 just over 1% of students there had Hispanic surnames. MacDonald and Garcia speculated that enrollment of Latinos/Latinas was higher in Arizona, New Mexico, and Colorado because Latinos/Latinas there were more affluent and politically powerful (as descendants of Spaniards rather than Native peoples). Indeed, in 1886 the University of Arizona had one Latino member on its first board of trustees (MacDonald & Garcia).

In contrast to exceedingly limited enrollment in public universities, Latino/Latina students were a strong presence at the many Catholic colleges founded in the Southwest following the Mexican-American War, for which

Spanish-speaking students were actively recruited (MacDonald & Garcia, 2003). One women's college offered courses in English and Spanish, and "even report cards and bills were printed in Spanish" (MacDonald & Garcia, p. 22). As a whole, however, Latinos/Latinas had little access to higher education in the Southwest. Multiple factors made earning an education in preparation to attend a university difficult: Primary and secondary schools were taught only in English, forcing out most Latino/Latina students long before they were ready for college; students faced discrimination; and those whose families were migrant workers moved often (Olivas, 1989).

The acquisition of Puerto Rico as a territory of the United States in 1898 at the close of the Spanish-American War marks a decidedly different aspect of the history of the higher education of Latinos/Latinas in the United States. Almost immediately, the University of Puerto Rico was founded with a focus on teacher training. Additionally, the U.S. government sent a few Puerto Rican students to colleges on the mainland, almost all of them restricted by statute to HBCUs with an industrial/agricultural focus. A select few were sent to elite universities for training to govern the new colony (MacDonald & Garcia, 2003).

The many Puerto Ricans who moved to the mainland in the 1930s through 1950s rarely attended colleges or universities. Public schools were taught only in English, and Puerto Rican students were often kept behind their grade level or placed in remedial courses. Not surprisingly, few had the opportunity or encouragement to complete the requirements for college entrance (MacDonald & Garcia, 2003).

From the late 1920s through the years following World War II, Latinos/Latinas enrolled in higher education in numbers sufficient in some places to start their own student organizations and newspapers (MacDonald & Garcia, 2003). The extent of enrollment remains unknown but likely was concentrated in the Southwest, New York, and Chicago. MacDonald and Garcia attributed this small growth in Latino/Latina enrollment to encouragement from Latino/Latina youth organizations, individual mentors, community foundations in the Latino/Latina community, and the GI Bill.

The 1960s and 1970s saw an explosive growth in Latino/Latina American enrollment (although Latino/Latina students remained heavily clustered in community colleges) and in Latino/Latina student activism. Latino/Latina students formed numerous organizations that spanned institutional boundaries, advocating for increased Latino/Latina enrollment, culturally relevant curricula and scholarship on Latino/Latina issues from a Latino/Latina perspective, and services to support retention. Some of these groups merged in 1969 to form Movimiento Estudiantil Chicano de Aztlán (n.d.), which is still active on many campuses. Similar activism among Puerto Rican and African American college students in New York City led the City University of New York to move to an open admissions policy in the early 1970s, more than tripling the numbers of Puerto Rican students. Protests in other urban centers led to the founding of Chicano and Boricua (Puerto Rican) studies programs and student centers (MacDonald & Garcia, 2003), as well as the establishment of Hostos Community College, "the first historically Puerto Rican college to be established in the continental United States" (Olivas, 1989, p. 565).

In 1973 the U.S. government classified Hispanics as a single panethnic group rather than many different peoples. While a great deal of cultural variation is lost in this agglomeration, and the controversy over it has continued from its first use in 1973 until today, it "signaled unprecedented recognition and attention" (MacDonald & Garcia, 2003, p. 34) and made it possible to evaluate the progress of Latino/Latina students.

The Higher Education Act of 1965 recognized HSIs, degree-granting colleges and universities with at least 25% Hispanic enrollment, although that definition was revised in 1998 to specify that at least 50% of Hispanic students must come from below the poverty line (Gasman, 2008). Only three universities were founded specifically to serve Hispanic students, "all established as a result of the Civil Rights Movement in the 1960s and 1970s" (Gasman, p. 23), meaning that most HSIs do not have, or did not have at their founding, an explicit mission to educate Latino/Latina students. HSIs are growing rapidly with the expansion of the Latino/Latina population in the United States, and their original concentration in urban areas is expanding as they become more geographically dispersed (Gasman). HSIs include public and private institutions as well as two- and four-year institutions.

While the previous discussion focuses on Chicano and Puerto Rican college access, the demographic portrait of the Latino/Latina community is far more diverse. Chicanos and Puerto Ricans still constitute the majority of Latinos/Latinas in the United States today (roughly 60% and 10% of the Latino/Latina population; Torres, 2004). The remaining 30% includes immigrants and their descendants from across the Caribbean, Central America, and South America who arrived in the United States for varied reasons (e.g., economic opportunity, political asylum, to escape war), have a variety of educational and economic resources, and came at different points in time.

In closing this section, it should be noted that a significant enrollment gap remains between Latino/Latina students and White students. "In 2001, around 65 percent of white 16- to 24-year-olds had enrolled in college compared to . . . just under 50 percent of Hispanics of the same age" (Bowen et al., 2005, pp. 75–76). Latinos/Latinas who do enroll in college do so disproportionately at community colleges (MacDonald & Garcia, 2003). Still, Latino/Latina's proportional enrollment in higher education almost tripled between 1976 and 2007, growing from 4% of the college-going population to 11% (NCES, 2009, p. 2).

Native Americans

As B. Wright (2002) so clearly noted, the primary goal of British (and European) colonization was the conversion of Native peoples to Christianity. It is no surprise then that the early colonial colleges that accepted Native American students did so for the purpose of cultural assimilation (American Indian Higher Education Consortium, 2000; Institute for Higher Education Policy [IHEP], 2007) and conversion—to raise funds from European donors interested in converting "heathens," rather than for the educational goals of Native people (Carney, 1999). Many people may be surprised that "three of the nine original colonial colleges included educating Native Americans in their original statements of purpose or mission" (McClellan, Tippeconnic Fox, & Lowe, 2005, p. 8); perhaps more telling of the educational environment at those colleges is that only 4 of the 47 Native Americans who enrolled in higher education before the Revolutionary War actually graduated (McClellan et al.). Over the course of numerous treaties between the newly formed U.S. government and Native American nations, what little attention that was given to the education of Native Americans was focused primarily on vocational education (Carney), with the goal of "lower-echelon assimilation . . . [with] a minimum level of funding provided for Indian students to attend eastern colleges" (p. 50).

As with other preparatory schools and academies that evolved into colleges and universities during the 1800s, many primary and secondary schools whose original purpose was the education of Native Americans grew into colleges. However, with this evolution came increasing need for revenue, almost invariably leading to an expansion of the colleges' missions to include educating White students and then to lessening, if not discarding, their original missions of educating Native American students. In fact, "none evolved into exclusively Native American colleges" (Carney, 1999, p. 82). Only two universities exist today that were founded to serve Native Americans: Bacone College and Pembroke University (now the University of North Carolina at Pembroke) (Carney; McClellen et al., 2005).

While Native American students attend most types of higher education institutions in the United States, a disproportionate number are educated at tribal colleges and universities (TCUs), which have developed over the last 30 years "as institutions of higher learning created by American Indians for American Indians" (IHEP, 2007, p. 8). They were created as part of the American Indian Movement, an effort for self-determination among U.S. Native people. Most TCUs are community colleges, offering two-year degrees with a focus on the needs of the local communities. They serve multiple functions, including "preserving native cultures, traditions, and languages" (p. 15), providing education to "geographically isolated tribal communities" (p. 8), and developing economic opportunity as well as preparing students for transfer to four-year institutions and for the workforce.

Despite doubling enrollment in higher education between 1976 and 2002, Native American enrollment in and completion of higher education still lags behind all other racial/cultural groups in the United States (IHEP, 2007; Ogunwole, 2006). Though TCUs now offer a means for cultural preservation, the low enrollment of American Indians in higher education perpetuates the cultural xenophobia that began hundreds of years ago.

African Americans

Even during slavery, some African Americans were able to obtain an education. Holmes (1934/1969) wrote that "a considerable number of persons of color received academic instruction in varying degrees, ranging from the rudiments of reading and writing to skill in . . . foreign languages and mathematics" (p. 8). Only with the slave rebellions of the early 1800s, led by people who could read and write, were laws passed in the South "forbidding the instruction of Negroes in reading, writing, and arithmetic" (p. 10). In some states those laws applied to all African Americans, in others only to slaves (Holmes). This meant that by the time of the Civil War, while there were educated African Americans in the South, their numbers were few.

The first known Black graduate of a U.S. institution of higher education earned his degree in 1823 from Middlebury College, followed by two students in 1826 at Amherst College and Bowdoin College ("Timeline of Affirmative Action," 2007). From its founding in 1833 Oberlin College enrolled African American women and men as well as White women (and men), and by 1861 "several white institutions were admitting Negro women and men" (Noble, 1956, p. 19). A small number of colleges for African Americans were founded in the North between the late 1840s and the beginning of the Civil War (Drewry & Doermann, 2001; Lucas, 2006). Despite these options, there is no evidence of more than 28 African Americans receiving bachelor's degrees in the United States before the Emancipation Proclamation in 1863 (Drewry & Doermann; Lucas).

Following the Civil War, a number of private colleges for African Americans were founded in the South. Like most early colleges in the United States, these included primary and secondary education as well as truly collegiate divisions, with far greater enrollment in the preparatory divisions (Holmes, 1934/1969). Still, these private colleges were the primary source of higher education for Blacks in the South. More than their private counterparts, however, the 23 publicly funded Black colleges in the South (by 1915) were "colleges or normal schools in name only" (Anderson, 1988, p. 238).

The private colleges were funded by three major sources: White northern missionary groups, whose "goals in establishing these colleges were to Christianize the freedmen . . . and to rid the country of the 'menace' of uneducated African Americans" (Gasman, 2008, p. 19); Black religious organizations; and beginning in the 1880s, White northern industrialists wanting to create a low-wage workforce with the skills the industrialists desired (Holmes, 1934/1969). Many of these colleges had a focus on agricultural and industrial education (as did many other institutions whose students were poor or immigrant), because of the desires of funders and because of a common sentiment that practical education would best serve Black people's immediate financial needs. This philosophy was "that higher education ought to direct black boys and girls to places in life that were congruent with the South's racial caste system" (Anderson, 1988, p. 248).

However, strong challenges to these vocationally focused institutions arose from within the Black community by individuals, primarily from Black missionary societies (Anderson, 1988), who favored a liberal arts curriculum and standards of the best White universities (Drewry & Doermann, 2001). This push led to the development of Black universities whose focus was on the education of the "talented tenth" (DuBois, 2011), the academic elite of the African American community, who would "become the leaders of their people" (Anderson, p. 241) in political and civic life.

This split between practical and classical education played out even more markedly for African American women. While almost all Black colleges were coeducational, women students were being prepared for lives as homemakers and teachers. Curricula had a heavy focus on morality, and Black women college students' behavior was highly regulated, more so than that of their White female peers or their Black male classmates. Noble (1956) wrote:

> It appears that many of the Negro women's rules and regulations may possibly have been predicated on reasons relating to her foremother's sex role as a slave. Overnight she was to so live that by her ideal behavior the sins of her foremother's [sic] might be blotted out. Her education in many instances appears to have been based on a philosophy that implied that she was weak and immoral and that at best she should be made fit to rear her children and keep house for her husband. (p. 24)

Public higher education for African Americans was greatly influenced by the passage of the second Morrill Act in 1890 (Agricultural Act of 1890), which provided opportunities for Blacks to be educated at universities receiving land-grant funds. However, this legislation left the states with the option of providing integrated universities or setting up separate segregated universities, which all southern and border states did, leading to the existence of 17 states with two land-grant institutions. While the provision of the 1890 Morrill Act called for equal funding in states with dual systems, in reality, Black universities typically received only about two thirds of the funding that new White universities did (Holmes, 1934/1969).

In 1896 the U.S. Supreme Court heard the case of *Plessy v. Ferguson*. Although the case was about the constitutionality of segregated transportation, the court's findings that separate but equal facilities did not violate the Fourteenth Amendment's guarantee of equal privileges of citizenship were subsequently applied to higher education. One consequence of the *Plessy v. Ferguson* decision was *Berea College v. Commonwealth of Kentucky* (1908), which had educated Black and White students together since its founding in 1859. Kentucky had enacted "a law requiring segregation in all state schools, both public and private" (Drewry & Doermann, 2001, p. 21). The case went to the U.S. Supreme Court, which found for Kentucky, "permitting states to outlaw voluntary as well as obligatory contact between the races" (Drewry & Doermann, p. 21) across the country.

These legal decisions only codified what was already happening in practice. "In 1899–1900, no more than eighty-eight blacks were awarded degrees from white colleges (most of them from Oberlin) and there were an estimated 475 graduated from predominantly black colleges" (Lucas, 2006, p. 215). At the turn of the 20th century, southern schools attended by Black students were overwhelmingly private (Anderson, 1988). In 1915 only 1 of the 12 Black land-grant colleges, Florida A&M, actually taught college-level courses, and it enrolled only 12 students (Drewry & Doermann, 2001; Lucas). Another 40 Black students attended Black public universities established outside the land-grant program (Drewry & Doermann). The private institutions were economically marginal and struggling but offered the only opportunity most African Americans had for a substantial higher education curriculum.

In 1910 "at least 5 percent of all whites aged 18 to 21 were attending college; the figure for blacks stood at less than one-third of 1 percent" (Lucas, 2006, p. 216). By 1950, 5.18% of White Americans over 14 years old had completed four or more years of college, while 1.71% of African Americans had. However, for African American women that value was 1.94%, still far behind their White women counterparts, of whom 4.44% had completed college. This number far surpassed that of Black men, only 1.49% of whom had completed college (calculations based on raw data in Noble, 1956). African American women also earned more master's degrees than men, but not doctorates (Noble). Noble provided several hypotheses for why Black women were more educated than Black men when the reverse was true for White women. In particular, she pointed out that while White women had occupational choices of moderate income that did not require a college degree, such as sales clerks and secretaries, Black women were barred from those jobs. The only jobs above menial and domestic labor open to African American women were teaching positions, and in the 20th century, these increasingly required bachelor's degrees and sometimes master's degrees.

Funding for public Black colleges slowly increased, as did their enroll-ment. Still, Black Americans were for the most part restricted to Black uni-versities. Even in the mid-1930s almost all Blacks were attending Black universities, either public or private. African American students attending White universities in most cases faced social isolation and discrimination from fellow students and from faculty members and the administration. For example, in 1912, President Abbot Lawrence Lowell of Harvard, known for his elitism and favoritism of wealthy White Protestants, removed Black stu-dents from housing at Harvard, despite official university policy that "no one was to be excluded 'by reason of his color'" (Lucas, 2006, p. 217), because he believed they made the White students uncomfortable.

Leadership at Black universities, and most faculty positions, remained White, with most institutions appointing their first Black presidents in the 1940s and 1950s (the first was in 1906), long after sufficient numbers of highly educated African Americans qualified for those positions. These prac-tices were particularly evident at institutions still receiving funding from White philanthropists who generally appointed White trustees (Drewry & Doermann, 2001) and continued their emphasis on preparing workers for their industries and leaders within the Black community who would encour-age the acceptance of a lesser status for African Americans.

In the 1920s, to ensure funding from prominent northern industrialists, the president of Fisk, one of the leading elite Black universities, "attempted to repress student initiative, undermine their equalitarian spirit, and control their thinking on race relations so as to produce a class of black intellectuals that would uncomplainingly accept the southern racial hierarchy" (Ander-son, 1988, p. 268). These policies created a powerful response. Protests by students, alumni, and the local Black community led to the president's ouster a year later. While northern philanthropists continued their support of major Black universities that had long focused on vocational education, change happened in these universities as well. As southern states began to require teachers to have bachelor's degrees, these universities phased out their primary and secondary education programs and enrolled greater numbers of collegiate-level students. These students took their education seriously and protested the inferior academic skills of their instructors, "specifically reject-ing the Hampton-Tuskegee Idea and its philosophy of manual training and racial subordination" (Anderson, p. 274).

By the 1930s increasing numbers of African Americans were pursuing graduate degrees. However, nine southern states had no graduate programs at their Black universities, and another nine paid for their Black residents to attend graduate programs out of state. In 1938 an African American applied to the University of Missouri's law school and was denied because of his race. The case went to the U.S. Supreme Court, which wrote, "the State was bound to furnish [to African Americans] *within its borders* facilities for . . . education substantially equal to those which the State has afforded to a person of the white race" (Hill, 1985, p. 11). States had the option to either integrate their educational programs or establish separate programs, the latter of which is what happened in most southern states (Hill; Lucas, 2006), although at the graduate level a number did quietly acquiesce to integration (Thelin, 2004).

While the GI Bill is widely credited with expanding access to higher education for working-class veterans of the Second World War, it is less known that it had far fewer benefits for African American veterans. Because of discrimination Black soldiers faced during World War II, they received disproportionate numbers of dishonorable discharges, so they were thus disproportionately ineligible for benefits (Maher & Tetreault, 2007). Vastly disparate levels of funding for Black and White children's education in the South meant that far fewer Black veterans had the academic skills to enroll in higher education (Bowen et al., 2005). Moreover, because awarding benefits most often occurred at the state and local levels, discriminatory practices were legal and existed in many areas (Maher & Tetreault). Black veterans returning to the South were for the most part restricted to Black universities, whose limited economic resources prevented them from being able to meet the demand for those who were academically qualified and who had been able to secure GI benefits. In their analysis of the consequences of the GI Bill, Turner and Bound (cited in Bowen et al., 2005) concluded "the G.I. Bill exacerbated rather than narrowed the economic and educational differences between blacks and whites" (p. 33).

"Prior to the 1950s, black public and private colleges were, with rare exception, the only colleges accessible to black Americans" (Drewry & Doermann, 2001, p. 1), enrolling about 90% of all Black collegians, most studying either teaching or ministry. According to Hill (1985),

> In 1961 black students had been admitted to only 17 percent of public white institutions in the South. By 1965, it is estimated that the traditionally white

colleges enrolled about one-fourth of the black students in the South; by 1970
this had increased to 40 percent. (p. xiii)

Desegregation of southern universities in the two decades following the
Brown v. Board of Education (1954) decision occurred in fits and starts,
often with violent resistance from the universities themselves, most visibly
at the University of Alabama, University of Georgia, and University of
Mississippi. Black students attempting to enroll at these universities were
expelled for "conspiring to aid in rioting" or "disturbing the peace," or
they were sent forcibly to mental hospitals for "lunacy hearings" (Lucas,
2006, p. 261). In other places desegregation was "largely a matter of half-
hearted, token compliance" (Thelin, 2004, p. 304). "Overall only 17 percent of the public white institutions in the South had admitted black
students by 1961" (Hill, 1985, p. 14). The few African American students
managing to enroll in southern White universities experienced overt and
subtle discrimination and isolation, as "segregation and exclusion often
continued in dormitories, dining halls, and classroom seating arrangements" (Thelin, p. 304). Consequently, "black students remained marginal
and proportionately underrepresented at almost all racially desegregated
campuses in the United States" (p. 305).

The Brown decision raised difficult challenges for Black universities, particularly those that were publicly funded. Although the Brown decision was
implemented only very slowly, calls for the closure of public Black universities began by the late 1960s, pointing to their poor facilities, poorly paid
faculty, and low academic standards. Those arguing in favor of closing these
institutions insisted that public funds go to support White universities,
which were, if only nominally, open to all students (Drewry & Doermann,
2001). In response, a few public Black universities closed or merged with
White institutions (U.S. Department of Education Office for Civil Rights,
1991). Advocates of Black colleges and universities pointed out that these
institutions had educated and continued to educate students who had poor
preparation but great ability, that their graduates had made exceptional contributions to social and political movements, and that their graduates earned
advanced degrees in exceptional numbers (Robinson & Albert, 2008). These
arguments continue to the present, with ongoing calls for the closure or
mergers of HBCUs in the South ("Unlikely Backer for Black College
Merger," 2010).

A number of factors have contributed to the tremendous increases in college and graduate school attendance by African Americans over the past 50 years. Vast increases in high school graduation rates, a growing Black middle class, the elimination of legally sanctioned discrimination, the expansion of many forms of financial aid, and Affirmative Action policies all have contributed. Still, a significant enrollment gap remains between African American students and White students. "In 2001, around 65 percent of white 16- to 24-year-olds had enrolled in college compared to about 55 percent of African Americans" (Bowen et al., 2005, p. 75). The fact that African American students with diverse levels of preparation continue to graduate at much higher rates from HBCUs than from predominantly White institutions (PWIs) (Robinson & Albert, 2008) indicates that the climate for Black students at PWIs likely has an adverse impact on their success.

Hence, over 260 years after the Emancipation Proclamation, enrollment and graduation rates of African Americans lag behind those of their White counterparts. Chances of earning a degree are still far greater for African American students at HBCUs than at PWIs.

Students With Disabilities

No comprehensive history of people with disabilities in higher education exists, although surely at least a few disabled veterans from the Civil War must have attended college. The institution now known as Gallaudet University was founded in 1857 as Columbia Institution for the Instruction of the Deaf and Dumb and the Blind (Drezner, 2008), and the institution received authorization to grant bachelor's and master's degrees in 1864 (Gallaudet University, 1997); Gallaudet continues in its mission to serve deaf and hard-of-hearing students today. Possibly the best known early case of collegiate attendance by a person with a disability was Helen Keller, who in 1904 graduated from Radcliffe College (American Federation for the Blind, 2011).

According to Madaus (2000), there was "minimal to non-existent" (p. 5) progress on access to higher education for students with disabilities between the founding of Gallaudet and the close of World War I. However, with the return of thousands of disabled veterans, Congress passed the Vocational Education Act in 1917, leading to the establishment of the Federal Board

for Vocational Education. The passage of the act provided funding for vocational education to states, which included funding for veterans with
disabilities.

The return of World War II veterans resulted in explicit documentation
of and support for college students with disabilities. While accommodations
were made and support was provided for disabled veterans, the changes made
on campuses opened doors to other students with disabilities. The GI Bill
and the Disabled Veterans Vocational Rehabilitation Act of 1943 provided
funding for veterans with disabilities to attend higher education. On a few
campuses, the veterans affairs offices worked in conjunction with community veterans affairs offices and rehabilitation programs to make the campus
physically accessible, although other accommodations were rarely made
(Madaus, 2000). Still, according to Madaus, "The prevailing attitude among
administration and faculty in higher education was summarized by Nugent
(1978) . . . that 'to include severely handicapped students in regular college
programs would be a waste of time and effort'" (p. 6).

During the rest of the 1940s and 1950s campuses slowly added disability
services. In 1968 a study by the U.S. Department of Health, Education, and
Welfare found only "200 institutions with some degree of accessibility for
students with orthopedic disabilities" (Madaus, 2000, p. 7). No significant
expansion of services for students with disabilities or reenrollment of students with disabilities occurred until the disability rights movements of the
early 1970s and subsequent substantive changes in federal laws.

The Civil Rights Movement of the 1960s, and in particular the theory of
self-determination, greatly influenced people with disabilities. Most notable
were the Rolling Quads, a group of University of California, Berkeley students who advocated for and received increased independence over their
own lives, including the ability to determine their own living situations as
well as obtaining greater physical access to the university (Madaus, 2000).
They believed that "people with disabilities are the best people to serve other
people with disabilities," seeing themselves as "empowered people rather
than patients" (Lewis & Rosa, 2003, p. 1).

Section 504 of the 1973 Rehabilitation Act was the first piece of federal
legislation that mandated equal educational opportunity for people with disabilities in all programs receiving federal assistance. This "was the first time
that those with differing abilities were accorded civil rights with respect to

education" (Drezner, 2008, p. 59), and it was no longer legal to deny admission solely on the basis of disability or to counsel students into or out of careers because of their disability. The rights of students with disabilities were extended in 1990 with passage of the Americans With Disabilities Act, which provided a definition of disability and guidelines for accessibility (Pliner, 2002).

These two pieces of legislation have substantially increased the enrollment of people with disabilities in higher education. According to Pliner (2002), "Since the 1970s, the number of students with disabilities attending college has tripled" (p. 245), and although the exact number is difficult to determine, estimates are between 8% and 9% of undergraduate students (Pliner), with the values slightly lower when only students attending four-year institutions are considered (Henderson, 2001). Significant differences by gender and race are evident by type of disability, with women and people of color more likely to report chronic health disabilities and men more likely to identify themselves as having learning disabilities (Henderson; Pliner).

Despite this growth, students with disabilities still do not enroll in college at rates their high school graduation levels predict, nor are their retention rates equal to those of students in the general population (Izzo, Murray, & Novak, 2008). This lack of retention likely has many causes. However, a campus environment that defines disability as deviant and unqualified surely plays a major role. Students with disabilities continue to report campus climates where it is assumed they do not belong, where requests for legally required accommodations are treated as illegitimate requests for unfair advantages, and where support services are typically understaffed (Belch, 2000; Schuck & Kroeger 1993; Wilson, Gretzel, & Brown, 2000).

Lesbian, Gay, Bisexual, and Transgender Students

The history of higher education documenting the experiences of lesbian, gay, bisexual, and transgender (LGBT) people before the middle of the 20th century is somewhat limited and almost absent before the 20th century. There are many reasons for this, but a critical one is that the concept of an identity as an LGBT person (as compared to being in love with or having sex with a person of the same sex) did not take hold until well into the 20th century (Broido, 1999; Dilley, 2002). However, there is strong documentation of enduring romantic relationships between women in the late 1800s and early 1900s, particularly in women's colleges (Faderman, 1991). It was not uncommon for senior women administrators and faculty to openly live with other women and be treated as a couple, and for students to have crushes on one another and on women faculty (Faderman; Gibson & Meem, 2005). These "long-term partnerships between women were seen as neither unnatural nor immoral, and therefore . . . they could be treated with the kind of openness and respect characteristic of married heterosexual couples" (Gibson & Meem, p. 4).

Intimacy between women became suspect only with the popularization of Freud's ideas about sex and the increasing awareness of women's sexuality. As Faderman (1991) wrote, "By the end of World War I the tolerance for any manifestations of what would earlier have been considered 'romantic friendship' had virtually disappeared" (p. 35). MacKay (1993) noted the change at Vassar between the 1920s and 1930s in attitudes toward intimate relationships between women. Attitudes moved from casual acceptance to condemnation and awareness of the need to hide same-sex attraction. In a review of accounts of the lives of gay male students in the 20th century, Dilley (2002) concluded, "Non-heterosexual students were on college campuses throughout the twentieth century; they did not always identify along collective social or political identities on campuses but rather often had lives (positive and negative) that were different from [those of] their heterosexual peers" (p. 16).

Into the 1960s, students caught in gay bars or associating with known homosexuals could be, and often were, dismissed from their universities, required to attend counseling, received disciplinary sanction, or experienced social rejection (Dilley, 2002; MacKay, 1993). While some had social contact with other homosexuals, many lived isolated lives. In fact, numerous LGBT people chose to deny their sexual orientation and presented a heterosexual persona to the campus community to avoid social stigma, a practice that continues today.

However, by the late 1960s and early 1970s some gay and lesbian students began to challenge conventional assumptions about the shameful nature of same-sex desire and publicly claimed an affirmative identity as well as demanded recognition by (and funding from) the university. The first gay student organization was founded in 1967 at Columbia University; a number of others followed quickly on the heels of the Stonewall Rebellion in

New York City in 1969 (Dilley, 2002). Advocating for "equality and inclusion" (p. 167), these organizations provided support and counseling, social activities, political advocacy, as well as encouragement for what would 30 years later become known as queer studies. These efforts frequently did not meet with success. Many campuses denied recognition or funding to nascent gay student organizations, "but by 1996, there were more than 2,000" (p. 175).

In the 1990s and into the 21st century, gay and lesbian student groups expanded to include bisexual and transgender individuals as well as heterosexual allies and those who preferred not to use labels to define their sexual orientation. Students continue their political advocacy, focusing on adding sexual orientation and gender identity to university nondiscrimination clauses, advocating for domestic partner benefits, and protesting the exclusion of openly gay and lesbian students from campus ROTC programs.

While LGBT students were less often subject to overt hostility and physical abuse on campus, contemporary measures continue to show widespread negative attitudes toward them (e.g., Holley, Larson, Adelman, & Treviño, 2007; Rankin, 2004). Rankin's survey of the campus climate for LGBT people in the first decade of the 21st century found, on what could easily be considered one of the most welcoming campuses in the United States for LGBT people, that "within the last 12 months nearly 30 percent of the respondents have personally experienced harassment due to their sexual orientation or gender identity. Sixty percent felt that queer people were likely to be the targets of harassment on campus" (p. 18). Obviously such stigma and harassment hinders inclusion on campuses. The openness and respect offered lesbians at women's colleges in the 19th century offers a model for educators to replicate today.

Socioeconomic Class

While many students attending the colonial colleges were sons of the economic elite (Thelin, 2004), from the start "opportunities for a poor but ambitious youth to attend college and thereby advance himself remained open" (Lucas, 2006, p. 108), particularly at more rural colleges (Bowen et al., 2005). Thelin estimated that in the early 1800s, at some colleges "25–40 percent of the students were receiving some form of missionary fund scholarship" (p. 63). Allmendiger "estimat[ed] that in the early 19th century between one-fourth and one-half of the students at . . . New England colleges relied on charity funds or had to teach school in order to cover tuition and other expenses" (as cited in Bowen et al., p. 13). Universities "devised [class schedules] that allowed some poor students to work their way through college by teaching school on a part-time basis" (Lucas, p. 108), while at Mount Holyoke College, all students and faculty had domestic responsibilities at the college to reduce tuition. At Oberlin all students had mandatory work assignments (Solomon, 1985).

As the number of colleges expanded in the early 1800s, those not in the most elite tier struggled to fill seats, using various forms of tuition discounts, scholarships, altered course schedules, and other means to attract students (Bowen et al., 2005). Consequently, "segregation by social class became increasingly common in the forms of off-campus room and board arrangements" (p. 16).

Following the Civil War primary and secondary education expanded rapidly, along with a huge increase in the need for teachers. Many states instituted *normal* (teacher training) colleges, which in many cases charged no tuition if students committed to teach upon graduation. These normal colleges provided opportunities for students, primarily women, to gain a college education they otherwise would not have had access to. Normal schools educated predominantly women students, including many African Americans and immigrants (often Irish).

At the start, women attending higher education institutions in the United States were likely to come from modest economic backgrounds; their best opportunities for economic success would come from education, while their wealthier peers relied on marriage for economic success. Upper-middle-class and wealthy women began attending college in large numbers only well into the 1900s (Horowitz, 1984, 1987).

The federal government took on a significant role at the end of World War II in increasing access to college for those of limited economic means. Whatever its faults in implementation (in particular, denying eligibility to African Americans), the GI Bill made a college education economically feasible for that "significant percentage of the college-age population [that] had the ability and the interest but lacked the resources to attend college" (Bowen et al., 2005, p. 31). The rise of junior and community colleges also expanded educational opportunities for students from lower-income families because of their significantly lower tuitions and flexible course schedules, allowing students to study while holding down full-time jobs.

> In the mid-1960s, . . . national legislation tied economic progress directly to college attendance for poor youth and provided the financial aid to do so. As a result, the proportion of students entering higher education from the lowest segments of the economy nearly doubled, from 12 to 22 percent. (Walpole, 2002, p. 357)

Today, students from low socioeconomic backgrounds are more likely to attend college than they were in the past. However, their enrollment still lags far behind that of their wealthier peers. According to data from the College Board, "Only 54 percent of high school graduates from the lowest income quartile enroll in college compared to 82 percent of those with incomes above [the top quartile]" (Bowen et al., 2005, p. 74). Disturbingly, that gap appears to be widening since 1992 (Bowen et al.). Only 43% of college-qualified high school graduates from the lowest income quartile are likely to earn a bachelor's degree, whereas 80% of college-qualified, top-income-quartile students are. This gap is exacerbated because eighth graders from the lowest income quartile are only about half as likely as their top-quartile peers to become college qualified (47% vs. 86%) (Advisory Committee on Student Financial Assistance, 2006). The discussion in this section illustrates additional ways campuses remain exclusive.

Religious Minorities

Higher education in the early years of the American colonies was in most places explicitly religiously denominational, and those denominations were protestant. Religious disputes between the faculty and leaders of colonial colleges led to a number of abrupt departures and foundings of new institutions. However, any denominational requirements applied only to the faculty and only in the founding years of the college.

In general, in the 18th and 19th centuries there were few religious outliers among students or faculty to threaten the dominant religious orders, and thus there was no need to develop restrictions based on religious affiliation, which later became common after World War I (Bowen et al., 2005). Georgetown University, founded in 1789, was the first Catholic institution of higher education in the United States, but "by 1900 there were 152

Catholic colleges for men and only the beginnings of an effort to provide a higher education for Catholic women" (Schier, 2002, p. 18).

As part of a nationwide growth in anti-immigrant sentiment, administrators of elite universities worried about the increasing numbers of Jewish students in the immediate aftermath of World War I. Indeed, the 1918 meeting of the Association of New England Deans was devoted to discussion of "the rapid increase of the 'foreign element'" (Karabel, 2005, p. 75), code for Jewish students. The response to the rise in Jewish enrollment contrasted with the response to comparable increases in Irish Catholic enrollment, as Catholic students were believed to be able to "assimilate into American society" (Takaki, 1993, p. 161). New admissions criteria were instituted with the explicit intent to curb Jewish enrollment. These criteria shifted from being purely academic, which were leading to the overrepresentation of undesirable students who were seen as "culturally alien" (p. 75), to criteria that evaluated potential students' character, their "potential as business and social leaders" (p. 100), their athletic ability, or their regional diversity.

With the specific intent of identifying Jewish students, in 1922 Harvard began asking applicants for photographs and their "race and color, religious preference, birthplace of father" (Karabel, 2005, p. 94), and any change made to the family's last name. Furthermore, applicants' school principals and headmasters were asked to identify candidates' religions. While explicit ceilings on Jewish enrollment and blatant discrimination were controversial, and at Harvard a committee to address admission criteria unanimously recommended "no departure be made from . . . the policy of equality opportunity for all regardless of race and religion" (p. 101), this subtler way of discriminating gained hold, eventually forming the basis of modern admission criteria for today's highly selective universities. Even during the Great Depression, when universities were struggling to fill seats, "there was an acceleration in the adoption of policies limiting the number of Jewish students" (Bowen et al., 2005, p. 30).

While many would like to believe that discrimination on university campuses against religious minorities is a thing of the past, there is strong evidence to the contrary. A scan of *The Chronicle of Higher Education* indicates that discrimination and physical attacks against students who are Muslim, or are thought to be Muslim, are frequent. Anti-Semitism is so prevalent that in 2006 the U.S. Office of Civil Rights released a report and developed a program to address it (U.S. Commission on Civil Rights, 2006). Discrimination against non-Christians at the Air Force Academy is another example of religious intolerance that received a great deal of publicity in 2005 (Lipka, 2005).

We have identified how religion in addition to race, gender, sexual orientation, disability, and socioeconomic class have historically been conditions of exclusion. We have also offered examples of ways campuses continue to be exclusive. How can this information add complex meaning to diversifying higher education?

THE EVOLVING MEANING OF DIVERSITY

While the history of higher education with respect to access of various groups and the changing composition of the student body is well documented, the meaning of diversity—or *difference* (Manning, 2009)—is more challenging to place in a historical context. Indeed, conceptions of diversity have changed over the history of the student affairs profession, but there are many dimensions, layers, and intersections to these overlapping notions. For some, the meaning of diversity rests in numbers and demographic statistics, for others it embraces recognizing cultural differences and celebrating common bonds, and for others it is the challenge of acknowledging the differential access to social power that gives privileges to some groups and not others. Likewise, the definition of inclusion continues to evolve and build on itself. Inclusion can mean creating programs and policies to increase diversity on campuses; it can mean incorporating different cultural values, perspectives, and goals in practice and processes; and it can mean recognizing and dismantling power structures that continue to give some identity groups advantages and systematically marginalize others.

A variety of circumstances and variables has influenced what diversity has come to mean. As such, there is no simple way to define or understand diversity since the concept is ever changing and evolving. As Smith (1995) noted, "Framing discussions in terms of the evolution of our understanding of the concept, rather than presenting a concrete definition, can potentially illuminate what diversity has come to mean while still allowing for the continuing evolution of the term" (p. 222). Therefore, in this section, we attempt to put the meaning of diversity into a historical context, in the hope that we can fully appreciate the breadth and depth of this sometimes elusive term.

Absence of Awareness of Difference

Ironically, while Gomez stated that "the history of educational inequality in the United States is older than the nation itself" (as cited in Turner et al., 2002, p. xiv), the use of the term *diversity* did not become part of the lexicon of the academy until the 1980s (Baez, 2000). The earliest evidence of the term *diversity* (referring to race or ethnicity) did not appear in higher education literature until the early 1970s.

In 19th-century higher education, the concepts of diversity, inclusion, and equity simply did not exist—certainly not in the way we talk about them today (Bowen et al., 2005). If one were to ask any graduate student to characterize the diversity of college students from the colonial period through the early 20th century, the response would likely be that there was none; students were all wealthy White males. And for the most part, such characterizations are accurate. However, diversity exists in any enterprise whenever differences are present, and in higher education (as noted earlier in this chapter), even from its early years, women, African Americans, Native Americans, people with disabilities, members of the working class, Jews, and gay men and lesbians were earning baccalaureate degrees.

So why has it taken so long for the notion of diversity to take hold and evolve? Smith's (1995) analysis of research phases in higher education may provide a useful perspective for identifying the emergence of the concept of diversity in higher education. Smith said this phenomenon may be explained in part by the White male European perspective, which assumed that those who participated in higher education (or who should have participated) were limited to the majority, although exceptions were noted. Perhaps more than this, however, was a paradigm in higher education where objectivity and universal applicability were favored over variation and differences (which, incidentally, were viewed as irrelevant or flawed). In pursuit of understanding and explaining human beings in higher education, it made more sense to control for or ignore differences. Perhaps a more generous perspective is offered by Manning (2009), who suggested that for some, the "color-blind perspective" (p. 13) prevailed. Here, the goal is not to account for or eliminate human differences in pursuit of an objective reality, but to view all humans as equal, thereby making their differences not worth considering. Finally, in telling a story about a training program Levine (1999) conducted for senior administrators, he offered insight into why diversity may have been (and continues to be) overlooked or ignored: It can be a frightening and vexing problem. When he asked the administrators what they would like to see happen with the issue of diversity, he reported that "regardless of the race, gender, or age of the person, the answer was usually the same, 'I want it to go away'" (p. 9).

Diversity Means Increasing Difference

By the 1960s, largely as a result of the Civil Rights Movement, higher education began to view diversity in perhaps its most basic form: the numerical representation of various racial and ethnic groups. This view persists today and is commonly referred to as "structural diversity" (Hurtado, Milem, Clayton-Pederson, & Allen, 1999, p. 19). This view insists that increasing access to underrepresented groups is the right thing to do to remedy past wrongs that have created economic disadvantages and social immobility for minorities (Blimling, 2001). *Minority*, at this time, referred to racial minority and Black students in particular (Levine, 1999), and to a lesser extent, White women (Smith, 1995). In response to achieving this goal of diversity, affirmative steps were taken to recruit, admit, and enroll a greater number of racial minority students. Eventually, the push for great numbers of underrepresented groups expanded from students to also include staff, faculty, administrators, and trustees (including women at these levels) and from just increasing numbers to increasing numbers comparable to the regional or national population (Levine). So, to the extent that more underrepresented groups were now on campus, diversity was achieved. Manning (2009) argued that this view of diversity has benefits and liabilities. While increased numbers have the potential to change power structures and equality (the degree to which needs are recognized and addressed and how decisions are made), there is no guarantee this will take place when numbers alone are the ultimate goal.

Diversity Means Responding to Difference

As the student demographics began to change, marking progress in terms of structural diversity, attention in the 1970s and into the 1980s began to turn from the quantity of racial minority students experiencing college to the quality of that experience (Smith, 1995). Administrators did not know how—or did not wish—to respond to incoming minority students their institutions were not designed for (Fleming, 1984; D. J. Wright, 1987). As a result, colleges and universities became preoccupied not only with access of minority students but with their retention, graduation, and experiences of marginalization and discrimination. This may explain why the climate on college campuses for students of color and women was characterized as unwelcoming, chilly, and even inhospitable (Pope, 1992; Terrell, 1988; Yang, 1992). Diversity took on a new meaning in this context: the nature of the response to the concerns of the quality of students' experiences. As Levine (1999) noted, "a cornucopia of activities" (p. 5) emerged, including remedial services, support groups, specialized cocurricular activities and student groups, and a growth of academic programs in African American and women's studies. Not only did the response broaden in terms of the activities, but also for the groups affected by those activities, as the definition of minority expanded beyond race, ethnicity, and gender to also include other underrepresented groups according to religion, sexual orientation, ability, class, and nationality. The recognition of this broader definition of diversity dictated that more attention be focused on the overall campus ethos, climate, and response to the pervasive attitudes and acts of intolerance (Smith). As a result, institutions experienced the emergence of diversity training in the form of workshops that highlight tolerance, the value of diversity, and sensitivity training. Mohanty (1993) argued that while these workshops became ubiquitous on college campuses, they remain limited in their effectiveness because they did little to address and change the institutional and structural forms of inequality.

Diversity Means Incorporating Differences

The previous conceptualizations viewed diversity as an add-on to higher education, which warranted appropriate responses to prevent this growing diversity from negatively affecting the campus (Levine, 1999). Less attention was given to what this growing diversity meant for higher education and how (or even *if*) higher education would need to change. As a result, a new understanding of diversity began to emerge in the 1980s. In addition to diversity's being about numbers and responses, diversity came to be about incorporating new students into the fabric of the institution. As Levine (1999) put it, "The minority population has grown, and must be grafted into the existing college community" (p. 5). This view represents the embryonic stages of cultural pluralism or multiculturalism—the idea that the entire community benefits from recognition of the differences and the commonalities among all groups on campus, acknowledging and appreciating both the *pluribus* and the *unum* (Levine; Manning, 2009). From this perspective, a host of programs appeared on campus that celebrated the many contributions of diverse populations, including food and fashion festivals, week- or month-long celebrations of certain groups, or recognition of the way different cultures celebrated the winter holidays. The benefit of this view was that it resulted in diverse populations' feeling more recognized, valued, and welcomed as part of the community. On the other hand, it still did little to address structural inequality and may even have led to voyeurism of groups and co-opting of a culture's goods and practices for personal gain (Manning).

Diversity Means Learning About Difference

Another perspective on diversity emerged in the 1980s as well; this one had an emphasis on the curriculum. Indeed, from the inception the educational dimension of diversity and programs in ethnic studies and women's studies were important because they attempted to create a more inclusive curriculum for diverse students who were attending institutions in growing numbers (Smith, 1995). However, as the demographics of the country began to change, as corporate America began to focus on "managing diversity" in the workplace, and as the United States needed to turn its attention toward a global economy and geopolitical issues, it became evident that all students needed knowledge and skills to work with diverse groups and ideas (Blimling, 2001; Katz, 1989; Smith). As a result, by the early 1990s, many campuses with general education and liberal arts curricula began to require students to take courses in world civilizations, domestic diversity, and multiculturalism (Levine & Cureton, 1992). This new and substantial view of diversity had a more pragmatic benefit to it but still did not address social inequality.

Diversity Means Understanding the Complexity of Difference

As higher education moved into the 1990s, and the notion of diversity (and all its meanings) attracted a great deal of attention, new dimensions and lenses were added to the understanding of the term *diversity*. The basic conceptualizations of increasing, responding to, and incorporating differences persisted and had become so ingrained in the institutional psyche that they continued to influence policy, practice, programs, and research. However, new and more complex ways of thinking about diversity were introduced. One of the newer ones was a move from segmented ways of understanding diversity to a more integrated way, in which people do not have a single identity or separate identities (e.g., Black or female or Muslim), but their identity is multidimensional (Black and female and Muslim) (Jones & McEwen, 2000; Reynolds & Pope, 1991; Weber, 1998). In addition, there was a growing recognition that diversity as a concept was limited when understood from the dominant group's perspective; diversity meant the other (people of color, women, gays and lesbians). Diversity began to be viewed as a relative term; people are all diverse in relation to one another. Therefore, diversity needed to include the majority or privileged groups, namely, White students, heterosexual students, Christian students, and male students. The benefit of this broadened perspective, one, which was pointed out by Hoffman (2004), was that when educators fail to pay attention to and learn about majority group members, they may "inadvertently perpetuate the status of minority group members as the 'other,' as the ones who need explaining" (p. 375).

Diversity Means Acknowledging the Power in Difference

Another significant challenge to notions of diversity that emerged in the 1990s was that diversity, while about difference, also had to address the element of power. Diversity is a social construction; differences just are. It is the meaning attached to those differences that is significant, and an important part of that is power (or privilege) extended to some groups over others. Although terms like *racism*, *sexism*, and *classism* have long been part of the dialogue on diversity, their real meaning was not revealed until the language of oppression, power, and privilege entered the conversation. When educators address issues of oppression in our discussions on diversity, we are in effect transforming our understanding of diversity (Katz, 2003; Manning, 2009; Smith, 1995) and more actively and deliberately pursuing social justice. Diversity is no longer only about increasing differences, responding to differences, and understanding and appreciating differences; it is also about interrupting systems that give privileges to some groups and confronting the reluctance to dismantle those systems. Reason and Davis (2005), for example, proposed a perspective on diversity that underscores the goals of social justice where resources are equitably distributed, decision making is shared, and the system and culture of social inequality is dismantled.

WHAT WE HAVE LEARNED

The historical review of diversity in higher education presented in this chapter offers some important lessons that can inform our perspectives and practices today. In this section we examine some of the lessons learned, exploring how history has shaped our present and the potential it has for our future in creating inclusive campuses.

Diversity Defined

Clearly a lesson learned from this review is that the definition of diversity, while sometimes regarded as elusive, is certainly evolving. But we have also come to appreciate the elasticity of the term—its ability to "expand to embrace more categories" (Association of American Colleges and Universities [AAC&U], 1995a, p. 62). According to the AAC&U, "The term diversity, in fact, came into existence largely because race or gender or sexual orientation would no longer serve to adequately describe this expanded understanding" (p. 21). This can serve as an important reminder that while today we may believe we have exhausted all possible categories for inclusion of diversity, the future may introduce new categories never considered before. Throughout history, groups that were previously never considered as part of diversity became incorporated into the definition. For example, in the 1990s, gender expression and variance as well as religious groups outside the Judeo-Christian belief system (not to mention the nonreligious) were hardly regarded as part of the mosaic of diversity. We believe history has taught educators not to be afraid of the expanding notion of diversity—a lesson we may need to take courageously into the next century.

Community in a Pluralistic Society

An important lesson from this history is a bit more elusive but no less powerful. As college campuses have become more diverse, concerns have been raised about balkanization on campus or, as Levine and Cureton (1992) called it, the "mitosis" (p. 85) of the campus community. Some bristle at the notion of a multitude of student groups (e.g., the Korean Marketing Association) or particular courses of study (e.g., Islamic studies) or specialized student services (e.g., Gender and Sexuality Center). These concerns are reminiscent of the perplexed lament that Tatum (1997) analyzed: Why are all the Black students sitting together? Smith (1995) suggested that educators focus less on the (normal and developmentally appropriate) behavior of students and more on the history and characteristics of institutions that for a long time maintained policies and practices of marginalization and segregation. Educators need to create a vision of campuses where differences coexist in a pluralistic community that is built on "multiple memberships and crossover memberships" (p. 238).

MOVING BEYOND REPRESENTATION

History is replete with intentions, goals, events, and policies to increase the number of underrepresented people who serve in and are served by higher education. Simultaneously, the notion of diversity has expanded. We believe this growth and expansion has been positive for higher education. Nonetheless, history has shown that a mightier challenge has existed and continues to exist: addressing the institutional cultures and structures that perpetuate systems of inequality. As the AAC&U (1999) noted, "Diversifying students is only the beginning of a longer, more complex process" (p. 21). This is not limited only to the students. As Smith (1995) suggested, our history of diversifying faculty and administration has certainly begun to address representational diversity, but for any institution to achieve its espoused goals of diversity, it must also address issues of decision making, curriculum, scholarship, and images and standards of quality (and who defines them).

From the Problem to the Benefits of Diversity

Over the history of higher education, diversity has been a double-edged sword. On the one hand, it has been a goal and an aspiration of those in higher education to increase access to a wider range of students in pursuit of the benefits of education. On the other hand, diversity has often been regarded as a problem needing a solution. AAC&U (1995b) challenged educators to look at their history and consider how to view diversity not as a problem but as a resource. Maruyama, Moreno, Gudeman, and Marin (2000), for example, noted that almost 200 years ago White institutions began providing access to the possibilities and gains of higher education to women and people of color. The assumption undergirding these acts of inclusion was that educational opportunities enjoyed largely by White males were being extended to others. However, "Now we know that education is a two-way exchange that benefits all who participate in the multicultural marketplace of ideas and perspectives" (p. 5).

Diversity and Multicultural Competence

The complexities of diversity, its challenges and opportunities, must be understood, appreciated, addressed, and nurtured. This requires a specialized skill set for which student affairs scholars and professionals have advocated for more than 20 years (Cheatham, 1991; Ebbers & Henry, 1990; Fleming, 1984; McEwen & Roper, 1994; Nuss, 1996; Pope & Reynolds, 1997; Talbot, 1996). Pope and Reynolds introduced the term *multicultural competence* to the student affairs profession as a core competency, arguing that creating and maintaining diverse and affirming campuses will not happen by the sheer will of well-intentioned professionals or well-paid consultants. Instead, it must be deliberate and infused into practice by all professionals, grounded in specific knowledge about cultural groups and identities as well as the dynamics of oppression, self-awareness and awareness of our interpersonal relationships, and the ability to use that knowledge and awareness to inform practice. Multiculturally competent professionals not only acknowledge the presence and benefits of diversity on campus, they promote and make diversity work on campus through their practice (Pope, Mueller, & Reynolds, 2009).

CONCLUSION

Because of space limitations for this chapter, we recognize that the richness, pain, and victories of higher education's history with respect to diversity and inclusion is reduced to a limited glimpse of what actually has occurred. We acknowledge that identities have been addressed piecemeal, and, in particular, the rapid changes of the last 40 years have been addressed in only the briefest and sometimes overly simple form. Still, presenting this historical context is a powerful act in that it frames our past in such a way that allows educators to more fully appreciate current assumptions, values, ideas, and identities. Enlightened by this history, we can more fully comprehend and learn from challenging situations and outcomes resulting from, for example, a cultural error made by even the most well intentioned among us (as described at the beginning of this chapter). This historical context becomes an important part of the process of guiding individuals and groups through difficult conversations because it provides an opportunity to explore the phenomenon that who we were influences who we are. This chapter provides the setting for how educators today can honor and welcome others in the context of a past in which educators did not.

REFERENCES

Advisory Committee on Student Financial Assistance. (2006). *Mortgaging our future: How financial barriers to college undercut America's global competitiveness.* Washington, DC: Author.

Agricultural College Act of 1890, 7 U.S.C. § 321 *et seq.* (1890).

American Federation for the Blind. (2011). *Helen Keller biography.* Retrieved from http://www.afb.org/Section.asp?SectionID=1&TopicID=129

American Indian Higher Education Consortium. (2000). *Creating role models for change: A survey of tribal college graduates.* Washington, DC: Author.

Anderson, J. D. (1988). *The education of Blacks in the South: 1860–1935.* Chapel Hill: University of North Carolina Press.

Asian Pacific Americans and Immigration Law. (2010). Retrieved from the University of Dayton School of Law website: http://academic.udayton.edu/race/02 rights/immigr05.htm

Association of American Colleges and Universities. (1995a). *Diversity in higher education: A work in progress.* Washington, DC: Author.

Association of American Colleges and Universities. (1995b). *Liberal learning and the arts of connection for a new academy.* Washington, DC: Author.

Association of American Colleges and Universities. (1999). *To form a more perfect union: Campus diversity initiatives.* Washington, DC: Author.

Austin, A. W. (2004). *From concentration camp to campus: Japanese American students and World War II.* Urbana: University of Illinois Press.

Baez, B. (2000). Diversity and its contradictions. In C. S. Turner, a. l. antonio, M. Garcia, B. V. Laden, A. Nora, & C. L. Presley (Eds.), *Racial and ethnic diversity in higher education* (2nd ed., pp. 383–388). Boston, MA: Pearson Learning Solutions.

Belanger, C. (2006). What is the meaning of "historical context"? *Quebec history encyclopedia.* Retrieved from http://faculty.marianopolis.edu/c.belanger/quebec history/Historicalcontext.html

Belch, H. A. (Ed.). (2000). *Serving students with disabilities.* (New Directions for Student Services No. 91). San Francisco, CA: Jossey-Bass.

Berea College v. Commonwealth of Kentucky, 211 U.S. 45 (1908).

Blimling, G. S. (2001). Diversity makes you smarter [Editorial]. *Journal of College Student Development, 42*(6), 517–519.

Bowen, W. G., Kurzweil, M. A., & Tobin, E. M. (2005). *Equity and excellence in American higher education.* Charlottesville: University of Virginia Press.

Broido, E. M. (1999). Constructing identity: The nature and meaning of lesbian, gay, and bisexual identity development. In R. M. Perez, K. A. DeBord, & K. J. Bieschke (Eds.), *Handbook of counseling and therapy with lesbians, gays, and bisexuals* (pp. 13–33). Washington, DC: American Psychological Association.

Brown v. Board of Educ., 347 U.S. 483 (1954).

Carney, M. C. (1999). *Native American higher education in the United States.* New Brunswick, NJ: Transaction.

Chang, M. J., & Kiang, P. N. (2002). New challenges of representing Asian American students in U.S. higher education. In W. A. Smith, P. G. Altbach, & K. Lomotey (Eds.), *The racial crisis in American higher education: Continuing challenges for the twenty-first century* (Rev. ed., pp. 137–158). Albany, NY: SUNY Press.

Cheatham, H. E. (1991). *Cultural pluralism on campus.* Alexandria, VA: American College Personnel Association.

The Chronicle of Higher Education. (2011, August 26). *Almanac Issue, 57*(1).

Civil Rights Act of 1964, 78 § 241 (1964).

Daniels, R. (1988). *Asian America: Chinese and Japanese in the United States since 1850.* Seattle: University of Washington Press.

Dilley, P. (2002). Queer man on campus: A history of non-heterosexual college men, 1945–2000. New York, NY: RoutledgeFalmer.

Disabled Veterans Vocational Rehabilitation Act of 1943, 29 U.S.C.A. § 31 *et seq.* (1943).

Drewry, H. N., & Doermann, H. (2001). *Stand and prosper: Private Black colleges and their students.* Princeton, NJ: Princeton University Press.

Drezner, N. D. (2008). Arguing for a different view: Deaf-serving institutions as minority-serving. In M. Gasman, B. Baez, & C. S. V. Turner (Eds.), *Understanding minority-serving institutions* (pp. 57–70). Albany, NY: SUNY Press.

DuBois, W. E. B. (2011). *The talented tenth.* Retrieved from http://www.webdubois .org/dbTalentedTenth.html

Ebbers, L. H., & Henry, S. L. (1990). Cultural competence: A new challenge to student affairs professionals. *NASPA Journal, 27*(4), 319–323.

Faderman, L. (1991). *Odd girls and twilight lovers: A history of lesbian life in twentieth-century America.* New York, NY: Penguin Books.

Fleming, J. (1984). *Blacks in college: A comparative study of students' success in Black and White institutions.* San Francisco, CA: Jossey-Bass.

Fourteenth Amendment to the Constitution. (1868). Retrieved from http://www .archives.gov/exhibits/charters/constitution_amendments_11-27.html

Gallaudet University. (1997). *The beginnings.* Retrieved from http://pr.gallaudet .edu/GallaudetHistory/page1.html

Gasman, M. (2008). Minority-serving institutions: A historical backdrop. In M. Gasman, B. Baez, & C. S. V. Turner (Eds.), *Understanding minority-serving institutions* (pp. 18–27). Albany, NY: SUNY Press.

Gibson, M., & Meem, D. T. (2005). Introduction. *Journal of Lesbian Studies, 9*(4), 1–12.

Guido-DiBrito, F. (2002). Women students: Overview. In A. M. Martinez Aleman & K. A. Renn (Eds.), *Women in higher education: An encyclopedia* (pp. 249–262). Santa Barbara, CA: ABC-CLIO.

Hall, R. M., & Sandler, B. R. (1984). *Out of the classroom: A chilly campus climate for women.* Washington, DC: Association of American Colleges.

Henderson, C. (2001). *2001 college freshmen with disabilities: A biennial statistical profile.* Washington, DC: HEATH Resource Center and American Council on Education. Retrieved from ERIC database. (ED458728)

Higher Education Act of 1965, Pub. L. No. 89-329 Cong. (1965)

Hill, S. T. (1985). *The traditionally Black institutions of higher education 1860 to 1982.* Washington, DC: National Center for Education Statistics.

Hoffman, R. M. (2004). Conceptualizing heterosexual identity development: Issues and challenges. *Journal of Counseling and Development, 82*(3), 375–380.

Holley, L. C., Larson, N. C., Adelman, M., & Treviño, J. (2007). Attitudes among university undergraduates toward LGB and five ethnic/racial groups. *Journal of LGBT Youth, 5*(1), 79–101. doi:10.1300/J524v05n0107

Holmes, D. O. W. (1969). *The evolution of the Negro college.* New York, NY: Teachers College, Columbia University. (Original work published 1934)

Horowitz, H. L. (1984). *Alma mater: Design and experiences in the women's college from their nineteenth-century beginnings to the 1930s.* Boston, MA: Beacon Press.

Horowitz, H. L. (1987). *Campus life: Undergraduate cultures from the end of the eighteenth century to the present.* Chicago, IL: University of Chicago Press.

Hurtado, S., Milem, J., Clayton-Pederson, A., & Allen, W. (1999). *Enacting diverse learning environments: Improving the climate for racial/ethnic diversity in higher education.* Washington, DC: George Washington University.

Immigration and Naturalization Act of 1965, 79 § 911 (1965).

Institute for Higher Education Policy (2007). *The path of many journeys: The benefits of higher education for Native people and communities.* Washington, DC: Author. Retrieved from www.aihec.org/resources/documents/ThePathOfManyJourneys.pdf

Izzo, M. V., Murray, A., & Novak, J. (2008). The faculty perspective on universal design for learning. *Journal of Postsecondary Education and Disability, 21*(2), 60–72.

Jones, S. R., & McEwen, M. K. (2000). A conceptual model of multiple dimensions of identity. *Journal of College Student Development, 41*(4), 405–414.

Karabel, J. (2005). *The chosen: The hidden history of admission and exclusion at Harvard, Yale, and Princeton.* New York, NY: Houghton Mifflin.

Katz, J. H. (1989). The challenge of diversity. In C. Woolbright (Ed.), *Valuing diversity on campus* (pp. 1–21). Bloomington, IN: Association of College Unions International.

Katz, J. H. (2003). *White awareness: Handbook for anti-racism training.* Norman: University of Oklahoma Press.

Levine, A. (1999). Diversity [President's essay]. *Teachers College, Columbia University: Annual Report.* New York, NY: Teachers College, Columbia University.

Levine, A., & Cureton, J. (1998). The quiet revolution: Eleven facts about multiculturalism and the curriculum. *Change, 24*(1), 25–29.

Lewis, C., & Rosa, C. (2003, July). *"Back to the future": Understanding our history to refine our vision of higher education and disability.* Paper presented at the meeting of the Association on Higher Education and Disability, Dallas, TX. Retrieved from http://www.ahead.org/conferences/past/2003

Lipka, S. (2005, April 21). U.S. Air Force Academy hit with allegations of pervasive religious intolerance. *The Chronicle of Higher Education.* Retrieved from http://chron
icle.com/article/US-Air-Force-Academy-Hit/120481/

Lucas, C. J. (2006). *American higher education: A history* (2nd ed.). New York, NY: Palgrave Macmillan.

MacDonald, V., & Garcia, T. (2003). Historical perspectives on Latino access to higher education, 1848–1990. In J. Castellanos & L. Jones (Eds.), *The majority in the minority: Expanding the representation of Latina/o faculty, administrators and students in higher education* (pp. 15–43). Sterling, VA: Stylus.

MacKay, A. (Ed.). (1993). *Wolf girls at Vassar: Lesbian and gay experiences 1930–1990.* New York, NY: St. Martin's Press.

Madaus, J. W. (2000). Services for college and university students with disabilities: A historical perspective. *Journal of Postsecondary Education and Disability, 14*(1), 4–21.

Maher, F. A., & Tetreault, M. K. T. (2007). *Privilege and diversity in the academy.* New York, NY: Routledge.

Manning, K. (2009, May–June). Philosophical underpinnings of student affairs work on difference. *About Campus, 14*(2), 11–17.

Maruyama, G., Moreno, J. F., Gudeman, R. H., & Marin, P. (2000). *Does diversity make a difference? Three research studies on diversity in college classrooms.* Washington, DC: American Council on Education & American Association of University Professors. Retrieved from http://www.eric.ed.gov/ERICWebPortal/search/detail mini.jsp?_nfpb=true&_&ERICExtSearch_SearchValue_0=ED444409&ERIC ExtSearch_SearchType_0=no&accno=ED444409

McClellan, G. S., Tippeconnic Fox, M. J., & Lowe, S. C. (2005). Where we have been: A history of Native American higher education. In M. J. Tippeconnie Fox, S. C. Lowe, & G. S. McClellan (Eds.), *Serving Native American Students.* (New Directions for Student Services No. 109, pp. 7–15). San Francisco, CA: Jossey-Bass.

McEwen, M. K., & Roper, L. D. (1994). Incorporating multiculturalism into student affairs preparation programs: Suggestions from the literature. *Journal of College Student Development, 35*(1), 46–53.

Mohanty, C. T. (1993). On race and voice: Challenges for liberal education. In B. W. Thompson & S. Tyagi (Eds.), *Beyond a dream deferred: Multicultural education and the politics of excellence* (pp. 41–65). Minneapolis: University of Minnesota Press.

Morrill Act of 1862, 7 U.S.C. § 301 *et seq.* (1862).

Movimiento Estudiantil Chicano de Aztlán. (n.d.). *About us.* Retrieved from http://www.nationalmecha.org/about.html

Nakanishi, D. T. (2002). Asian Pacific Americans and colleges and universities. In C. S. Turner, a. l. antonio, M. Garcia, B. V. Laden, A. Nora, & C. L. Presley (Eds.), *Racial and ethnic diversity in higher education* (2nd ed., pp. 73–90). Boston, MA: Pearson Learning Solutions.

Newcomer, M. (1959). *A century of higher education for American women.* New York, NY: Harper & Brothers.

Ng, J. C., Lee, S. S., & Pak, Y. K. (2007). Contesting the model minority and perpetual foreigner stereotypes: A critical review of literature on Asian Americans in higher education. *Review of Research in Education, 31*, 95–130. doi:10.3102/0091732X07300046095

Nidiffer, J. (2002). Overview. In A. M. Martinez Aleman & K. A. Renn (Eds.), *Women in higher education: An encyclopedia* (pp. 1–15). Santa Barbara, CA: ABC-CLIO.

Noble, J. L. (1956). *The Negro woman's college education.* New York, NY: Teachers College, Columbia University.

Nuss, E. M. (1996). The development of student affairs. In S. R. Komives & D. B. Woodard, Jr. (Eds.), *Student services: A handbook for the profession* (3rd ed., pp. 22–42). San Francisco, CA: Jossey-Bass.

Ogunwole, S. (2006). *We the people: American Indians and Alaska Natives in the United States.* Washington, DC: U.S. Census Bureau. Retrieved from http://www .census.gov/prod/2006pubs/censr-28.pdf

Olivas, M. A. (1989). Indian, Chicano, and Puerto Rican colleges: Status and issues. In L. F. Goodchild & H. S. Wechsler (Eds.), *ASHE reader on the history of higher education* (pp. 559–576). Needham Heights, MA: Gin Press.

Park, J. J., & Teranishi, R. T. (2008). Asian American and Pacific Islander serving institutions. In M. Gasman, B. Baez, & C. S. V. Turner (Eds.), *Understanding minority-serving institutions* (pp. 111–126). Albany, NY: SUNY Press.

Pensionado women. (n.d.). Retrieved from http://filam.si.edu/curriculum/u3-part-02b.html

Plessy v. Ferguson, 163 U.S. 537 (1896).

Pliner, S. M. (2002). Women with disabilities. In A. M. Martinez Aleman & K. A. Renn (Eds.), *Women in higher education: An encyclopedia* (pp. 244–246). Santa Barbara, CA: ABC-CLIO.

Pope, R. L. (1992). *An analysis of multiracial change efforts in student affairs.* Unpublished doctoral dissertation, University of Massachusetts, Amherst.

Pope, R. L., Mueller, J. A., & Reynolds, A. L. (2009). Looking back and moving forward: Future directions for diversity research in student affairs. *Journal of College Student Development, 50*(6), 640–658.

Pope, R. L., & Reynolds, A. L. (1997). Student affairs core competencies: Integrating multicultural awareness, knowledge, and skills. *Journal of College Student Development, 38*(3), 266–277.

Rankin, S. R. (2004, Winter). Campus climate for lesbian, gay, bisexual and transgender people. *The Diversity Factor, 12*(1), 18–23.

Reason, R. D., & Davis, T. L. (2005). Antecedents, precursors, and concurrent concepts in the development of social justice attitudes and actions. In R. D. Reason, T. Davis, N. J. Evans (Eds.), *Developing social justice allies.* (New Directions for Student Services No. 110, pp. 5–15). San Francisco, CA: Jossey-Bass.

Reynolds, A. L., & Pope, R. L. (1991). The complexities of diversity: Exploring multiple oppressions. *Journal of Counseling and Development, 70,* 174–180.

Robinson, B. B., & Albert, A. R. (2008). HBCU's institutional advantage: Returns to teacher education. In M. Gasman, B. Baez, & C. S. V. Turner (Eds.), *Understanding minority-serving institutions* (pp. 183–199). Albany, NY: SUNY Press.

Rudolph, F. (1990). *The American college and university.* Athens: University of Georgia Press.

Schier, T. (2002). Catholic women's colleges. In A. M. Martinez Aleman & K. A. Renn (Eds.), *Women in higher education: An encyclopedia* (pp. 17–21). Santa Barbara, CA: ABC-CLIO.

Schuck, J. & Kroeger, S. (1993). Essential elements in effective service delivery. In S. Kroeger & S. Schuck (Eds.), *Responding to disability issues in student affairs* (New Directions for Student Services, No. 64, pp. 59–68). San Francisco, CA: Jossey-Bass.

Section 504 of the 1973 Rehabilitation Act, 29 U.S.C. § 701 *et seq.* (1973).

Servicemen's Readjustment Act, P.L. 78–346, 58 Stat. 284m § 1707–24 (1944).

Smith, D. G. (1995). Organizational implications of diversity in higher education. In M. M. Chemers, S. Oskamp, & M. A. Constanzo (Eds.), *Diversity in organizations: New perspectives for a changing workplace* (pp. 220–244). Thousand Oaks, CA: Sage.

Solomon, B. M. (1985). *In the company of educated women.* New Haven, CT: Yale University.

Somers, P. (2002). Title IX. In A. M. Martinez Aleman & K. A. Renn (Eds.), *Women in higher education: An encyclopedia* (pp. 237–243). Santa Barbara, CA: ABC-CLIO.

Suarez-Balcazar, Y., Orellana-Damacela, L., Portillo, N., Rowan, J. M., & Andrews-Guillen, C. (2003). Experiences of differential treatment among college students of color. *Journal of Higher Education, 74*(4), 428–444.

Takaki, R. (1993). *A different mirror: A history of multicultural America.* Boston, MA: Little, Brown.

Talbot, D. M. (1996). Multiculturalism. In S. R. Komives & D. B. Woodard, Jr. (Eds.), *Student services: A handbook for the profession* (3rd ed., pp. 380–396). San Francisco, CA: Jossey-Bass.

Tatum, B. D. (1997). *"Why are all the Black kids sitting together in the cafeteria?" And other conversations about race.* New York, NY: Basic Books.

Terrell, M. (1988). Racism: Undermining higher education. *NASPA Journal, 26*(2), 82–84.

Thelin, J. R. (2004). *A history of American higher education.* Baltimore, MD: Johns Hopkins University Press.

Timeline of Affirmative Action: JBHE chronology of major landmarks in the progress of African Americans in higher education. (2007). Retrieved from the *Journal of Blacks in Higher Education* website: http://www.jbhe.com/timeline.html

Title IX of the Educational Amendments of 1972, 29 U.S.C. § 1681-1688 (1972).

Torres, V. (2004). The diversity among us: Puerto Ricans, Cuban Americans, Caribbean Americans, and Central and South Americans. In A. M. Ortiz (Ed.),

Addressing the unique needs of Latino American Students (New Directions for Student Services No. 105, pp. 5–16). San Francisco, CA: Jossey-Bass.

Turner, C. S., antonio, a. l., Garcia, M., Laden, B. V., Nora, A., & Presley, C. L. (Eds.). (2002). *Racial and ethnic diversity in higher education* (2nd ed.). Boston, MA: Pearson Learning Solutions.

Unlikely backer for Black college merger. (2010, January 28). *Inside Higher Ed.* Retrieved from http://www.insidehighered.com/news/2010/01/28/qt#218696

U.S. Commission on Civil Rights. (2006). *Public education campaign to end campus anti-Semitism.* Washington, DC: Author. Retrieved from http://www.eusccr.com/

U.S. Department of Education Office for Civil Rights. (1991). Historically Black colleges and universities and higher education desegregation. Washington, DC: Author.

Vocational Education Act of 1917, 29 U.S.C. 31 *et seq.* (1917).

Walpole, M. B. (2002). Socioeconomic status. In A. M. Martinez Aleman & K. A. Renn (Eds.), *Women in higher education: An encyclopedia* (pp. 355–358). Santa Barbara, CA: ABC-CLIO.

Weber, L. (1998). A conceptual framework for understanding race, class, gender, and sexuality. *Psychology of Women Quarterly, 22*(1), 13–32.

Whitmire, R. (2007, July 7). The latest way to discriminate against women. *The Chronicle of Higher Education, 53*(46), B16. Retrieved from http://chronicle.com/article/The-Latest-Way-to-Discrimin/34773/

Wilson, K., Gretzel, E., & Brown, T. (2000). Enhancing the post-secondary campus climate for students with disabilities. *Journal of Vocational Rehabilitation, 14*(1), 37–50.

Wolf-Wendel, L. (2002). Women's colleges. In A. M. Martinez Aleman & K. A. Renn (Eds.), *Women in higher education: An encyclopedia* (pp. 61–67). Santa Barbara, CA: ABC-CLIO.

Wright, B. (2002). The "untameable savage spirit": American Indians in colonial colleges. In C. S. Turner, A. L. Antonio, M. Garcia, B. V. Laden, A. Nora, & C. L. Presley (Eds.), *Racial and ethnic diversity in higher education* (2nd ed., pp. 122–134). Boston, MA: Pearson Learning Solutions.

Wright, D. J. (1987). Minority students: Developmental beginnings. In D. J. Wright (Ed.), *Responding to the needs of today's minority students* (New Directions for Student Services No. 38, pp. 5–21). San Francisco, CA: Jossey-Bass.

Yang, J. A. (1992). *Chilly campus climate: A qualitative study on White racial identity development attitudes.* Unpublished manuscript, Shippensburg University, Shippensburg, PA.

4

The Influence of Institutional Context and Culture

Raechele L. Pope and Lucy A. LePeau

ERHAPS IT WAS THE HOT PINK FLYER advertising National Coming Out Day sponsored by the Gay, Lesbian, Bisexual Student Alliance that caught her eye. Or maybe it was just the messy appearance of the bulletin board—a myriad of flyers carelessly arranged on top of each other, large and small, some handwritten and others professionally designed, held in place by staples, pushpins, even masking tape. For whatever reason, on this day the provost stopped to examine a bulletin board in front of the food court in the student union to read a sampling of the various postings: Need Work?—Job Fair Next Week; International Student Discussion Group; Open Casting Call for *The Vagina Monologues*; Annual Latino/a Student Leadership Conference; Military Scholarship Available; Don't Miss the Upcoming Campus Drag Show; Earn up to 6 Spanish Credits in 2 Weeks Over the Summer; Symposium Monday: How Healthcare Reform May Affect College Students; Spring Break Island Adventure—Only $500; Eating Disorder Support Group; Chinese 101—Class meets M-W-F 8:00–9:00 AM; Join the College Republicans; Summer Institute in Advance Statistics and Methods.

Intentional or not, the messages on the flyers present a composite image of the institution and are viewed differently by various members of a higher education institution. Such perceptions are undoubtedly influenced by the reader's multiple identities, expectations, and relationships with the institution. In addition, every institution has its own spoken and unspoken culture or context that influences not only its policies and public image but also how the institution is perceived by others. The purpose of this chapter is to explore how institutional culture and context are shaped by campus climate and the presence or absence of cross-cultural dialogue.

Culture is a lens through which individuals view experiences, work, education, and themselves (Pope & Thomas, 2000). Such a lens, when critically examined, can uncover underlying assumptions, values, and practices that motivate and propagate most institutional standards, policies, and practices (Fried, 1995; Minnich, 2004). In higher education, culture can be "an interpretive framework for understanding and appreciating events and actions in colleges and universities" (Kuh & Whitt, 1988, p. 3). Kuh (2003) identified various outcomes (i.e., artifacts, values, and assumptions) within this framework that constitute institutional culture. Schein (1985) suggested that several properties are essential to understanding culture, including observable behavioral practices, dominant values expressed by the organization, social norms, guiding philosophy, and rules for getting along with others. Insight into the underlying cultural values and assumptions for any institution of higher education can be obtained through a cultural audit or other form of assessment to gather relevant information about the espoused and enacted culture and mission of a college or university. Fried has been critical of this approach to culture by recommending that educators move from an object analysis of culture (e.g., examining the various artifacts or policies) to a more transactional dynamic whereby we examine the influence the institution has on members of the environment and ways those same members can or do shape the institution.

As educators, deciphering institutional culture through the various lenses of institutional mission, institutional type, and culture alone is shortsighted without also examining the campus climate for underrepresented and often underserved students, staff, and faculty representing numerous others. As defined previously in this book, *others* refers to those individuals often seen as outside the mainstream and not the norm or dominant group in terms of race, ethnicity, sexual orientation, religion, and social class, to name a few. Ostensibly, many college or university mission statements include appreciation of diversity, inclusion, and multiculturalism as central tenets; however, the words often fall short when a climate of inclusion for students, faculty, and staff from different racial and ethnic groups is not created (Harper &

Quaye, 2009; Kuh, 1993; Kuh & Love, 2000; Quaye & Harper, 2007). The perceptions, expectations, and attitudes of students, faculty, and staff of differing races and ethnicities regarding the campus climate toward racial and ethnic diversity must be taken into account when assessing institutional culture (Hurtado, Milem, Clayton-Pedersen, & Allen, 1999; Kuh & Love). The same can be said for other underrepresented groups like lesbian, gay, bisexual, and transgender (LGBT) individuals. Therefore, the unavoidable intersection of the institutional context with individual and collective university cultures is why the presence or absence of cross-cultural dialogue is a critical element for making sense of institutional culture. Institutional culture that may or may not encourage the presence or absence of cross-cultural dialogue helps to set the stage for examination of institutional context that includes institutional mission and culture, geographic location, zeitgeist, institutional type, and structural diversity.

INSTITUTIONAL MISSION AND CULTURE

The driving force behind the educational practices of any institution in higher education emanates from its mission. The fundamental question a mission statement addresses is: Whom and in what manner does the institution serve (Barr, 2000)? The mission relates to the espoused values of what an institution expects of its students, staff, administrators, and faculty associated with the various historical, philosophical, and religious underpinnings of the institution (Kuh, 1993; Kuh, Kinzie, Schuh, & Whitt, 2005; Kuh & Whitt, 1988). Further, the enacted mission, or how the institution actually lives out its espoused mission, is key to understanding the real value and impact of an institutional mission. The enacted mission is based on delineated learning outcomes as well as for whom (i.e., student population[s], faculty, staff, and community) and for what types of education the institution seeks to provide (Kuh, 1993; Pike, Kuh, & Gonyea, 2003). The mission and philosophy is embedded within institutional culture (Kuh; Kuh et al., 2005; Kuh & Whitt). Predicated by the fact that almost all institutions of higher education have a mission statement, the institutional culture—defined as persistent patterns of norms, values, practices, beliefs, and assumptions that shape the behavior of individuals and groups in a college or university, and provide a frame of reference to interpret the meaning of events and actions on and off campus (Kuh & Whitt)—must be considered to capture the essence of an institution. The levels of culture based on "artifacts, perspectives, values, and assumptions" (Kuh & Hall, 1993, p. 4) encapsulate the interplay among students, faculty, and staff of the past and present as mutually shaping institutional culture. To this end, the physical setting of campus, stories and myths, rituals, and ceremonies are all incorporated into the physical, verbal, and behavioral artifacts of institutional culture (Kuh & Hall; Kuh & Whitt). Because students, faculty, and staff select specific organizations and academic departments to join, these organizations become subcultures that manifest their own unique attitudes and behaviors based on group membership. More complexly, the tacit perspectives of how things are done at a particular institution often influence the lived perspectives and assumptions of a campus. As such, the cultural view of institutional context takes on greater significance for students, faculty, and staff if the way things are done is incongruent with one's culture and values (Kuh & Hall; Kuh & Whitt). While many institutions of higher education espouse valuing diversity, members of the community who represent underserved or underrepresented groups and their allies are often very aware when an institution purports to support diversity initiatives but its behaviors, policies, and actions suggest otherwise (Quaye et al., 2008). Evidence of a disconnection between an institution's values and behaviors can encourage negative feelings and perceptions and ultimately disengagement from the campus community (Museus, 2008). For example, part of Brandeis University's (2010) mission statement is coupled with a diversity statement:

> Established in 1948 [in Waltham, MA] as a model of ethnic and religious pluralism, Brandeis University considers social justice central to its mission as a nonsectarian university founded by members of the American Jewish community. . . . Recognizes the need to analyze and address the ways in which social, cultural, and economic inequalities affect power and privilege in the larger society and at Brandeis itself.

An outsider to Brandeis, reviewing this mission/diversity statement, may infer that the Jewish heritage of the university may attract students and staff who identify themselves as Jewish even though Brandeis identifies itself as nonsectarian. Someone reviewing this diversity statement will expect institutional practices that implement reflection and action when individuals or groups experience inequities. It is incumbent upon administrators of institutions that espouse inclusive mission statements to be intentional in their efforts to ensure that what they say they value and what they do is consistent, which according to Harper and antonio (2008) "requires courage, consciousness, assessment, and planning" (p. 11).

INSTITUTIONAL CONTEXT: CONSIDERING GEOGRAPHIC LOCATION, ZEITGEIST, AND INSTITUTIONAL TYPE

While understanding institutional culture is important because it can provide insight into the spoken and unspoken expectations, mores, and values of a college or university, it is equally important to understand the context of an institution. Institutional context is a broader term that encompasses the various circumstances that influence and shape an institution, such as the setting or geographic location. In addition, the zeitgeist, or outlook and influence of a particular time period or generation, is also key to understanding institutional context. In other words, context is fluid and can evolve and change over time. The zeitgeist of the 1960s created a very different environment in higher education on racial diversity issues than is in the current era.

Institutions of higher education also vary by type in that they may share certain traits or characteristics that distinguish them as a group. For example, institutions are located in rural, urban, and suburban areas of the country and comprise residential and commuter, public and private, two-year and four-year institutions; community colleges; tribal colleges; comprehensive research institutions; liberal arts colleges; historically Black colleges and universities (HBCUs); religiously affiliated institutions; and Hispanic-serving institutions (HSIs; Barr, 2000; Ryu, 2008). The purpose of institutions of higher education according to Boyer (1990), using the lens of the zeitgeist of the early 19th and 20th centuries, is to serve the greater interests and needs of the community where the institution is based. However, it is important to remember that the needs and interests of an institution may be diametrically different based on the geographic location (Barr), backgrounds and values of community members, and the social and economic issues facing the institution (Kuh, 2003).

When considering the context of geographic location on the institutional culture, particularly as it relates to efforts toward inclusion and cross-cultural dialogue, it is important to consider the unique realities of rural, suburban, and urban campuses in terms of values, structural diversity, and the needs and realities of the surrounding communities. Rural and suburban campuses tend to have less structural diversity (e.g., prevalence of multiple racial and ethnic enclaves) than urban campuses, which influences their campus expectations and sensibilities. Urban campuses may offer students more structural diversity outside the university regardless of diversity on campus. Said another way, students may have more access to affinity groups outside the campus setting. However, the structural diversity of communities that surround rural campuses may closely resemble the campus community. Rural and suburban campuses may have to approach the process of creating inclusive environments for students in different ways than an urban campus community. Likewise, a campus's location in the United States also affects which issues and concerns are deemed important. Colleges in Mississippi, California, Montana, and New York will likely differ in the values, expectations, and mores their surrounding communities manifest and how that process occurs. Although the location of a campus cannot be changed, it is important to acknowledge that structural diversity is not required to enact an inclusive and diverse institutional culture.

Institutional type also has an effect on the individuals who work at and attend different types of campuses as well as on the culture they emanate. Predominantly White institutions (PWIs) are inherently different from campuses designed to or by default serve a majority of students of color (e.g., HBCUs, HSIs, and tribal colleges). Their populations differ so significantly because their missions, goals, and expectations are typically different as well. It is important that all campuses serve underrepresented groups; however, who is in that minority will vary depending on the campus population and mission. Meeting the needs of White students at an HBCU versus students of color at a PWI creates parallel challenges and circumstances for higher education professionals on both campus types.

Hirt (2006) outlined a conceptual framework after gathering data from over 1,100 student affairs professionals about the effect of the type of their institution on their professional work life. She applied seven metaphors to describe professional work life for student affairs administrators: liberal arts colleges as "The Standard Bearers," religiously affiliated institutions as "The

Interpreters," comprehensive colleges and universities as "The Generalists," research universities as "The Specialists," HBCUs as "The Guardians," community colleges as "The Producers," and HSIs as "The Change Agents." Although each and every campus environment had unique facets, the generalizations based on type are useful constructions for examining explicit and implicit expectations for educators working at these seven types of institutions.

The student populations and faculty departments at liberal arts colleges are small and change infrequently (Austin, 1990; Hirt, 2006). The Standard Bearers working on liberal arts campuses are often categorized as professionals highly attuned to the holistic development of students. According to Hirt, student affairs professionals at religiously affiliated institutions, The Interpreters, often view their work as a calling, become partners with faculty and parents in their work, and often must navigate church denominational politics. For example, how likely would students of a conservative religious college in the Deep South witness the following flyers on their campus: Casting Auditions for *The Vagina Monologues*, or Don't Miss the Upcoming Campus Drag Show? What impact would the invisibility of those issues have on the students who attend that college or the individuals who work there? Blurring the lines between the invisibility of productions such as *The Vagina Monologues* and the greater campus culture and climate, a prospective gay student may perceive the absence of the productions as a sign that he or she is not welcome on the campus. Likewise, a faculty member who conducts research pertaining to LGBT issues in higher education may question academic freedom on this campus. While such programming might not be openly embraced at small religious colleges in the Deep South, given the zeitgeist of the time and the characteristics of the current generation of students, it is likely they will be aware of such issues even if they are not addressed on campus. And even though not every campus is open to all students, it seems harder to pigeonhole current students as being only conservative or only religious. This generation of college students tends to dismiss labels used to describe them collectively and prefer to be seen as individuals (Howe & Strauss, 1993; Levine & Cureton, 1998), and it is important that campuses address that reality.

At HBCUs, primarily located in the southeastern part of the United States, The Guardians are focused on upholding the mission to educate Black students because of their devotion to Black history and culture (Hirt,

2006). Faculty and staff at HBCUs, often educated themselves at HBCUs as undergraduates, capitalize on already formed relationships, create educational and programmatic activities for students with limited resources, and navigate through highly politicized environments. HSIs, primarily clustered in six states (Arizona, California, Florida, Illinois, New York, and Texas) and growing from 163 institutions in 1995 to 341 in 2005, are characterized as such because at least 25% of the study body identifies itself as Hispanic (Hirt; Ryu, 2008). Because of exploding enrollment, limited financial resources, and populations of students from distinct Hispanic cultures at HSIs, student affairs professionals are expected to react to ongoing organizational change by continuing to define and redefine missions and practices that meet the rapidly evolving student populations. While not included in Hirt's conceptualization, students and educators at tribal colleges consider collectivist cultural values with a high commitment to the community exemplified by present time orientation, sharing, spirituality, and cooperation as guides to professional work life (Guardia & Evans, 2008; Pavel, Inglebret, & Banks, 2001).

Faculty members at community colleges typically take on extensive teaching loads and provide considerable remedial assistance to their students; student learning is a paramount value for faculty at a community college (Austin, 1990; Hirt, 2006). Called The Producers, student affairs professionals at community colleges find themselves in ever-evolving environments with small staffing structures working with many students from underserved populations (Hirt). The Generalists at comprehensive colleges and universities are often located at regional or state institutions, highly bureaucratized, open to change, and collaborative across student affairs and disciplines (Hirt). Faculty members at state colleges often grapple with balancing research demands with the needs of students in the classroom (Austin). The Specialists at research universities find the nature of work to be highly bureaucratized but slow to change (Hirt). The work of student affairs professionals at research universities is often fast paced, competitive, and identified as creative and full of risk taking (Hirt), while faculty striving to fulfill research agendas are of primary interest to the institution (Austin). For instance, an educator at a comprehensive institution in Michigan may think differently about a job fair for students seeking part-time or full-time employment while contemplating budget cuts and the loss of jobs on and off campus during the economic recession than an educator working at an urban community college in Florida. If one of the primary functions of the comprehensive institution is to serve the community (Barr, 2000; Boyer, 1990), but the community is struggling economically, the geographic setting will have an impact on the institution and will be a primary consideration when planning a job fair on campus. For instance, a career center staff member in Michigan may turn to inviting employers outside the state to recruit graduates at a job fair because of the lack of jobs locally, but this decision may be complicated. If the mission of the institution is to graduate students who will economically support the community, but jobs are not available because of a recession, then educators must contemplate how to meet the needs of the students but also uphold the institutional mission. Local employers may still be invited to the job fair, but collecting résumés may be the only opportunity the employers can provide at a time of recession. The invitation of local employers not only symbolically demonstrates to students that the campus community values students' applying their educational capital in the community, but also exposes students to the reality that immediate opportunities to work in the community are limited.

Although the snapshot approach of examining an institution's context is informative, the analysis falls short without consideration of institutional climates, especially in regard to structural diversity. Further, educators identifying themselves as change agents within these professional environments may see their work as an opportunity to modify or challenge the status quo in view of the changing demographics of students attending their respective institutions (Hurtado et al., 1999; Torres, Howard-Hamilton, & Cooper, 2003). The proclivity for an educator to consider institutional context and institutional type when selecting a place to work cannot be ignored, because an educator's values and cultural orientation(s) often guide selection of workplace environment (Hirt, 2006). Educators must wrestle with the confluence of institutional location, mission, campus environment, and campus culture interacting with the ways students experience the institutional context.

Hurtado, Milem, Clayton-Pedersen, and Allen (1998) provided a framework for examining campus environments based on historical, structural, psychological, and behavioral racial and ethnic climate that is "actual reports of general social interaction, interaction between and among individuals from different racial/ethnic backgrounds, and the nature of relations between and among groups on campus" (p. 37). Infusing this framework with research pertaining to the (a) structural diversity of an institution based on the race and ethnicity of students, faculty, and staff; (b) psychological perceptions and attitudes based on the precollege cultures students, faculty, and staff bring to an institutional environment; and (c) behaviors of individuals contributing to cross-cultural dialogue enriches the application of the conceptual framework from Hurtado et al. and adds further clarity regarding the effect of institutional context and culture. According to Mayhew, Grunwald, and Dey (2006), the degree to which these various components of racial/ethnic climate "make diverse university constituents feel comfortable as welcome and belonging members of the campus community reflects one way a campus can achieve a positive climate for diversity" (p. 64).

STRUCTURAL DIVERSITY: RACE AND ETHNICITY OF STUDENTS, FACULTY, AND STAFF

The structural or racial and ethnic composition of the student body does affect opportunities for students to interact with individuals whose race or ethnicity differs from their own (Denson & Chang, 2009; Umbach & Kuh, 2006). The debate about policies and practices surrounding Affirmative Action or race-conscious admissions developed to increase numeric representations of underrepresented students, particularly on campuses with longstanding White dominant cultures, is ongoing (Chang, 1999, 2002; Hurtado et al., 1999); however, research is increasingly finding support for the educational value and positive influence such structural diversity has on student learning (Chang, 1999; Gurin, Dey, Hurtado, & Gurin, 2002; Milem, 2003). Campuses continue to become more racially and ethnically diverse (Ryu, 2008); however, increasing numbers of students, faculty, and staff representing a spectrum of race, class, genders, sexual orientations, and disabilities alone does not address how structural diversity does or does not increase the likelihood of students' engaging in meaningful cross-cultural dialogues. Increasing structural racial and ethnic diversity on a given campus does not occur in a vacuum; the geographic location and institutional mission and type of the institution can have a profound influence. Further, the commitment of the institution toward increasing enrollment of students based on race and ethnicity in relation to the particular campus context necessitates deep understanding of the climate for students, faculty, and staff from different backgrounds (Hurtado et al., 1999).

INFLUENCE OF ATTITUDES AND VALUES OF STUDENTS, FACULTY, AND STAFF ON INSTITUTIONAL CULTURE

The perceptions students have about the assumptions, values, and beliefs of an institution's culture influences their perceptions about racial tensions on campus (Chang, 2002; Hurtado et al., 1999). A campus culture is mutually shaped by the people already present and by individuals who join the institutional community (Kuh & Love, 2000). When students matriculate they bring their multiple identities, such as race, ethnicity, sexual orientation, and religious group membership; their affiliation with various other social groups based on neighborhoods, churches, and social classes; and their expectations about the various groups they hope to join including social, academic, and cultural organizations (Kuh & Love). The assumptions that students bring based on their precollege experiences shape their views and expectations of these various groups. Depending on the campus climate for faculty, students, and staff identifying with different racial and ethnic groups, the initial feelings of sense of belonging vary (Hurtado et al., 1999; Torres et al., 2003). Scholars (cf. Hurtado, 1994; Hurtado et al., 1998; Milem, 2001) reported that a positive racial climate included (a) a meaningful number of students, faculty, and administrators of color; (b) a curriculum that infuses multicultural issues; (c) programs that support the recruitment, retention, and graduation of students of color; and (d) a mission statement that supports and centralizes an institutional commitment to diversity and pluralism. A negative racial climate does not incorporate these multicultural components and ultimately has a detrimental effect on the overall campus culture and the academic success for students of color (Rankin & Reason, 2005). This type of racial climate profoundly and negatively affects the well-being of students of color. Similar realities have been reported for other underserved and underrepresented groups (Brown, Clarke, Gortmaker, & Robinson-Keilig, 2004; Evans, 2002; Mayhew et al., 2006; Waldo, 1998; Wilson, Getzel, & Brown, 2000).

Kuh and Love (2000) developed eight propositions pertaining to students' cultural perspectives of a campus community and possible rationales for student departure. Museus and Quaye (2009) examined those eight propositions through a qualitative study using a sample of 30 students of color at a large public research PWI the researchers labeled as Mideastern University. Viewing the literature in tandem, Kuh and Love's and Museus and Quaye's propositions for understanding the cultural perspectives of faculty, students, and staff about institutional contexts is worth further consideration. First, students' cultural systems of making meaning, or interpretations, of how their cultures are represented on campus are different because students experience the same environment in multiple ways (Kuh & Love; Museus & Quaye). If several students of color are elected to student government offices, many White students might believe their campus is affirming to all students, whereas some students of color may feel those students are merely tokens and they commonly feel left out and on the periphery of student life. Museus and Quaye illustrated how students of color in the study whose precollege experiences were in a predominantly White environmental culture often perceived Mideastern as highly diverse, whereas students whose precollege experiences were in highly mixed racial and cultural environments perceived Mideastern as more homogeneous. Applying this theme in their research to the example in the beginning of the chapter, a student of color from a predominantly White background of origin enrolled on a campus like Mideastern may perceive the announcement "International Student Discussion Group" as an example of the racial and cultural diversity on the campus. However, a student of color from a diversified background of multiple cultures of origin may see the same announcement and perceive it as an example of how difficult it might be for an international student to find support. Students' perceptions may be based on their prior understanding of collegiate experiences when making these inferences about the campus culture.

Second, students' precollege cultures determine the importance they associate with attending or graduating from college, in addition to the expectations they have about interacting with diverse peers on a campus environment (Kuh & Love, 2000; Museus & Quaye, 2009). The third proposition relates to knowledge of diverse racial groups and opportunities for cultural immersion on campus and their influence on students' abilities to make meaning and possibly negotiate perceptions of the institutional environment's openness to their cultural group (Kuh & Love; Museus & Quaye). For example, a student or an educator viewing the flyer Register for the Annual Latino/a Student Leadership Conference may have varying ideas about the visibility of Latino/Latina students on campus. Based on their racial or cultural identity, not all Latino/Latina students would be interested in participating in such an event, while others will be committed to it. Students who are not Latino/Latina may pay little or no attention to the flyer, assuming it has no relevance to their lives. The remaining propositions from Kuh and Love and Museus and Quaye are that the cultural dissonance that students face on campus may present barriers to persistence, and that students of color who experience great dissonance may need to find cultural agents or allies who are able to validate their culture of origin and encourage educational attainment.

STUDENT, STAFF, AND FACULTY CONTRIBUTIONS TO CROSS-CULTURAL DIALOGUE

Alongside the perceptions of the campus climate in relation to structural diversity, the behaviors students exhibit when engaging in cross-cultural interactions on campus are important. So too are the cues they receive from faculty and peers about the importance of engaging in educational efforts to learn about content interconnected with race and ethnicity (Denson & Chang, 2009; Quaye & Harper, 2007). Denson and Chang used a sample of 20,178 students from the Cooperative Institutional Research Program "to examine the relationship between diversity and student development" (p. 329) by focusing on three outcomes of personal efficacy, academic skills, and social- or racial-culture domains. In the primary findings, students who engaged in diversity workshops and interacted with individuals of different races reported higher self-efficacy scores. Also, regardless of their own involvement in diversity workshops or activities, students at institutions with course work related to diversity issues had higher levels of academic skills, and students who attended campuses where the student population as a whole engaged in diversity issues demonstrated higher levels of knowledge and the ability to get along with people of different races and cultures. Denson and Chang's research adds to the body of literature demonstrating positive cognitive and affective benefits of students' own interactions with individuals from different cultures and races other than their own, but also the potentially distal benefits of diversity initiatives on a campus even if students are not involved in the academic workshops and activities. Denson and Chang suggested that the meaning of these findings will be shaped by students' experiences in specific institutional contexts. The far-reaching benefits of diversity initiatives on students' perceptions are documented (Denson & Chang) but at the same time expose the need for meaningful cross-cultural dialogues on college campuses.

Given the scholarly demands and sometimes philosophical opposition to diversity efforts in higher education, many faculty members have not been actively involved in contributing to diversity initiatives, even though Milem and Umbach (2008) suggested that "faculty members may be the campus constituency best positioned to assess how diversity influences teaching and affects student learning" (p. 156). Research has shown that "faculty emphasis on diversity in courses has positive effects on students' openness to racial understanding and overall satisfaction with college" (Smith, 1997, p. 32). First and foremost, faculty members can contribute to or inhibit cross-cultural dialogue in the classroom. Quaye and Harper (2007) offered three primary suggestions for faculty to engage in practices that intentionally relate to creating inclusive pedagogy and curricula in the classroom: (a) continuing to update and alter the literature base for classes that reflects cultural congruence for students and also using peers in respective departments to identify multicultural texts; (b) encouraging professors from dominant cultures to hold themselves accountable for learning and applying culturally inclusive pedagogical techniques; and (c) calling on faculty to continually self-reflect in regard to biases, assumptions, and prejudices they have about student learning and how those biases influence their teaching. Milem and Umbach suggested that given the resistance and limited competence regarding diversity matters among faculty members, "student affairs educators can play an important role in helping faculty understand the opportunities for teaching and learning that campus diversity provides, and help them to develop the skills they need to achieve these benefits in the classroom" (p. 167). Student affairs professionals are often the leaders in multicultural education on college campuses and set important examples by actively promoting diversity initiatives and participating in campus diversity dialogues. When student affairs professionals have the skills to facilitate difficult dialogues, it would be useful for them to offer training for faculty to assist in their efforts in addressing these important issues in their classroom.

Staff members and administrators on college campuses also have an important role regarding diversity initiatives. Jenkins and Walton (2008) suggested moving beyond planning campus cultural events to creating "educationally meaningful cultural programs" (p. 91). Pope (1993) suggested that many multicultural programs or change efforts focus on awareness-oriented cultural programs, which often make individuals feel good about diversity but probably do not influence the campus climate. However, programs that focus on deeper learning and awareness are more able to create a paradigm shift that can help participants change the way they view themselves and others who may be culturally different. Such efforts mean creating programs that are comprehensive, intentional, logistically efficient, and generationally relevant. Self-reflection and development of multicultural competence is necessary for student affairs professionals before they engage with diversity initiatives (Pope, Reynolds, & Mueller, 2004).

It is essential that students, faculty, and staff take active responsibility for engaging in cross-cultural dialogue. Chang (2002) noted, "A transformative discourse makes it clear that the diversity agenda is inextricably linked to the advancement of student learning and the democratization of institutions" (p. 135). Therefore, a need exists to consider how cross-racial and intercultural dialogues occur based on institutional context. Because examining institutional context and culture requires an intricate web of students, faculty, and staff inhabiting institutions of unique missions, educational philosophies, subcultures, and climates located in different regions of the country, educators and students often struggle to engage in meaningful cross-cultural dialogue. However, constructive dialogues can unfold based on intentional processes that situate educators amid institutional context and culture.

CREATING AN INSTITUTIONAL CLIMATE AND CULTURE THAT VALUES DIVERSITY AND DIALOGUE

Hurtado et al. (1998) offered a framework for understanding campus climate and its ability to facilitate or hinder the development of communities that value inclusion. While their work focused specifically on racial climate, it is possible to apply this same framework to other underserved and underrepresented groups on campus. The four dimensions are (a) an institution's history regarding racial inclusion or exclusion, (b) the effects of structural diversity on students, (c) psychological climate including perceptions and beliefs about diversity, and (d) behaviors of individuals contributing to cross-cultural interaction. Many campuses choose to focus merely on the structural diversity of numbers when addressing diversity issues even though research suggests the numbers alone do not ensure a link between diversity and positive climate (Hurtado et al., 1999; Milem, 2001). Hurtado et al. (1999) identified two key issues to explore

> when considering the success of efforts to improve the campus racial climate: (a) How diverse does the campus look in its representation of different cultural groups, and (b) To what extent do campus operations demonstrate that racial and ethnic diversity is an essential value? (p. 297)

Their latter point highlights the issue of institutional climate and whether campus administrators endorse and enact a diversity-affirming perspective in all aspects of the institution or whether their diversity efforts are more uncoordinated and limited in scope. For example, an individual considering attending Brandeis University might review the mission statement and look for examples of intergroup dialogues focused on intersectional approaches to power and privilege (e.g., conversations about race, religion, class, gender) inside and outside the classroom. The individual may look to see where intergroup dialogues are happening: conversations in the residence halls, academic departments, or student organizations. The individual could also evaluate staffing across campus. Who are the leaders in positions of power, and what visible identities do they represent? How are faculty members rewarded in different academic disciplines (e.g., pay structures across academic disciplines)? The confluence of these issues and the communication across campus regarding diversity efforts will demonstrate more coordinated, rather than isolated, efforts.

Harper and antonio (2008) stated unequivocally that institutions as well as individual educators must be intentional in their efforts to create campuses that embrace diversity values and practices. It is not enough, as many scholars have asserted, to merely focus on adding structural diversity to a campus (Chang, 2002; Harper & antonio; Pope, 1995) without also creating a plan for cross-cultural engagement (Museus, 2008) and multicultural organizational change (Grieger, 1996; Pope et al., 2004). For the purposes of this discussion on creating an institutional climate and culture that values diversity and dialogue, two distinct yet overlapping approaches are explored in greater depth: cross-cultural engagement and multicultural organizational development (MCOD). While one might suggest that all multicultural initiatives, including a campuswide program on cross-cultural engagement, could fall under the rubric of multicultural organizational change, the paradigm shift necessary for true transformation of higher education requires diverse approaches micro and macro in scope. Cross-cultural engagement occurs on the microlevel and encourages institutions to value the smallest interpersonal exchange that can occur on a campus and envision it as part of a larger institutional effort to improve cross-cultural interaction. On the macrolevel, MCOD change efforts can occur on multiple organizational levels and affect policies, practices, and procedures in individual programs and departments and across the campus as a whole.

Cross-Cultural Engagement

Given that research shows intergroup relationships may have a positive impact on retention, college satisfaction, and other measures of academic and social success (Smith, 1997), it seems that any effort to create campuses that value diversity and dialogue need to include opportunities for cross-cultural engagement. The purpose of this chapter is to emphasize the interplay among institutional mission, climate, culture, structural diversity, and other factors that simultaneously influence students and educators when trying to engage in cross-cultural dialogue. In fact, research has shown that diversity alone, even without having intact cross-cultural engagement or intergroup relations programs, increases the likelihood that students will interact with individuals who are different from them (Chang, 2001). Such efforts toward dialogue and cross-cultural engagement need to occur in the context of an ongoing and intentional programmatic effort that involves students, faculty, and staff from across campus. Such efforts can occur within student affairs units (i.e., residential life program or leadership training through student life) or in the classroom through learning communities or other educational interventions. Additional research does suggest that classroom environments can do much to enhance those interactions with active pedagogical approaches that incorporate and stimulate cross-cultural interaction and engagement (Hurtado, 2001). Socializing across difference, actively discussing those differences, and maintaining diverse friendships have been shown to offer beneficial effects on vital cognitive and affective dimensions (Harper & antonio, 2008).

Hurtado (2001) stated that "it may be that the college peer group provides the opportunity to experience this knowledge [of diversity] firsthand and learn how to negotiate differences" (p. 200). It is important to acknowledge that measuring the effects of diversity on college campuses is challenging because the outcomes may not always be visible or what is expected or desired (Chang, 1999). Student affairs professionals need to consider what their desired outcomes are and then create programs and services meant to create such outcomes. Poignantly, when the effects of diversity on college students were examined more closely by Hu and Kuh (2003), the benefits appeared to be much more positive for White students. Intentionality in the design of any intergroup effort is essential in benefitting all students. In this case, intentionality means consulting the target of one's multicultural change efforts and other campus and community constituents to determine their needs and wants. Upon completion, it is essential to evaluate the effectiveness for the various groups who participated.

Parker, Archer, and Scott (1992), based on the work by Barna (1988), identified a variety of barriers that interfere with cross-cultural engagement. Specifically, Barna suggested that assumed similarity, nonverbal misinterpretations, preconceptions and stereotypes, tendency to evaluate, and high anxiety all interfered with the ability or willingness of individuals to engage in what they perceived to be challenging interdialogues. When individuals assume universality or when individuals overemphasize similarities, the unique contributions of specific cultures are minimized, thus creating a barrier to effective and meaningful cross-cultural dialogue. This is further complicated by the tendency for individuals to misinterpret nonverbal behavior by evaluating its meaning based solely on their own cultural backgrounds. For example, to assume that everyone has the same expectations for physical space and contact may mean that some individuals will be perceived to be distant or disinterested because they are more physically removed while others may be viewed as aggressive or rude because they move past an individual's comfort zone. Such assumptions can profoundly affect communication. Preconceptions and stereotypes also influence cross-cultural engagement by blocking meaningful and genuine communication. The tendency to evaluate rather than understand others' belief systems can make it difficult to connect with others who have different cultural experiences and identities. Parker et al. identified additional barriers to cross-cultural engagement: (a) lack of cultural knowledge, (b) language differences, (c) stereotyping, (d) lack of tolerance, (e) self-disclosure, and (f) denial of racism.

Although Parker et al. (1992) suggested that the "foundation for multicultural relations on campus is effective communication" (p. 121), other scholars (D'Andrea & Daniels, 2007; Henry et al., 2007; Jones, 2008) proposed that individual and institutional resistance and backlash may occur as a result of efforts to engage in difficult dialogues and cross-cultural engagement. Jones explored causes and various strategies for working through student resistance; she suggested that "fully engaging the resistance that emerges in cross-cultural learning is challenging work, [but] essential to the learning process itself" (p. 81). It is vital to address resistance not only on the individual level but on the institutional level as well. On an individual basis that means moving out of one's comfort zone and facing any biases, prejudices, and assumptions about various cultural groups. Such individual risk taking also includes reaching out to form relationships and engage with others even if it is difficult. On an institutional level, there are always stakeholders, leaders, and other interested parties who will be threatened or disinterested in any type of cross-cultural engagement and may attempt to block change. Creating opportunities for institutional change by developing a multicultural strategic plan for one's department or division is an example of risk taking. By blending the microapproach of cross-cultural engagement with the macroapproach of MCOD, educators and student affairs professionals alike will be best equipped to have a transformative effect on their campuses.

MCOD

Pope et al. (2004) and others have suggested that without the use of systematic organizational and cultural change efforts, it is difficult to move away

from the sporadic and uncoordinated multicultural programmatic and educational interventions that have long been the focus of multicultural endeav-
ors in higher education. A variety of models for multicultural organization
change have been developed over the past 20 years to address this void.
Regardless of the particular theories or approaches used, most scholars highlight the necessity of leadership commitment and visible support for diversity
initiatives at the highest levels of the institution (Grieger, 1996; Manning &
Coleman-Boatwright, 1991; Pope, 1995; Smith, 1997). Leadership from the
top of the institution is necessary but not enough; comprehensive theories
and specific strategies and tools to guide multicultural change efforts are
necessary.

Relying on the work by Jackson and Holvino (1988) and Jackson and
Hardiman (1994) on MCOD as a model or tool for creating multiculturally
sensitive environments, Pope (1995) introduced MCOD theory and applications to the field of student affairs. According to Jackson (2006), the three
major elements of MCOD are an MCOD goal, MCOD developmental
stages, and an MCOD process. Becoming a multicultural organization or
institution "involves achievement of social justice (an anti-exclusionary
objective) and social diversity (an inclusionary objective)" (p. 143); in other
words, a multicultural organization strives to address issues of structural
diversity as well as incorporate social justice values and practices to ensure
the fair and just treatment of all who participate in the institution. It is not
enough to give everyone a seat at the table unless all participants are fairly
treated and their voices are included in the decision-making process. By
addressing multicultural issues at this organizational level, higher education
institutions are more able to create an institutional culture and climate that
embraces diversity at every level.

Jackson (2006), along with Katz (1989), suggested that there is a developmental process to becoming a multicultural organization, and to make progress, an institution must assess where it is on the continuum. In addition,
Garcia et al. (2001) suggested that assessment may document and evaluate
diversity initiatives, communicate issues with various stakeholders, and
enhance the overall diversity plan. In addition to assessment, Jackson highlighted other components of the multicultural change process, including
assembling an internal multicultural change team that can lead all aspects of
the plan. It is vital for this leadership to be internal so there is ownership of
the process. Once the data have been gathered and evaluated, a concrete

strategic plan must be developed to guide and structure the multicultural change effort. In addition, this group is typically charged with building support for the multicultural plan and assessing the readiness level of the organization. According to Reynolds and Pope (2003), "Without such frameworks it is difficult to assess the strengths and weaknesses of an organization, develop the necessary and appropriate interventions, and help those involved know whether their efforts have been successful" (p. 375).

To illustrate the planning process and envision how to create a multicultural strategic plan, an organizational development checklist was created by Grieger (1996). This checklist is based on MCOD principles and can be easily adapted to individual programs, departments, or institutions to assist in the creation of concrete and comprehensive strategic plans. Essential institutional areas such as mission statement, policy review, recruitment and retention of diverse staff, multicultural competency expectations and training, and physical environment are just a few of the items included in the checklist. For more insight into how to use such a tool, consult Reynolds and Pope (2003) for an example in a college counseling center.

An alternative approach to the Grieger (1996) checklist has been a heuristic model, the multicultural change intervention matrix (MCIM), developed by Pope (1995) to conceptualize and plan multicultural interventions. The MCIM consists of two primary dimensions: targets of multicultural interventions including the individual, group, and institution; and type of change consisting of first- or second-order change (see table 4.1). First-order change occurs without altering the core structure of a given system, while second-order change is more focused on fundamental transformation of the system. This matrix provides six ways to conceptualize and structure multicultural

Table 4.1   Multicultural Change Intervention Matrix

	Type of Change	
Target of Change	*1st Order Change*	*2nd Order Change*
INDIVIDUAL	A. Awareness	B. Paradigm Shift
GROUP	C. Membership	D. Restructuring
INSTITUTIONAL	E. Programmatic	F. Systemic

Note. ©Raechele L. Pope (1992)

change that increases the possible areas for intervention and types of activities, strategies, and tools available. For example, many multicultural change
efforts are targeted toward short-term individual awareness programs (Pope,
1993) when research has shown that more sustained opportunities for inter-
actional diversity have significant effects on cognitive and affective outcomes
(Harper & antonio, 2008). Through use of this matrix as an assessment tool,
administrators of an institution can gather vital information on where most
interventions are targeted and what areas require further attention.

Together, these MCOD tools or methods—the MCOD checklist and the
MCIM—offer varied approaches to address and alter the institutional culture and climate. Through the use of the systematic process of the checklist
and the strategic planning it supports, important artifacts can be evaluated
for multicultural sensitivity, such as realizing that important campus docu-
ments are available only in English or vital community spaces on campus
are not wheelchair accessible. Using the MCIM provides another way of
conceptualizing multicultural change efforts to ensure they are comprehensive and multifaceted. By focusing on the value of first- and second-order
change, college and university administrators can consciously create interventions targeting individuals, groups, and organizational units to enhance
the likelihood of multicultural transformation. These MCOD tools create
opportunities for intentional cultural change, and by engaging in such
efforts, it is truly possible for institutions to make the structural changes
necessary to ensure that multiculturalism is an institutional foundation.
These multicultural change efforts create opportunities for cross-cultural dialogue at all levels of the institution. When those dialogues occur, the campus
climate can also grow and change in ways that are affirming for all individuals and members of the community.

CONCLUSION

To create campus environments where all students can succeed and grow, it
is essential that all educators and student affairs professionals have the necessary awareness, knowledge, and skills to effectively address issues of culture
in the interpersonal and institutional complexity in higher education. Such
competence involves understanding how institutional culture is shaped by
campus climate and the presence or absence of cross-cultural dialogue on

campus. In this chapter we examined the various components of institutional culture and context, which include institutional mission and culture, geographic location, zeitgeist, institutional type, and structural diversity, and how they may influence multicultural change efforts in higher education. Exploration of the literature in cross-cultural engagement and MCOD provide a backdrop for some of the strategies that can be implemented to transform higher education into a collaborative, engaging, and open environment where students can learn and be validated.

REFERENCES

Austin, A. E. (1990). Faculty cultures, faculty values. In W. Tierney (Ed.), *Assessing academic climates and cultures* (New Directions for Institutional Research No. 68, pp. 61–74. San Francisco, CA: Jossey-Bass.

Barna, L. M. (1988). Stumbling blocks in intercultural communication. In L. Samovar & R. E. Porter (Eds.), *Intercultural communication: A reader* (5th ed., pp. 337–347). New York, NY: Wadsworth.

Barr, M. J. (2000). The importance of the institutional mission. In M. J. Barr & M. K. Desler (Eds.), *The handbook of student affairs administration* (2nd ed., pp. 25–36). San Francisco, CA: Jossey-Bass.

Boyer, E. L. (1990). *Scholarship reconsidered: Priorities of the professoriate.* Princeton, NJ: Carnegie Foundation for the Advancement of Teaching.

Brandeis University. (2010). *Mission statement.* Retrieved from http://www.brandeis .edu/about/mission.html

Brown, R. D., Clarke, B., Gortmaker, V., & Robinson-Keilig, R. (2004). Assessing the campus climate for Gay, Lesbian, Bisexual, and Transgender (GLBT) students using a multiple perspectives approach. *Journal of College Student Development, 45*(1), 8–26.

Chang, M. J. (1999). Does racial diversity matter? The educational impact of a racially diverse undergraduate population. *Journal of College Student Development, 40*(4), 377–395.

Chang, M. J. (2001). The positive educational effects of racial diversity on campus. In G. Orfield (Ed.), *Diversity challenged: Evidence on the impact of affirmative action* (pp. 175–186). Cambridge, MA: Harvard Education Publishing Group.

Chang, M. J. (2002). Preservation or transformation: Where's the real educational discourse on diversity? *Review of Higher Education, 25*(2), 125–140.

D'Andrea, M., & Daniels, J. (2007). Dealing with institutional racism on campus: Initiating difficult dialogues and social justice advocacy interventions. *College Student Affairs Journal, 26*(2), 169–176.

Denson, N., & Chang, M. J. (2009). Racial diversity matters: The impact of diversity-related student engagement and institutional context. *American Educational Research Journal, 46*(2), 322–353.

Evans, N. J. (2002). The impact of an LGBT safe zone project on campus climate. *Journal of College Student Development, 43*(4), 522–539.

Fried, J. (1995). *Shifting paradigms in student affairs: Culture, context, teaching and learning.* Washington, DC: American College Personnel Association.

Garcia, M., Hudgins, C. A., Musil, C. M., Nettles, M., Sedlacek, W. E., & Smith, D. G. (2001). *Assessing campus diversity initiatives: A guide for campus practitioners.* Washington, DC: Association of American Colleges and Universities.

Grieger, I. (1996). A multicultural organizational development checklist for student affairs. *Journal of College Student Development, 37*(5), 561–573.

Guardia, J. R., & Evans, N. J. (2008). Student development in tribal colleges and universities. *NASPA Journal, 45*(2), 237–264.

Gurin, P., Dey, E. L., Hurtado, S., & Gurin, G. (2002). Diversity and higher education: Theory and impact on educational outcomes. *Harvard Educational Review, 72*(3), 330–366.

Harper, S. R., & antonio, a. l. (2008). Not by accident: Intentionality in diversity, learning, and engagement. In S. R. Harper (Ed.), *Creating inclusive campus environments for cross-cultural learning and student engagement* (pp. 1–18). Washington, DC: National Association of Student Personnel Administrators.

Harper, S. R., & Quaye, S. J. (2009). Beyond sameness, with engagement and outcomes for all. In S. R. Harper & S. J. Quaye (Eds.), *Student engagement in higher education: Theoretical perspectives and practical approaches for diverse populations* (pp. 1–15). New York, NY: Routledge.

Henry, W., Cobb-Roberts, D., Sherman, D., Exum, H. A., Keller, H., & Shircliffe, B. (2007). When the dialogue becomes too difficult: A case study of resistance and backlash. *College Student Affairs Journal, 26*(2), 160–168.

Hirt, J. B. (2006). *Where you work matters: Student affairs administration at different types of institutions.* Lanham, MD: University Press of America.

Howe, N., & Strauss, B. (1993). *13th gen: Abort, retry, ignore, fail?* New York, NY: Vintage Books.

Hu, S., & Kuh, G. D. (2003). Diversity experiences and college student learning and personal development. *Journal of College Student Development, 44*(3), 320–334.

Hurtado, S. (1994). The institutional climate for talented Latino students. *Research in Higher Education, 35*(1), 21–41.

Hurtado, S. (2001). Linking diversity and educational purpose: How diversity affects the classroom environment and student development. In G. Orfield (Ed.),

Diversity challenged: Evidence on the impact of affirmative action (pp. 187–203). Cambridge, MA: Harvard Education Publishing Group.

Hurtado, S., Milem, J., Clayton-Pedersen, A., & Allen, W. (1999). *Enacting diverse learning environments: Improving the climate for racial/ethnic diversity in higher education.* Washington, DC: George Washington University, Graduate School of Education and Human Development.

Hurtado, S., Milem, J. F., Clayton-Pedersen, A. R., & Allen, W. R. (1998). Enhancing campus climates for racial/ethnic diversity: Educational policy and practice. *Review of Higher Education, 21*(3), 279–302.

Jackson, B. W. (2006). Theory and practice of multicultural organization development. In B. B. Jones & M. Brazzel (Eds.), *The NTL handbook of organization development and change: Principles, practices, and perspectives* (pp. 139–156). San Francisco, CA: Pfeiffer.

Jackson, B. W., & Hardiman, R. (1994). Multicultural organizational development. In E. Y. Cross, J. H. Katz, F. A. Miller, & E. W. Seashore (Eds.), *The promise of diversity: Over 40 voices discuss strategies for eliminating discrimination in organizations* (pp. 231–239). Boston, MA: McGraw-Hill.

Jackson, B. W., & Holvino, E. (1988). Developing multicultural organizations. *Journal of Applied Behavioral Science and Religion, 9*(2), 14–19.

Jenkins, T. S., & Walton, C. L. (2008). Student affairs and cultural practice: A framework for implementing culture outside the classroom. In S. R. Harper (Ed.), *Creating inclusive campus environments for cross-cultural learning and student engagement* (pp. 87–101). Washington, DC: National Association of Student Personnel Administrators.

Jones, S. R. (2008). Student resistance to cross-cultural engagement: Annoying distraction or site for transformative learning. In S. R. Harper (Ed.), *Creating inclusive campus environments for cross-cultural learning and student engagement* (pp. 67–85). Washington, DC: National Association of Student Personnel Administrators.

Katz, J. H. (1989). The challenges of diversity. In C. Woolbright (Ed.), *Valuing diversity on campus* (pp. 1–21). Bloomington, IN: Association of College Unions International.

Kuh, G. D. (1993). Appraising the character of a college. *Journal of Counseling and Development, 71*(6), 661–668.

Kuh, G. D. (2003). Organizational theory. In S. R. Komives & D. B. Woodard, Jr. (Eds.), *Student services: A handbook for the profession* (4th ed., pp. 269–296). San Francisco, CA: Jossey-Bass.

Kuh, G. D., & Hall, J. E. (1993). Cultural perspectives in student affairs. In G. D. Kuh (Ed.), *Using cultural perspectives in student affairs* (pp. 1–20). Lanham, MD: University Press of America.

Kuh, G. D., Kinzie, J., Schuh, J. H., & Whitt, E. J. (2005). *Assessing conditions to enhance educational effectiveness: The inventory for student engagement and success.* San Francisco, CA: Jossey-Bass.

Kuh, G. D., & Love, P. G. (2000). A cultural perspective on student departure. In J. M. Braxton (Ed.), *Reworking the student departure puzzle* (pp. 196–212). Nashville, TN: Vanderbilt University Press.

Kuh, G. D., & Whitt, E. J. (1988). *The invisible tapestry: Culture in American colleges and universities.* Washington, DC: George Washington University, Graduate School of Education and Human Development.

Levine, A., & Cureton, J. S. (1998). *When hope and fear collide: A portrait of today's college student.* San Francisco, CA: Jossey-Bass.

Manning, K., & Coleman-Boatwright, P. (1991). Student affairs initiatives toward a multicultural university. *Journal of College Student Development, 32*(4), 367–374.

Mayhew, M. J., Grunwald, H. E., & Dey, E. L. (2006). Breaking the silence: Achieving a positive campus climate for diversity from the staff perspective. *Research in Higher Education, 47*(1), 63–88.

Milem, J. F. (2001). Increasing diversity benefits: How campus climate and teaching methods affect student outcomes. In G. Orfield (Ed.), *Diversity challenged: Evidence on the impact of affirmative action* (pp. 233–250). Cambridge, MA: Harvard Education Publishing Group.

Milem, J. F. (2003). The educational benefits of diversity: Evidence from multiple sectors. In M. J. Chang, D. Witt, J. Jones, & K. Hakuta (Eds.), *Compelling interest: Examining the evidence on racial dynamics in higher education* (pp. 126–169). Palo Alto, CA: Stanford University Press.

Milem, J. F., & Umbach, P. D. (2008). Understanding the difference diversity makes: Faculty beliefs, attitudes, and behaviors. In S. R. Harper (Ed.), *Creating inclusive campus environments for cross-cultural learning and student engagement* (pp. 155–172). Washington, DC: National Association of Student Personnel Administrators.

Minnich, E. K. (2004). *Transforming knowledge* (2nd ed.). Philadelphia, PA: Temple University Press.

Museus, S. D. (2008). Focusing on institutional fabric: Assessing campus cultures to enhance cross-cultural engagement. In S. R. Harper (Ed.), *Creating inclusive campus environments for cross-cultural learning and student engagement* (pp. 205–234). Washington, DC: National Association of Student Personnel Administrators.

Museus, S. D., & Quaye, S. J. (2009). Toward an intercultural perspective of racial and ethnic minority college student persistence. *Review of Higher Education, 33*(1), 67–94.

Parker, W. M., Archer, J., & Scott, J. (1992). *Multicultural relations on campus: A personal growth approach.* Philadelphia, PA: Accelerated Development.

Pavel, D. M. S., Inglebret, E., & Banks, S. R. A. (2001). Tribal colleges and universities in an era of dynamic development. *Peabody Journal of Education, 76*(1), 50–72.

Pike, G. R., Kuh, G. D., & Gonyea, R. M. (2003). The relationship between institutional mission and students' involvement with educational outcomes. *Research in Higher Education, 44*(2), 241–261.

Pope, R. L. (1993). *An analysis of multiracial change efforts in student affairs.* Unpublished doctoral dissertation, University of Massachusetts, Amherst.

Pope, R. L. (1995). Multicultural organization and development: Implications and applications for student affairs. In J. Fried (Ed.), *Shifting paradigms in student affairs: Culture, context, teaching, and learning* (pp. 233–249). Lanham, MD: American College Personnel Association.

Pope, R. L., Reynolds, A. L., & Mueller, J. A. (2004). *Multicultural competence in student affairs.* San Francisco, CA: Jossey-Bass.

Pope, R. L., & Thomas, C. D. (2000). Cultural dynamics and issues in higher education. In R. T. Carter (Ed.), *Addressing cultural issues in organizations: Beyond the corporate context* (pp. 115–129). Thousand Oaks, CA: Sage.

Quaye, S. J., & Harper, S. R. (2007). Faculty accountability for culturally inclusive pedagogy and curricula. *Liberal Education, 93*(3), 32–39.

Quaye, S. J., Lin, D. K., Buie, C. R., Abad, M., Labonte, A., Greenberg, J., & Hall, J. W. (2008). Student voice and sensemaking of multiculturalism on campus. In S. R. Harper (Ed.), *Creating inclusive campus environments for cross-cultural learning and student engagement* (pp. 19–44). Washington, DC: National Association of Student Personnel Administrators.

Rankin, S. R., & Reason, R. D. (2005). Differing perceptions: How students of color and White students perceive campus climate for underrepresented groups. *Journal of College Student Development, 46*(1), 43–61.

Reynolds, A. L., & Pope, R. L. (2003). Multicultural competencies in counseling centers. In D. B. Pope-Davis, H. L. K. Coleman, W. M. Liu, & R. L. Toporek (Eds.), *Handbook of multicultural competencies in counseling and psychology* (pp. 365–382). Thousand Oaks, CA: Sage.

Ryu, M. (2008). *Minorities in higher education 2008: Twenty-third status report.* Washington, DC: American Council on Education.

Schein, E. H. (1985). *Organizational culture and leadership.* San Francisco, CA: Jossey-Bass.

Smith, D. G. (1997). *Diversity works: The emerging picture of how students benefit.* Washington, DC: Association of American Colleges and Universities.

Torres, V., Howard-Hamilton, M. F., & Cooper, D. L. (2003). Identity development of diverse populations: Implications for teaching and administration in higher education. *ASHE/ERIC Higher Education Report, 29*(6).

Umbach, P. D., & Kuh, G. D. (2006). Student experiences with diversity at liberal arts colleges: Another claim for distinctiveness. *Journal of Higher Education*, *77*(1), 169–192.

Waldo, C. R. (1998). Out on campus: Sexual orientation and academic climate in a university context. *American Journal of Community Psychology*, *26*(5), 745–774.

Wilson, K., Getzel, E., & Brown, T. (2000). Enhancing the post-secondary campus climate for students with disabilities. *Journal of Vocational Rehabilitation*, *14*(1), 37–50.

5

Moving Beyond the Talk

From Difficult Dialogue to Action

Sherry K. Watt

In the word question, *there is a beautiful word*—quest. *I love that word. We are all partners in a quest. The essential questions have no answers. You are my question, and I am yours—and then there is dialogue. The moment we have answers, there is no dialogue. Questions unite people.*

—Elie Wiesel (Winfrey, 2000)

MANY COLLEGE CAMPUSES in the United States are striving to increase the number of students of color, provide course offerings that help all students learn about cultural difference, and introduce experiences that will help prepare students to be successful in a diverse society. Administrators at some institutions are pursuing these efforts because they are motivated by the basic principle that diversity is good, which requires only a surface-level understanding of systematic oppression. A cursory understanding of systematic oppression leads campus administrators to focus on outcomes without assessing the underlying problems that contribute to a marginalized and a less satisfactory college experience. Systematic oppression uses embedded, integrated, and interacting "contexts and social roles" (Cecero, 2010, p. 498) that "stigmatizes and violates the targeted group" (Hardiman, Jackson, & Griffin, 2007, p. 6) through unwanted domination and repression. Such systems can and do include families,

131

schools, religious organizations, and institutions. "Systems of oppression are woven into the social fabric so that their processes and effects become normalized" (Hardiman et al, p. 37). For instance, officials of a higher education institution might primarily focus on increasing the number of students of color without seriously evaluating the quality of their existence on campus. Other institution administrators are striving to embrace strategies that disrupt systematic oppression on a deeper level, shifting their view to demonstrate that diversity matters as a central and integrative dimension rather than a required and marginalized part of the college experience. Higher education institutions moving in this direction are embracing diversity as a value. Nonetheless, these institutions are situated in a society that has historically devalued difference, and therefore the change to embrace diversity as a value is often met with resistance. Maneuvering the resistance to change should involve difficult dialogues on how valuing diversity is actually manifested in the day-to-day life of a higher education institution. It also involves earnest reflection about what actions are needed to change the organization at the cultural level. The process of embracing diversity as a value requires that campus leaders find a thoughtful balance between dialogue and action.

This chapter focuses on describing the nature of difficult dialogues; the dynamics and impact that power, oppression, and privilege have on these dialogues; the role of dialogue in the organizational change process for higher education institutions; and practical strategies student affairs professionals can employ to address social justice issues from a human and an environment perspective. As an overall approach to moving beyond talking about diversity to action steps that work toward actual social change on college campuses, I describe how student affairs professionals can use dialogue on meaningful questions as a strategy to guide faculty, staff, and students to face the challenges together related to embracing and enacting diversity as a value. Specifically, this chapter addresses the following questions: What is a difficult dialogue? How do the dynamics of power, oppression, and privilege affect dialogue? What is the role of dialogue in the organizational change process of inclusion? And what are the key conditions needed for a productive dialogue?

WHAT IS A DIFFICULT DIALOGUE?

As student affairs professionals, we spend the majority of our time engaged in dialogue with colleagues, faculty, and students. Dialogue is defined as a conversation between two or more individuals (Patterson, Grenny, McMillan, & Switzler, 2002). Often, learning in college involves an active pursuit of knowledge through students' engaging in dialogue with classmates, faculty, staff, and student affairs professionals. Therefore, being able to continue to engage in dialogue without becoming overwhelmed by feelings of anger, hurt, or fear (Patterson et al.) is important to learning. Dialogue often becomes difficult because of personal and social investments, but also communication is complicated by the historical and structural dynamics of the relationship between marginalized and dominant identities of those involved in the conversation. Communication between, for instance, an African American and a White person is rarely completely without the historic memories that are associated with being raised in a society with unequal distribution of power because of race. And of course, there is the unique slant on any communication because of the particular individual's personal and family history as well as personality characteristics. A *difficult dialogue* "is a verbal or written exchange of ideas or opinions between citizens within a community that centers on an awakening of potentially conflicting views of beliefs or values about social justice issues (such as racism, sexism, ableism, heterosexism/homophobia)" (Watt, 2007, p. 116). These dialogues are difficult because they involve an awakening to different views individuals have of ideas that have roots in the interrelationship of power, oppression, and privilege for marginalized and dominant groups in this society.

HOW DO THE DYNAMICS OF POWER, OPPRESSION, AND PRIVILEGE AFFECT DIALOGUE?

The impact of historical and structural dynamics of power, oppression, and privilege is ever present in dialogue between members of dominant and marginalized groups (Reason & Davis, 2005; Spring, 2010). Power addresses the sociopolitical processes that characterize one group's interaction with another (Pharr, 1997). Specifically, institutional and economic power defines the relationship individuals have with each other. For example, marriage for most of the United States is an institution reserved for heterosexual couples that leads directly to economic power in the form of tax benefits. Therefore, the right for heterosexual couples to get married defines their position of higher power in relation to a gay or lesbian partnership. A gay or lesbian couple's existence is restricted by institutional laws that in many states deny nonheterosexuals the right to marry, which has direct implications on their economic capacity in the society. Where people are situated in the power dynamic characterizes their view and experience, which likely frames the perspective or lack thereof when in dialogue with another. A heterosexual person engaging in dialogue with others might unearth awakenings about power, oppression, and privilege that he or she has enjoyed based on heterosexual privilege. While the outcomes of this privilege have limitations on the lives of all individuals regardless of their sexual identity, direct limitations are placed on the day-to-day life of a gay or lesbian person. Resultantly, the dialogue between a heterosexual person and a gay or lesbian individual is situated within that context.

Oppression is defined by a system that limits power, interests, or opportunities of those who are members of marginalized groups. Oppression is not just random acts by individuals but involves a comprehensive set of interrelated attitudes and behaviors that are normalized (Hardiman, Jackson, & Griffin, 2007). Pharr (1997) pointed out a direct connection between power and oppression. For instance, Pharr highlighted connections between all oppressions (e.g., racism, sexism, heterosexism, ableism), such as promoting a defined norm or "a standard of rightness and often righteousness wherein all others are judged in relation to it" (p. 53), creating the other. The process of "othering" results in creating an unproductive dynamic perpetuated between dominant and oppressed groups as well as within and across oppressed groups that reinforces and promotes invisibility, distortions, stereotyping, blaming the victim, internalized oppression/self-hate, horizontal hostility, isolation, assimilation, tokenism, and individual solutions. Common elements such as these serve to maintain the economic power and control of a system by promoting the message of othering through media advertisements (e.g., negative or single-focused or a lack of representation of people of color, while the depictions of Whites are textured and widely varied on television shows and commercials) and in laws (marriage between a man and a women with children results in a tax benefit). Imprinting the image of a group as against the norm or as the norm for the entire culture does determine whether a person is considered to be lacking, deviant, or not fully human. Or images are imprinted as sufficient and valued, as the standard of success, and almost superhuman. The imprint society has of a group leads to choices that determine whether people are deemed worthy enough to be involved in decisions that affect their lives. The link between power and oppression limits the lives of all members of this society, but most especially marginalized groups. The dominant groups may not consciously feel the direct impact on them by having privilege, which results in having more power and control in their lives. And yet, they certainly have advantages from these bequeathed benefits, which ultimately have consequences that shape the dynamics of dialogue.

Peggy McIntosh's (1997) well-known article "White Privilege and Male Privilege: A Personal Account of Coming to See Correspondences Through Work in Women's Studies" defined *privilege* as "an invisible package of unearned assets which [she could] count on cashing in each day" (p. 291). However, privilege goes beyond race and can include other identities in dominant society, such as being heterosexual, middle or upper class, or able-bodied (Watt, 2009). Raising awareness of diversity involves exploration on a personal and political level where one's own privileged identities are considered in relation to racism, sexism, ableism, classism, and so on (Watt, 2007). Dialogue becomes emotionally charged because this type of exploration requires individuals to ask themselves a central human-life question— Who am I?—which necessitates fundamentally examining related questions such as, What do I believe? What was I taught? What is my truth? Whom do I love? How am I existing in this society? and What must I give up for the greater good? This interconnected examination naturally has the potential to raise complex feelings, such as rage, sadness, powerlessness, pride, joy, endearment, guilt, fear, and resentment, particularly for people who enjoy privileged identities. Engaging in emotionally charged, difficult dialogue with others about changing the climate of our higher education institutions is risky. As faculty, staff, and students it is risky to be involved in a process that not only requires an examination of professional and academic relationships where one's livelihood/future is largely determined, but also necessitates revisiting and potentially deconstructing personal and familial relationships.

Logically, the angle taken to explore social oppression matters and contributes to the tension often present in the dialogue. For a marginalized identity, feelings of rage, powerlessness, and sadness might take center stage when examining change in social oppression, while for a privileged identity feelings of fear, entitlement, and defensiveness might come to the forefront. Attacking or defending privileged identity is often the kindling for difficult dialogues (Watt, 2007). More specifically, contemplation of a marginalized identity may involve coming to terms with the reality that an immutable characteristic has influenced many social interactions, while struggling with the idea that if it were not for the psychological and structural restrictions endured, one might have been more successful in life. Consideration of a privileged identity might require one to reflect on what it means to leave the secure socialization of everyday interactions with the self, friends, and family that has reinforced agency in life, while also wrestling with whether one's position and status in society was truly earned. The paradoxes inherent in reflecting on one's marginalized and privileged identity can stretch the mind and heart to their limits. The reflection can become even more mind-boggling and heart wrenching when complicated by the fact that many people's complete identity likely comprises a mix of privileged and marginalized identities. These multiple identities as well as potential contemplations and considerations determine how one filters information while engaging in dialogue on organizational change. Conflict can arise because many of these campus community members come from different perspectives and may disagree on what is valued at the institution as well as the process used to change the organization.

It is important to recognize that discussions about diversity are extremely complex and are always situated in the context of historical and structural oppression; laced with multifaceted dynamics of power, oppression, and privilege; and deeply connected to personal and familial relational traditions that are central to identity (Jones & McEwen, 2000; Watt, 2009). These difficult dialogues are common when attempting to change the culture of an organization.

WHAT IS THE ROLE OF DIALOGUE IN THE ORGANIZATIONAL CHANGE PROCESS?

According to the American Council on Education, organizational change can be described as embracing ideas: "Change is deep, pervasive, intentional, and long term; it is organic and requires holistic and integrated thinking; and it entails new approaches to student affairs, faculty development, pedagogy, assessment, and community involvement" (as cited in Woodard, Love, & Komives, 2000, p. 61). Exploring meaningful questions in dialogue is a significant part of an organization's transformation process. Sustaining change involves talking about critical questions that reexamine basic assumptions campus members use in reaffirming or modifying policies and practices so that policies and practices align with the idea of diversity as a core value. This leads to behavior changes in faculty, staff, and students (Woodard et al.). As Lewin's classic equation $B = f(P \times E)$ implies, higher education institutions are social systems made up of evolving human (P) and environmental (E) factors that interact ($\times$) and result (f) in behaviors (B) (as cited in Huebner & Lawson, 1990). Therefore, to embrace diversity as a value, institutions must use a process whereby behavior is (re)shaped and answers are organically discovered that are responsive to the evolving nature of these aspects of organizations. The use of effective oral and written communication among members of the campus community is central to this process. Finding ways to have productive dialogue about how to change the organization that balances thought with action involves campus community leaders' nurturing certain key environmental conditions.

WHAT ARE THE KEY CONDITIONS NEEDED FOR A PRODUCTIVE DIALOGUE?

For a higher education institution that has been established for many years, it is likely that there are many senior faculty who take pride in the intellectual community they have built, alumni whose financial giving is wrapped up in the institution's carrying on certain traditions, knowledgeable staff who hold the institutional memory and have been dedicated to maintaining practices and procedures for decades, and students who are attending the institution because of its established reputation. It is difficult to simultaneously address the needs of each of these constituencies while questioning the institution's foundation. Many opportunities for missteps and defensive behavior will probably arise during discussions about this type of organizational change (see Watt, 2009), and for the dialogue to derail while balancing these seemingly mutual values. Student affairs professionals need to be intentional about preparing the campus for the dialogue becoming difficult. Two conditions are essential in proactively setting up an environment for productive dialogue: *mutual purpose* and *mutual respect* (Patterson et al., 2002). In their book, *Crucial Conversations*, Patterson et al. discussed applying these conditions to personal as well as professional dialogue where risking or changing relationships is at stake. The following sections include the basic principles of these conditions along with an explanation of why it is necessary to have these certain elements in the environment when intentionally examining the assumptions behind institutional practices that were adopted in a society where historical and structural social oppression is pervasive.

Mutual Purpose

In preparation for conversation about organizational change, campus leaders need to begin the process by creating a shared meaning of the end goal. Campus leaders must converse about the espoused and lived mission of the institution, reflect on the direction the organization needs to take, and develop a vision for the end goal, which can be clearly articulated to the entire campus. As campus leaders are developing this vision, they need to consult with the different representative groups (e.g., faculty, staff, alumni, students) and make sense of what it would mean for their campus to embrace diversity as a value. Establishing a shared meaning of the end goal is critical when preparing the environment for productive dialogue. A clear vision provides members of the community with the opportunity to make a decision about the role they can play in the organizational change. It also allows those who are not in alignment with the direction the institution is taking to make a fully informed decision about whether they can remain with the organization. A shared end goal of diversity as a value might mean the institution will create new practices that are very different for daily work of faculty, staff, and students. Changing job descriptions and creating new responsibilities is stressful under normal circumstances, but transition induced from a dissection of the institution's values adds an additional layer of strain. In a situation that is already fraught with risk, it is critical that campus leaders consistently and transparently communicate their vision of the end goal and their best understanding of how that might affect individuals or constituency groups on campus. While the leaders may not be able to articulate the exact process for reaching the end goal, they must prepare the campus by persistently providing a shared meaning of their vision to the larger campus and acknowledging up front that the organic nature of the process will produce uncertainty at times.

Mutual Respect

Campus leaders need to support their words with actions that reassure campus community members that they will be treated fairly. Shifting the lens toward a focus on social oppression as the problem and away from a sole focus on how individuals experience racism, heterosexism, or ableism might engender fair treatment conditions. This lens allows those from privileged and marginalized groups to bear some responsibility for changing the foundational problem, whereas historically the burden for changing the organization in this way has largely been placed on the target group (e.g., people of color, gay men, or lesbians). Focus on addressing systemic change (racism, heterosexism, etc.) rather than helping individuals (those less fortunate) cope with oppression creates an environment in which all the constituents can come to the table with a contribution and a responsibility. To avoid dialogue that has an underlying message that campus community members are coming to this discussion, for instance, as "poor helpless Black people" or "mean and clueless White people," campus leaders need to intentionally communicate the shared responsibility. They must also directly acknowledge the potentially different angles from which members of the community might approach the conversation. Moreover, creating conditions for potentially productive dialogue assumes a learning ethos. Learning ethos practices are guided by the assumption that each member comes to the table with goodwill as well as lessons to learn about the complex and interdependent nature of social oppression. And yet, those who are facilitating these dialogues need to handle gracefully the complications that will likely arise related to the ever present power dynamics that are inherent on a historical, social, and organizational level. Therefore, campus leaders must be intentional in thinking through and addressing the immediacy of the power, oppression, and privilege dynamics that exist between and within the relationships of campus constituents. An environment of learning ethos is more likely to occur when facilitators also pay attention to fundamental elements of relationship. Mutual respect is born out of attending to basic relational dimensions such as kindness; empathy; attention to the needs of others; and, most importantly, the capacity to allow colleagues and students to be who they are (marginalized and privileged) in the space of these dialogues. Finally, establishing a condition of mutual respect can also be achieved through the safety and security of having a consistent structure for when and how these dialogues will take place.

ASKING AND NOT ANSWERING: USING MEANINGFUL QUESTIONS TO GUIDE ACTION

As Elie Wiesel (Winfrey, 2000) pointed out, questions and dialogue are natural partners. Posing a thoughtful question can invite dialogue as well as guide a community on a journey of exploration that unites everyone in a common cause. Higher education institutions today are experiencing an economic downturn that is affecting our nation, and budgets are being significantly cut for many programs and services on campus. It is difficult to proceed with exploring questions under these circumstances, especially questions that appear to have elusive answers, and participants must trust the answers will be revealed as they move through the process. Yet, there is no final answer to how to go about changing the policies and practices of a higher education institution when its foundation is built from the roots of social oppression that are part of our nation's history. For that matter, faculty, staff, and students are part of an institutional and societal culture that requires change, and they may have difficulty thinking about transforming their campus climate while living in it. It might be said that it is like teaching fish how to see water. To teach campus community members to uproot socially unjust practices, they have to be invited to deconstruct their comprehension of power, oppression, and privilege as they relate to their institution. Deconstruction of this kind necessitates an active examination of the institutional and societal system that is informed from the marginalized and privileged perspectives. For these reasons investing more in a collaborative process of transformation by wrestling with meaningful questions that are at the foundation of the institution's policies and practices is a constructive process toward discovering innovative ways the organization can embrace diversity as a value.

USING MEANINGFUL QUESTIONS AS A GUIDE

A productive strategy to explore complex issues that are complicated by historical and structural dynamics and include individuals' investments in their personal and social identities is to use meaningful questions as a catalyst. Meaningful questions, for the purposes of this chapter, are posed about a challenge that either has no answers or has potentially multiple answers. Posing these types of questions to invested constituents about matters at their institution requires group members to wrestle with an issue that brings in their personal and social investments as well as to consider the historical and structural dynamics.

Campus leaders need to use resources from the larger higher education community as well as their own campuses to construct a meaningful question to guide dialogue about organizational change on diversity matters. To start, campus leaders should consult the latest higher education literature for research findings that inform practical approaches to campus climate change. The literature might provide useful definitions of cultural competence, cultural climate, and research findings that measure the impact of the climate on the environment and on individual student experiences. Specific attention should be paid to reading about strategies of institutions that have experienced some success in addressing diversity matters. A meaningful question arises from the body of scholarly research as well as from the campus community's best ideas about how to fit that information to its own environmental profile. A meaningful question invites campus community members to discuss the impact of social oppression on the environment in a way that moves the institution toward the change campus leaders envision. For example, meaningful questions might include, What is a diverse environment? What does that specifically mean for our campus? What would have to change for our community to interact in ways that overcome the impact of the historical and structural dynamics of power, oppression, and privilege in our society? How will our day-to-day practices change? How will we know we are making progress toward the cultural change we envision?

Discussing questions like these get to the source of the problem while guiding campus constituents toward new policies and practices. These questions fit the criterion of meaningfulness because they invite the campus community to a conversation with potentially multiple answers and no one right answer (discussed on p. 147 in Chapter 6). It also creates an opportunity for campus community members to ask themselves about their personal, professional, and social investments.

Once meaningful questions are constructed, campus leaders must decide on the process and forum to raise these queries. Raising a meaningful question that invites productive dialogue begins with vetting the question with smaller diverse groups of faculty, staff, and students. This helps campus leaders know whether their question has considered the needs of the different experiences of those represented on their campus. Ultimately, campus leaders will need to raise these questions in an open invitation to the campus and provide multiple opportunities for participation. To be certain the structure provides the safety and security needed for productive dialogue, care should be taken to invite skilled facilitators from on campus or an off-campus consultant. Thoughtfully selecting the facilitators communicates the importance campus leaders are placing on organizational change. It also provides some assurance that conversations will not get derailed but rather provide outcomes in the shared vision. Finally, it is very important that campus leaders manage the process in transparent ways. Providing summaries that report the progress and outcome of these essential dialogues will help confirm that different voices were captured and heard by the campus community during the process of wrestling with these questions. Summary reports also provide a record of the progress made. These reports will be needed if the group becomes discouraged, which is a reasonable reaction to a task as difficult as changing the cultural climate. Reports also record the agreements and commitments made to produce change in the campus community, which will help the community maintain the change. Again as Elie Wiesel said, the questions and the quest for answers unite people and can create a movement toward change that enriches the lives of the entire campus community.

Using this process as an approach to organizational change efforts in diversity has three important components: It is informed by the latest scholarly work in the area of diversity, it is an inclusive process that demands active involvement of all voices on campus, and it takes precautions to help the dialogue to move toward action. While members of the campus community may not know the answer and are certainly not immune from making mistakes, they will likely feel more competent in wrestling with these difficult issues. At least the transparency of the process used to arrive at the chosen course of action engenders trust. It is liberating to engage in a process that changes an organization, improves the life of campus community members, and has an impact on a society. As Harro (2000) pointed out, feelings such as self-love, balance, joy, and security, all essential elements in educating college students as healthy and responsible citizens, are at the core of liberation.

To create environments that are socially just and that move beyond conversations about diversity being good toward living diversity as a value, faculty, staff, and students must be led by student affairs professionals who engage in difficult dialogues guided by meaningful questions and invite all parties to take personal responsibility and commit to take action. Chapter 6 offers examples of such dialogues and action.

REFERENCES

Cecero, J. J. (2010). The spiritual exercises in counseling and therapy. In J. G. Ponterotto, J. Manuel Cases, L. A. Suzuki, & C. A. Alexander (Eds.), *Handbook of multicultural counseling* (3rd ed., pp. 479–501). Los Angeles, CA: Sage.

Hardiman, R., Jackson, B., & Griffin, P. (2007). Conceptual foundations for social justice. In M. Adams, L. Bell, & P. Griffin (Eds.), *Teaching diversity for social justice* (2nd ed., pp. 35–66). New York: Routledge.

Harro, B. (2000). The cycle of liberation. In M. Adams, W. J. Blumenfeld, R. Castañeda, H. W. Hackman, M. L. Peters, & X. Zúñiga (Eds.), *Readings for diversity and social justice: An anthology on racism, antisemitism, sexism, heterosexism, ableism, and classism* (pp. 463–469). New York, NY: Routledge.

Huebner, L. A., & Lawson, J. M. (1990). Understanding and assessing college environments. In D. G. Creamer & Associates (Eds.), *College student development: Theory and practice for the 1990s* (pp. 127–154). Alexandria, VA: American College Personnel Association.

Jones, S. R., & McEwen, M. K. (2000). A conceptual model of multiple identity development. *Journal of College Student Development, 41*(4), 405–414.

McIntosh, G. (1997). White privilege and male privilege: A personal account of coming to see correspondences through work in women's studies. In R. Delgado & J. Stefancic (Eds.), *Critical White studies: Looking behind the mirror* (pp. 291–304). Philadelphia, PA: Temple University Press.

Patterson, K., Grenny, J., McMillan, R., & Switzler, A. (2002). *Crucial conversations: Tools for talking when stakes are high.* New York, NY: McGraw-Hill.

Pharr, S. (1997). *Homophobia: A weapon of sexism.* Berkeley, CA: Chardon Press.

Reason, R. D., & Davis, T. L. (2005). Antecedents, precursors, and concurrent concepts in the development of social justice attitudes and actions. *New Directions in Student Services* (110), 5–15.

Spring, J. (2010). *Deculturalization and the struggle for equality: A brief history of the education of dominated cultures in the United States.* New York, NY: McGraw-Hill.

Watt, S. K. (2007). Difficult dialogues, privilege and social justice: Uses of the privileged identity exploration (PIE) model in student affairs practice. *College Student Affairs Journal, 26*(2), 114–126.

Watt, S. K. (2009). Facilitating difficult dialogues at the intersections of religious privilege. *New Directions for Student Services* (125), 65–73.

Winfrey, O. (2000, November 15). Oprah talks to Elie Wiesel. *O, The Oprah Magazine*. Retrieved from http://www.oprah.com/omagazine/Oprah-Interviews-Elie-Wiesel/7

Woodard, D. B., Jr., Love, P. G., & Komives, S. R. (2000). *Leadership and management issues for a new century*. (New Directions for Student Services No. 92). San Francisco, CA: Jossey-Bass.

6

Different Approaches to Real Issues

Matthew J. Weigand and Lucy A. LePeau

T HERE IS NO RIGHT WAY to initiate change to make our campuses welcoming, inclusive, and engaging for all students. Rather, essential elements of the process, outlined in earlier chapters of this book, help educators consider potential strategies for creating effective multicultural change in our work contexts. By presenting realistic case studies and responses from current student affairs professionals, we offer insight into how the elements of the critical reflection process described in this book may be applied to practice. In doing so, this chapter demonstrates the multiplicity of perspectives and approaches professionals dedicated to ongoing development of multicultural competence may adopt when they encounter situations in which power, oppression, or privilege are salient—situations that are inherently complex. Often in real-life situations we are not privy to understanding how campus stakeholders grapple with the complexities involved as they make decisions; rather we see only the outcome.

In addition to demonstrating there is no one right answer or outcome, our intent is to bring to light examples of ways professionals intentionally consider their own social identities, historical and institutional contexts, and other relevant situational factors as they propose solutions for resolving issues presented in two case studies, and how the convergence of those factors influences decision making. Ultimately, we hope this insight helps readers consider their own power, oppression, or privilege in meaningful ways in their everyday practice. We also hope this chapter encourages readers to initiate discussions with colleagues on difficult topics and empowers readers

145

to advocate for and work toward building inclusive environments. That is, we hope this chapter inspires readers to find the courage to practice the skills required to enact positive multicultural change on college campuses.

PRESENTING TWO CASE STUDIES: ENGAGING CONTRIBUTORS IN PERSONAL REFLECTION

The two case studies presented in this chapter are followed by responses from four professionals who represent a variety of social identities and professional roles in higher education. The cases are based on real-life experiences, and we wrote them as realistically as possible. The names of all involved are fictitious. While it is impractical to include all relevant background and contextual information about the cases, the information provided is sufficient to provoke thought and meaningful discussion. The student affairs professionals, graduate students, and faculty responding to the cases considered not only the situation or issue itself but also how the intersections of their own social identities, their personal and positional power, and the institutional context influenced their thinking and decision making. Specifically, each respondent was asked to provide a written response to the case, addressing the following:

- the problems, challenges, and issues raised in the scenario that should be considered;
- the stakeholders, their relative positions of power in this situation, and how possible responses may contribute to or challenge stakeholders' privileges or feelings of oppression;
- their own salient social identities, positional power, and emotions that have an impact on their responses to the situation; and
- how institutional and national contexts shape how they view and respond to the case.

Having access to the contributors' considerations in each of these areas provides insight into and depth to their responses. However, we chose to focus on the contributors' responses to the last two bullet points because of their relevance to the core ideas presented in this book. Refer to the appendix for a full list of the reflection questions provided for each respondent when reviewing the case.

The contributors' initial responses to the cases were structured in different formats based on their own personal preferences. Some respondents answered all the reflection questions, some adopted a positional role in the case and responded from that lens, and some responded in a hybrid format of the first two instances. After writing an initial draft of the chapter in which we synthesized and compared and contrasted responses, we followed up with most of the respondents to ask clarifying questions or to probe their responses more deeply. After making revisions, we sent a complete draft of the chapter to all respondents as a form of member checking.

As authors of this chapter, we were challenged to examine our own power in making decisions about what pieces of the responses to include and in making connections, interpretations, and inferences about contributors' responses. We recognize that our social identities and professional contexts played a role in how we made sense of the contributors' ideas. Our objective was to encourage respondents to work intentionally and purposefully from their perspectives even while knowing that all our perspectives are limited in one way or another. Therefore, responses are not meant to be judged as best or worst; instead, they illuminate the variety of ways professionals can actively work to create positive change for inclusion at colleges and universities.

As you read the responses, we encourage you to put yourself in the respondents' shoes and seek to truly understand their perspectives. Moreover, we encourage you to consider each of the cases from your own point of view, taking into account your own identity, power, and context. Finally, we strongly encourage you to share and discuss these cases and responses with colleagues on your campus. This is one strategy to initiate a potentially difficult dialogue in a relatively low-risk environment; after all, while the cases are meant to be realistic, they are in fact simulated situations with no real-life consequences. These conversations may lead to more thoughtful and effective responses to actual situations as they arise on your campus, to greater comfort talking with colleagues about the complexity of diversity, and ultimately to more inclusive college and university campuses and student affairs practice.

CASE 1—A DISAGREEMENT ESCALATES

When Kate Harris, director of student activities at Highbanks State University for the past 10 months, arrived at work on Friday morning, she learned from her staff about a verbal altercation between two students during a late-night event run by her office the previous evening. Her graduate assistant, Nick, was present at the event and filled her in on what happened. In short, Nick observed two students on the outskirts of the event yelling at each other, and one of them ultimately telling the other, "You'd better watch your back" and "I'm gonna take you down." Although the interaction was very brief, Nick took the threat seriously and called campus security. The officers talked to each of the students individually, took statements from them and a few witnesses, served the two students notices to appear before the campus judicial board, and escorted them back to their residence hall rooms.

Kate read the official report filed by campus security and was shocked when she learned who the students were. In her role as adviser to several student organizations, Kate worked closely with Toussaint Williams and Eric Chen, both presidents of large student clubs that were cosponsoring the event. Although it had been only a few weeks into the semester, Kate's interactions with both students led her to believe they were polite, intelligent, and respectful, so she was surprised by their behavior. The students' statements provided to campus security, as well as those of the witnesses, were fairly consistent. They had a disagreement about where their clubs' sponsorship signs should be posted, with Toussaint arguing that since his club provided more money and more members to work the event, he got to decide. The disagreement quickly escalated, they both raised their voices inappropriately, and Toussaint told the security officers that he shouldn't have lost his temper and threatened Eric.

Kate thanked Nick for handling the situation well and began thinking about how she might address the incident the next time she met individually with Toussaint and Eric. Other than those imminent conversations and possible judicial sanctions, she thought the incident was behind them all until the following weekend when she saw that Toussaint had posted his thoughts about the incident on Facebook. A new story emerged in which Toussaint claimed that his threat to Eric was provoked by a racial slur; he said Eric called him the N word and that's why he lost his temper and threatened him.

By Monday morning, numerous Facebook groups with hundreds of members were discussing the incident. The campus was abuzz with students sharing opinions with each other and fueling unprecedented tension between the Black Student Union (BSU) and the Asian Student Union (ASU), Toussaint's and Eric's organizations, respectively. The Lesbian Gay Bisexual Transgender (LGBT) Alliance took sides as well, deciding to support Eric, who was openly gay and a past officer of that organization. Eric also served as a student representative on the campus's diversity board, and there were calls for him to resign. Almost overnight, the incident went from a relatively minor disagreement between two student leaders who handled it poorly to a significant campus issue with racial undertones that could have lasting effects.

Kate urgently tried to set up a meeting with her direct supervisor, the dean of students, to discuss what to do. In the meantime, Eric showed up in her office wanting to talk. On the verge of tears, he denied calling Toussaint any name, especially the *N* word. He said that he knew he acted inappropriately that evening by yelling, but that their argument had nothing to do with race. He reminded Kate of all the work he had done on campus to promote cultural awareness and appreciation of diversity and said he was sickened by the accusation that he used a racial slur. Eric asked Kate to promise he wouldn't be kicked off the diversity board, because all of this was a lie. Feeling that she didn't have enough information to make promises, all Kate could say was that the incident would be investigated fully and that there would be a fair resolution. Eric left feeling hopeless, helpless, and alone—that no one was on his side.

About an hour later, Toussaint showed up at Kate's office. Although she didn't feel prepared to talk with him, she also couldn't turn him away. Toussaint recounted the incident as he wrote it on Facebook—not as it was written in the original statements and reports. He pleaded for Kate's support, suggesting that as a Black woman, she must be able to understand how he lost his temper and threatened Eric after being called the *N* word. He asked that Eric be removed from his position as president of the ASU and from the campus diversity board immediately. Kate told Toussaint that he needed to be patient and that she was sure the investigation would result in a fair outcome. He left feeling disgusted that Kate wouldn't support "one of her own."

Finally, that afternoon, Kate was able to talk with the dean of students but didn't know where to begin.

Responses

Four student affairs professionals, representing varying social identities and in positions ranging from entry level to senior level, responded to this case. Respondents included two midlevel professionals, one who works at a large midwestern state university and is also enrolled in a social justice doctoral program, and another who works at a small liberal arts college in the South; one senior-level administrator who works at a Jesuit institution; and one entry-level professional employed at an elite public university in the West. The institutional differences among student affairs professionals, along with their relevant social identities as described later, influenced their responses. The actual responses appear first, followed by a discussion of how respondents' institutional context and social identities shaped their responses. Collectively, respondents emphasized complex possible responses embedded in three topical areas: working with Kate; responding to the students, including discussion about restorative justice tactics; and considering broader student organizations and university community actions.

In their responses, three of the professionals addressed the importance of empowering and supporting Kate to act in this situation. A senior-level respondent discussed the importance of "affirming Kate's ability to work through the situation and empowering her to consider how she—and we—should respond." He supported this position by citing Kate's direct relationship with both of the students involved and her ability to consider her history with both students prior to the incident. He also noted that she became directly involved in the case once Toussaint expressed his disgust that as a Black professional she would not support "one of her own." The respondent wondered what Kate thought about hearing this response from Toussaint. Another respondent stated, "I want to show her that I will stand in solidarity with her. . . . I am careful not to offer or imply that she needs help because I know she is very capable, but instead to convey that I want to align with and support her." Finally, an entry-level respondent put it this way:

> Given my position within the organization and as a person with privilege as a White person, I would ask Kate if she wanted my help but I would not step in and take over. My belief is that Kate has more positional experience and lived experience in the context of racial slander. Why would I think that I know better than she does?

Also similar is the professionals' desire to address the incident directly with Toussaint and Eric. For one midlevel professional, fact finding was important. He said he "would meet with Toussaint again in an attempt to reconcile the fact that he gave two versions of the story at two different times." For this professional, determining whether the *N* word was used was essential to determining his response. If it was used, he recommended Eric's removal from the diversity board; if not, he considered action against Toussaint for the implication. Regardless of whether the *N* word was used, he mentioned talking separately with both students about the "inappropriateness of their exchange and interaction as campus and organizational leaders."

The other respondents stated that it is imperative to "hear their versions of what happened and the events or factors that may have led up to the incident." Two described using a restorative justice process for Eric and Toussaint, with the goal of understanding each student's perspective on what transpired, their feelings about it, and the personal responsibility each is willing to take. The second phase of a restorative justice approach includes working with all parties involved in an incident to consider action steps to try to develop ways to teach the community about the situation. This serves as a prevention technique for future incidents on the campus. If the students are willing to meet together, one respondent suggested that they

> explore the intended and unintended consequences of their actions, the impact on the community, and what they thought might be a good strategy from here on out. I would want to know what they thought would help each other and their communities heal.

Another discussed his desire to determine "the appropriateness of formal dispute resolution, convened as soon as possible, as a means to bring Eric and Toussaint together to discuss the incident and its aftermath." He continued,

> This may be followed by a restorative justice or circle process with some of the secondary stakeholders (those who witnessed or responded to the incident, some of the student organization officers who became involved in response or advocacy, etc.). The key objective, in each case, is to use honest dialogue not only as a means to defuse, and perhaps resolve, the situation, but also to use the situation as an opportunity to engage students in learning a constructive process for responding to and resolving conflict with civility and compassion.

Respondents also suggested addressing the student organizations involved and the broader university community with interventions such as organizing dialogue spaces on campus to discuss the issue and resolution deeply; working with the groups involved to provide closure and dissipate intergroup tension by focusing on the facts (i.e., emphasizing that this was more of a general disagreement and not a racially charged incident if that is what's determined after further investigation); and printing in the college newspaper a public statement describing the campus's response, stating that discrimination will not be tolerated, and encouraging students to make judgments based on fact rather than rumor. One respondent expressed her desire to discuss with members of the BSU and the ASU the "historical legacies of oppression that linger within the institution" as a way to inform and encourage the students involved with BSU and ASU to "build solidarity among the students and challenge the status quo that perpetuates oppression." Further, she suggested meeting with students across campus as well as colleagues to better understand how the racial climate might be a contributing factor in this incident.

One additional action proposed by the respondents to address this situation include working with those involved in the judicial process. Specifically, one respondent suggested meeting with campus security and judicial officers to learn their "plans and progress for continued investigation, follow-up, and/or formal charges," as well as their timeline given that the situation had escalated quickly. Another proposed meeting with colleagues in judicial affairs to discuss how "judicial and criminal systems are likely to unfairly and inconsistently hold minoritized students accountable while ongoing oppression perpetuated by dominant students and administrators goes without accountability or sanctions" and to plan a training session for judicial officers about working against this bias inherent in the judicial system.

Another respondent suggested reexamining student activities policies and practices to see whether a standard procedure existed for staff to handle such potential conflicts. Further, this respondent expressed concern that graduate assistant Nick may have been able to defuse the situation more effectively at the time of the incident if he had a working relationship with the leaders of the groups cosponsoring the event. Similarly, another respondent suggested discussing with Kate how to effectively follow up with Nick in the interest of supporting graduate students as they "develop the capacity to respond to incidents that occur at events they manage independently." And one respondent suggested checking in with Nick to hear more about his perspective of the situation since he was present during the event.

Finally, one midlevel respondent wanted to "develop a team that will be more proactive about identifying and responding to incidents on campus." The team would comprise a diverse group of stakeholders—diverse in terms of positions and reporting structures as well as social identities—to review and respond to incidents of bias. She continued,

> The group will have the role of reviewing specific incidents, responding to them, and supporting targets of discrimination. Additionally, and perhaps most importantly, this group will use the collection and review of incidents as information that speaks to the campus climate. [The group] will be charged with bringing issues of institutional bias and oppression to the attention of the Dean of Students and identifying plans for changing the ways business as usual occurs on campus.

Again, the proposed next steps for addressing the situation are complex and exemplify the interaction of the known and unknown factors identified in the written case study. While the student affairs professionals' responses and action steps are similar in many ways, there are also some differences as noted previously. There are also significant differences in how each of the professionals arrived at their proposed solutions.

Institutional Context, Salient Identities, Positional Power, and Emotions

As mentioned previously, the professionals who contributed responses to these cases were diverse not only in terms of their social identities but also in terms of their positions on campus and the types and cultures of the campuses where they work. Therefore, the confluence of institutional context, salient identities, positional power, and emotions is explored for a senior-level administrator and adjunct faculty member (James), two midlevel managers (Rashad and Shelby), and one entry-level professional (Olive). Each professional's reflections relate to the possible solutions to this complex case.

James. This respondent described himself as a heterosexual White male and acknowledged that these identities played a role in how he formulated his thoughts and how others interpreted his response to the case. He said, "I have to acknowledge my sexuality and race may not be at the forefront of how I do things but my relationships with those individuals involved in the situation could be influenced by that fact and anything I would do could be interpreted through that lens." He then related Toussaint's disgust that Kate didn't support "one of her own" in the case to ways students or colleagues may perceive his actions. He said, "Someone on campus could think, 'Of course you'll do that because you're White and male.' I might not make my decisions from that frame, but my social identities inform how my decisions can be interpreted and perceived."

He addressed his positional power by commenting that the "power inherent in a 'dean of students' title also carries expectations and perceptions, in addition to the chance that these layers of power and privilege could inhibit rather than enhance learning and resolution of the situation." He elaborated:

> There are two things at play: recognizing that some people may want or expect a dean of students to make a decision and resolve the situation in a more unilateral fashion to "take care of it." That might not be the most educational way to resolve the situation. The second thing is that the actions that I might take because of being a dean of students may carry more weight than similar actions that other people in the situation could take. Something that I do might be perceived differently coming from me as the dean of students rather than the same action coming from Kate as the director of student activities.

His awareness of his positional power and his care to not misuse that power is evident throughout his responses in his insistence on empowering, engaging, and consulting with others. For example, he noted affirming and supporting Kate's ability to appropriately handle the situation as the professional who is most directly involved; while asking judicial and security officials about their plans and timelines, he did not mention giving them direction or advice, and he determined "*in collaboration with the graduate and professional staff* [emphasis added], the appropriateness of formal dispute resolution."

James's commitment to collaboration and involving others in the decision-making process, as well as his suggestion that the "community should have the opportunity to engage in dialogue that directly addresses the complex social issues raised in the aftermath of the original incident," may also be a reflection of this respondent's employment at a Jesuit institution. He noted, "It is essential that this work is accomplished in a manner that respects Kate and Nick's professional capacities and growth while honoring the educational mission and values of the institution." The respondent stated that the mission and philosophy of the Jesuit institution where he has worked for over 10 years may naturally be reflected in his response to the case. For example, Jesuit ideals like *cura personalis* (care for the whole person) and faith-seeking justice are implied in the ways this respondent offers approaches that are congruent with the university's mission.

Moreover, James wrote,

> As someone who has spent considerable time studying and teaching issues of race, cross-cultural engagement, and social justice, I can't help but feel how unfortunate it is that the situation has escalated to the point it has and wonder if any form of early intervention might have alleviated the situation. I would want to work quickly to stem the tide of further growth of the problem.

This statement may imply a use of his positional power, in that as a senior administrator he is likely able to influence the timeline of the investigation, intervention, and other responses. In other words, he most likely has the ability to expedite the process to prevent additional incidents related to the original altercation between the students, which may tangentially reveal his power to relieve his own feelings about the way the situation escalated. James expressed sadness because he perceives the layers of the educational process are not working for these students at this point, and the situation is having negative effects on the campus community. Hence, this respondent emphasized a restorative justice approach to initiating action steps to move forward as a campus community. This statement about feeling sadness may also reveal the privilege he has as a White man—not having to face similar racially charged issues on a daily basis as a person of color might.

Finally, this same statement also reveals James's position as an adjunct faculty member. This role that is salient to him may help explain why he was the only respondent to include following up in a developmental way with Nick, the graduate student who witnessed the incident and made the initial report to campus security, as an essential step in this case.

Rashad. This second contributor identified himself as an African American man "sensitive to the experience of not only other Black students, but students of color in general." Specifically, he is mindful of possible experiences with racism the students involved may have encountered in the past.

Further, graduating from and working at predominantly White institutions (PWIs) sensitized him to the needs of students of color who attend PWIs. In his consideration of the stakeholders in this case, he stated that any response could "easily lead to a situation where students feel marginalized or like 'they don't matter'" especially in regard to whether Eric is allowed to remain on the diversity board, which is seen as a position of power. Rashad also stressed the importance of communicating the rationale for whatever action is ultimately implemented with the larger campus community. "Not having accurate or any information at all, especially when an administrative action is (or is not) taken, can contribute to potential feelings of hopelessness, unimportance, or any other feeling that comes with being left in the dark." It can also lead to the student body and campus community "creating or manufacturing 'truth or fact.'"

For example, the respondent suggested that if Eric was allowed to remain on the diversity board, but the rationale for the decision was not explained, Toussaint's (and other students') perception may be that his perspective was not heard or did not matter, and "he might feel as if he is not a valued member of the community because no one was held accountable for what happened to him." Similarly, if Eric was removed from the diversity board without adequate explanation, he "might easily assert that his removal was an overreaction or that he was treated unfairly." This respondent acknowledged that institutional factors such as size of the institution and campus climate (in this case particularly for members of underrepresented racial/ ethnic groups) influenced his thinking, suggesting that "it can be difficult (and dangerously foolhardy) to make decisions in a vacuum without considering institutional contexts and campus climate."

Finally, Rashad acknowledged that as a person of color, he is sensitive to instances of intolerance and would need to be mindful of the "visceral or emotional reaction" that the use of the *N* word might cause for him. Rashad's racial identity may help explain the extreme importance he placed on determining whether that derogatory word was said during the incident and reconciling the fact that Toussaint gave two different versions of the encounter at two different times. Moreover, Rashad is mindful of his emotional reaction to Toussaint's assertion that Kate was "not supporting my own." This compels Rashad to suggest having another conversation with Toussaint specifically about this issue, after the primary issues are resolved.

Rashad also named "student affairs professional" and "student organization advisor" as identities that were salient for him in this case. One of his priorities, then, was "to ensure that both students are supported and treated with care." This is evident by his suggestion that meeting the needs of stakeholders involves "listening, listening, listening."

> Taking the time to listen to each stakeholder to understand their perspective and story is crucial. Many times people feel valued if individuals simply take the time to listen to what they have to say. . . . Listening often serves to validate, and when people feel validated they feel respected and cared for.

At the same time he showed support for them, Rashad also responded in a way that is consistent with student affairs' commitment to holistic student development. That is, he held the students accountable for their actions and helped them "understand that there is an appropriate way for handling disagreements and yelling/arguing/threats is not the way to do that." According to Rashad, it is important that after speaking with both students, they "walk away from this having learned something about either themselves or working with others."

Similarly, as a student organization adviser, Rashad prioritized "deescalating the growing tension between the two student organizations" as a key issue to address in this case. As such, he suggested working with the advisers and leadership of all the student organizations involved to share information and provide closure. He also acknowledged the power that not only the two students (i.e., Toussaint and Eric) held in this situation, but also the BSU, ASU, and LGBT Alliance. He recognized the possibility of these groups' becoming major players in this campus situation, "whether it be through Facebook groups, letters to the campus newspaper, . . . or sit-ins or demonstrations."

Rashad viewed faculty/staff and the student activities office as having limited power in this case. "Beyond trying to sway or influence individual or small groups of students that they may interact with, I think both of these groups are limited in what they can do." This perspective may be a realistic reflection of a midlevel manager's influence over a situation in which many students and student organizations are involved and are operating on rumors or incomplete information. Other questions or concerns Rashad's response conjures include, What is the level of respect student affairs staff (or midlevel student affairs staff) have on this campus? Might this response be reflective of Rashad's experience being a minority (student and professional of color at PWIs) with perhaps limited power or influence?

Shelby. Juxtapose this stance with that of our third respondent, who described herself as a "White woman who is enrolled in a social justice [graduate] program." As a professional and White person, Shelby sees working with students as giving her an "opportunity to control the situation in ways that work for [her]." She wrote that in her position of relative dominance over students,

> I can decide when and how to approach the students, direct the conversations, end the conversation when I feel uncomfortable, and be somewhat assured that the racially minoritized students would follow my lead instead of expecting me to follow theirs.

The last comment acknowledges the power she has in this situation because she is a White student affairs professional. Another example of the power she holds is evident by her intention to plan training sessions for judicial officers on working against bias in the judicial system. She attributed this ability to challenge the status quo with little risk to herself to the fact that she is White.

> Because of my positionality as a white person, we know that I am more likely to be heard by upper-level administrators and that I face fewer risks of retribution as a result of engaging in a power struggle so I will take the lead challenging the dominant process.

Shelby also acknowledged some limits and cautions related to being White. For example, she recognized that she may be unaware of some of the contextual factors that may have influenced the events, such as the racial climate on campus that may negatively affect underrepresented students. (At the same time, she recognized that her ability to work on this campus without knowing the racial climate is a privilege she has because of being White.) She was also cautious in her interactions with Kate, stating,

> From my place of privilege, I need to be concerned about the historical domination of Black women by White women. I am careful not to offer or imply that she needs help because I know she is very capable, but instead to convey that I want to align with and support her.

Moreover, Shelby suggested that as a midlevel professional and a woman, her efforts to challenge the oppressive systems that may have contributed to this incident may be dismissed. She anticipated that some administrators would judge that she overreacted or that she is "too young to understand how the real world works." She anticipated being judged as too emotional and her desire to support students as coddling.

> In these ways, things that are important to me—connecting with students, engaging my emotions as well as my intellect, and responding to needs of students—will be summarily dismissed as unprofessional, which is code for not masculine.

Shelby was aware that this case elicits emotions in her that may influence her decisions and reactions. Specifically, she acknowledged insecurity when working with issues of difference and oppression as well as apprehension about making a mistake. She also recognized that working and connecting with students "feels good" to her and is aware that some decisions make her feel safe (i.e., within her comfort zone).

Shelby's role as a graduate student studying social justice is apparent throughout her response as well. From that training, she can "identify many factors of power, dominance, and oppression in this incident." In addition to addressing the immediate stakeholders and issues in this case, she attempted to analyze and address systems of dominance and oppression as well. For example, she recognized that "the judicial and criminal systems have a history of failing to understand the historical and institutional factors that created the context of oppression in the first place, placing the focus of blame on the subordinated body."

Thus, this respondent hopes that student affairs professionals will take systemic factors into consideration when working with students, rather than focus exclusively on students who find themselves in conflict as "problems" or "troublemakers" who need to be punished or corrected. In this case, she suggested that the administrators involved ask, "What is going on in the institution that led [Toussaint and Eric] to come into this conflict in the first place?"

Similarly, one of her responses was to discuss with the students and student organizations the "historical legacies of oppression that linger within the institution and our society" to help them come together to challenge the power structure rather than direct their frustration at each other. Moreover, while she planned to address the situation with the students specifically, she stated that as a graduate student studying social justice, she knows that "the response of connecting with the students often falls short of social change (Kivel, 2007). Addressing the needs of minoritized persons is important but is not complete without addressing the systems that oppress them in the first place."

She provided the following example to help illuminate her point:

> Eric may have perceived Toussaint to be a member of the group who has historically received more resources and attention to issues they raise; he may experience the ASU being marginalized on campus. The argument they had over the placement of the sign may have more specifically been an argument over who holds the positionality for resources on campus. As an organization with stronger historical roots and more members, the Black Student Union may have more history and relative power than the Asian Student Union.

She continued,

> This specific incident would likely have looked much differently if Toussaint and Eric had not been located in a historically rooted system of dominance and oppression. It would have been much easier for them to argue about where to place a sign, but in this situation, they were also asserting their need to be recognized and to have power to make decisions that impact them.

Related to this, Shelby placed considerable responsibility on herself to challenge what she identifies as oppressive systems, going beyond addressing the immediate issues and stakeholders involved in this incident. For example, Shelby suggested setting up a meeting with the associate dean of students to discuss issues related to potential inequities in funding for organizations, which may have been foundational to the conflict between ASU and BSU given the probability that they had limited resources. As Shelby put it, "White students are more likely to be involved with funded organizations [and] funded organizations are more likely to be able to fund their own events and not be forced to seek out co-sponsors." In other words, is the institutional context, specifically funding practices, creating an increased likelihood for conflict among students of color or members of clubs composed of traditionally underrepresented students, a situation that primarily White clubs can avoid?

Moreover, Shelby would explore why the campus police were called to an incident involving only a verbal squabble. She asked, "What is the context that promotes a graduate student to view two men of color as threatening?" and raised the question of whether the graduate student would have responded similarly if the students involved in the conflict were White. She acknowledged the probable good intentions of the individual graduate student while questioning the institutional "policies of education, practice, and evaluation for student affairs staff, faculty, and security personnel related to these known (researched) biases." Similarly, Shelby would "advocate that the institution investigate more about the environment [at the institution] that fosters racial epithets instead of assuming that this is an issue related to the individual student charged with the infraction."

Further, she proposed developing a team to more thoroughly respond to bias-related incidents in the future, as well as calling attention to any other issues of institutional bias and oppression and identifying plans to change them. The respondent emphasized the importance of continuing to practice self-reflectivity when attempting to create systemic change. Shelby said,

> I must be able to implicate myself individually first in order to take responsibility for my participation and to position myself within the system rather than outside of it (where I might prefer to think of myself). This process of co-implication can also be useful when speaking with others from the dominant groups in the administration so that I can position myself with them in this process of examining self/institution instead of seeming to be blaming the system/them and not implicating myself.

She concluded, "Individually, each of us does not need to be a racist, but by being part of an institution created to benefit those already with power, if we are not working to change it, we are likely perpetuating the oppression of the system." After reviewing her response, Shelby questioned how she lives and hoped she would enact the solutions she proposed. She said, "It is clear to me that I responded from an academic perspective and that negotiating the politics in a live situation is more tenuous and scary than when responding what I should do in a case study."

Olive. The final respondent to this case identified her salient identities as White, lesbian/gender queer, administrator, and entry level. Similar to the previous contributor, Olive's whiteness was salient in her interactions with

Kate. She felt "concerned about stepping on Kate's toes and questioning her response to the incident." After all, "This is Kate's shop," and the respondent would want Kate to know that she sees her as a capable and competent person who can handle the situation. It is likely that the respondent expressed concern about stepping on Kate's toes because of the historical power differential between Whites and Blacks and her desire to not perpetuate that legacy. Olive also noted that in her current context, Kate would be her boss. She said it is not only "about the historical context in terms of stepping on toes but it is also about the fact that she is above me and it would be weird to tell my boss what to do." This influenced her response to the case in that "before offering suggestions [to Kate], it would be important to see if [she is] needed in the first place." And if so, rather than give advice or provide suggestions, she would "ask questions that strive to help Kate run through her ideas, make decisions, and provide direction." Olive wrote that "as a White person, I know that despite my best efforts, I am going to miss a piece of the picture." She explained,

> I have to be careful because there are factors that I can attempt to empathize with, but will never really understand like the relationship between two African American or two Black people, but I can't feel it the same way that they feel it because I don't understand the intricacies of what they feel. They could think that some of what I find important is not salient in this situation.

Olive saw her identification as lesbian/gender queer as a way to connect with the LGBT students on campus, since she said she is likely to have an existing relationship with them. From a lesbian/gender queer experience lens, she also suggested her and students' perceptions of an altercation may be turned into identity politics in the case. Olive stated she would use her relationships with students to help "work on a collective understanding and process for addressing the issue." Moreover, her lesbian/gender queer identity—and the oppression and victimization she has experienced as a result of being misunderstood because of this aspect of her identity—may have contributed to her focusing her response to the case on facilitating genuine dialogue, understanding each student's perspective, and helping students "understand the impact of their beliefs and making conscious decisions about how they want to be in community with others who may have different value systems and ways of being." Her lesbian/gender queer identity also may have influenced the emotions that were evoked by this case: frustration, upset, concern, and fear. "Divisions and power struggles in marginalized communities certainly keep the focus off the power structures that may be causing the strife to begin with."

Olive's professional role as administrator was salient to her as well, particularly as the institutional context defines the relationship between students and staff. She acknowledged that on campuses where students see administrators as "mentors, guides, and confidants," this role likely gives her power in developing trust with the students. In contrast, in institutional contexts where there is a tradition of mistrust between students and administrators, her role as administrator gives her little power in this situation, in that students may view her as an enemy and distrust her and her intentions. In either case, though, Olive suggested speaking with the students directly involved, and "work[ing] to bring the community together to raise, face, and resolve the issue."

Olive felt she had little power in this situation as an entry-level professional. Although she was conscious of her position at the lowest level of the professional hierarchy, she still felt "comfortable sharing [her] authentic thoughts and feelings about this case with Kate." However, it may be because of her position level that her response does not include challenging "oppressive systems" as the previous respondent suggested. Finally, it is also possible that her position as an entry-level professional gives her a unique perspective for viewing the case. For example, Olive is the only respondent to consider that Kate's short tenure on the campus could have an influence in that she may not have had enough time to "understand the political landscape [and] historical relationship on campus, and build trusting relationships with the stakeholders in this case."

Each respondent viewed the case from slightly or vastly different perspectives, related to the differing intersections of social identities, institutional contexts, and positional power perceived (or not) for each person. The diversity of ideas about how to respond most effectively to this case affirms the mission of this chapter by illustrating there are no right answers for making sense of complex cases while providing possible solutions given the institutional culture(s), context, and climate represented by each respondent. Yet, all the respondents operated from a place of working in their own unique ways to create positive change on their campuses—enacting the core value of inclusion. The next case offers a different set of circumstances and real issues to explore.

CASE 2—DISRUPTIVE STUDENT THREAT?

As the director of the student conduct office, Derrick Dixon assembled a threat assessment team composed of faculty, administrators, and students to develop protocol for proactive approaches to preventing tragedies such as those at Northern Illinois University and Virginia Tech from happening on their campus. The objectives of the team are threefold: to empower the campus community to identify and report incidents of students who exhibit disruptive emotional and behavioral threats in the classroom and other campus spaces, enhance the development of a culture of care by taking proactive measures to maintain campus safety, and refer students who are exhibiting inappropriate behavior but may also be experiencing emotional or mental health concerns to the student conduct office and the counseling center. The team serves as a consulting group for members of the campus community for strategies to employ when encountering students who exhibit disturbing behavior inside and outside the classroom.

Dixon communicated a week ago via telephone with Professor Weston about the peculiar behavior of a student named Luis in Weston's course. During the telephone conversation, Weston expressed his concern that Luis invokes fear in his classroom environment by his presence because he stares inappropriately at women (two students complained to Weston during the class break). Other students avoid working with him during small-group activities in class. Furthermore, he keeps his Bible sitting on his desk during class discussions. Weston is a full professor of business law and a White man who has been teaching at the university for over 20 years. Weston sought advice from Dixon about what measures, if any, to take to address this situation, because in his years of teaching he had not come across a student who seemed so "disturbing." After hanging up the phone with Weston, Dixon checked Luis's disciplinary and academic records to ascertain whether previous complaints had been filed. There were no reports in Luis's file because he just transferred; this was Luis's first semester on campus. Dixon advised Weston to pay close attention to this situation and follow up with him if subsequent complaints from students about Luis are made. Dixon then mentioned the incident to other members of the threat assessment team.

Less than two weeks later, Dixon received an e-mail message from Weston. Within the first paragraph, Weston demanded campus police presence either inside or outside his classroom if Luis is to remain enrolled in the course. Weston attached a message from a student, Paulina, a 25-year-old married woman who had submitted a formal complaint to Weston about Luis. In Paulina's message, she attached information from Luis's "About Me" section of his Facebook page. Paulina noted that Luis's message, which read,

> I will not associate with anyone who is not like-minded and doesn't have a mind set to educate themselves for the good and grace of Jesus Christ my Lord and Savior. If you do not complement my goals and visions, don't let the door hit you on your way out

was quite unnerving. Paulina noted that Luis's incessant staring at her during class caused her great discomfort. The staring coupled with the messages on Luis's Facebook page made her and her husband concerned not only for her safety but also for the safety of the entire class.

Weston then said he returned the midterm exams to the students last week. Luis's performance was in his words "abysmal." In all his years of teaching, he had never had a student earn such a low grade, less than 25%, on the exam. When Weston talked with Luis about his exam, as opposed to admitting that he was unprepared, Luis stated, "I'll get a 95% on the next exam." Weston was shocked by Luis's "detachment from reality." He wrote to Dixon, "I want him out of my classroom." Weston then questioned how the university could have admitted a student who was clearly academically unprepared for work at this level.

Dixon consulted with the threat assessment team and then perused Luis's Facebook page. Dixon saw Luis's profile picture, a smiling, clean-cut Latino male with his mom and dog. Olivia Goldsmith, vice president for student affairs, advised Dixon to set up an appointment with Luis and let him know that his mother or another family member was welcome to attend the meeting with him. Dixon's next step was to call Luis into the office, but Luis didn't show up for the meeting. Per Weston's request, campus police were stationed outside the classroom for the next class period. Dixon then sent Luis a letter informing him that he would be receiving an interim suspension from the university until he complied with meeting with Dixon in the student conduct office.

After Luis's receipt of the letter, he and his mother scheduled a meeting with Dixon for the next day. When Luis and his mother arrived for the meeting, Dixon was immediately struck by Luis's gentle nature. Dixon asked Luis about his experience in the class. Luis was shocked by the reaction of his peers and professor. When Dixon asked Luis about his performance on the first exam, he said, "I'm not used to classes here yet." Luis's mother objected, "I thought you were earning an A in this course." During the course of the conversation, Luis agreed to see a counselor in the university counseling center to talk about his transition to life at the university; however, he adamantly wanted to finish the course without a late withdrawal because he'd completed most of the work.

When Luis left his office, Dixon considered the interactions with Weston and Luis and his mother. Luis wants to finish the class, but Weston and two other students in the course want him to withdraw from the course. What should happen next?

Responses

Like the first case, four student affairs professionals responded to this second one. Respondents were two midlevel professionals, one who works at a large public university and another at an Ivy League institution; a senior-level professional who works at a comprehensive public college; and one entry-level professional who works at an elite private institution. Again, the actual responses are presented first, followed by an explanation of how the respondents' institutional contexts and social identities shaped the response. Respondents offered suggestions pertaining to distinctions about when and how to intervene with Weston and Luis, approaches to working with the threat assessment team, and ways to incorporate dialogue (including application of student development theory) among stakeholders involved in the case. Moreover, issues pertaining to student affairs professionals' role as advocates for students, family members, and faculty were considered in the responses.

In responding to this case, a few of the contributors mentioned that situations very similar to this one play out on college and university campuses frequently. While this is not necessarily a new phenomenon, the attention paid to this aspect of student affairs work has increased dramatically since the tragic incidents at Virginia Tech and Northern Illinois University. One respondent poignantly compared student affairs professionals' role in responding to these incidents to the wizard in *The Wizard of Oz*:

> We are looked to as having all the answers to very difficult and complex problems that have no simple answers. Once we climb out from behind the curtain, we find that we only can give that which already exists and hope that we don't simply fly away on an uncharted course in our balloon. We could use a good witch Glinda to remind us that we need to stop and listen to our inner thoughts to find our way home.

The complexity of the responses offered suggests individual respondents listened to their inner thoughts when making decisions in a situation with many ambiguities. For instance, two of the respondents made distinctions between how they would have responded differently if they were involved in the case earlier, and how they would respond if they became involved where the case ends. The other two respondents assumed the ability to become involved early in the case, and their responses reflect this decision.

For the initial phone conversation with Weston, three respondents recommended gathering as much pertinent information as possible, including details about specific behaviors that invoked fear in the students, descriptions of what exactly was meant by "staring inappropriately," and necessary answers to questions of Weston to ascertain whether Luis ever threatened to harm himself or others. Further, the respondents suggested probing Weston to determine if there were potential violations of the student code of conduct. Respondents described the initial phone conversation as an opportunity to encourage Weston to converse directly with Luis to discuss his behavior.

Two respondents said they would use the information gathered during this phone conversation to determine the appropriateness of bringing the situation and relevant information to the threat assessment team. One of the respondents also discussed the importance of designing the processes used by the behavioral assessment team before the incident even occurred. If involving the threat assessment team was determined appropriate, one respondent suggested the team initiate further fact finding about Luis, such as "gathering police reports on campus or other relevant jurisdictions," contacting the conduct officer at Luis's previous campus to determine if reports had been made there, gathering academic records, and reviewing Facebook and other social networking sites. In addition, she suggested contacting staff of other campus offices and faculty to find out if they had relevant information to share, including academic advising, disability services, counseling, student health, other faculty members teaching Luis, and residence life professionals if he lived on campus.

All four respondents mentioned getting more involved in the case themselves at an earlier point, rather than allowing nearly two weeks to pass without any intervention. One respondent suggested attending Weston's class to directly observe the behaviors being described and possibly talking with Luis briefly after class to set up a meeting. This respondent and others mentioned the importance of meeting with Luis immediately to inform him of students' perceptions that his behavior is troubling and to determine if there may be underlying issues, with the goal of helping Luis meet behavioral expectations and succeed academically at his institution. Two of the respondents indicated that the meeting should not include Luis's family, one of whom pointed out that family issues may be part of a problem Luis is dealing with. During this meeting between Dixon and Luis, one respondent mentioned that Luis "should be explicitly told what he is doing that is scaring his professor and fellow students and asked to stop behaving in that manner." The respondent further stated that "Luis should also be made aware of the consequences, if any, for continuing to behave in the manner of concern." Another respondent suggested that this in-depth conversation between Dixon and Luis, without his mother present,

> may open the door to a "teachable moment," sharing with Luis the university's expectations of all students. Maybe Luis will feel comfortable enough to express feelings he may have regarding the professors, his fellow students, the class, and his role as a student within this particular institution.

Finally, the interim suspension imposed on Luis was troubling to some respondents. As one wrote, "Issuing an interim suspension to Luis was a terrible mistake." He suggested "there was no overt threatening or dangerous behavior" in this case, and "suspension should never be used for missing a meeting with a campus administrator if no threat or dangerous behavior has been demonstrated." Another respondent questioned whether an adequate attempt was made to inform Luis of the meeting with Dixon that he did not attend, including explaining the urgency of the meeting and potential consequences for not attending.

In responding to the case at the point where it ends, the contributors suggested slightly different approaches. Two began by consulting with other experts on campus, including the counseling center (after making sure Luis signed a release of information allowing a candid conversation) and a disability support office. These consultations were made in an effort to better understand why Luis might be exhibiting awkward behaviors and to determine whether Luis was a threat to himself or others. If he was considered a threat, one respondent noted the importance of meeting with Luis again (with his family member if he chose) to talk about voluntarily withdrawing from the university, "knowing that we have an involuntary withdrawal policy if we need to use it." If he was not considered a threat, other actions were recommended, including referring Luis to campus resources, following up with Weston and the students who expressed concern about Luis's behavior, and discussing options regarding Luis's completing Weston's course.

Specifically, one respondent mentioned referring Luis to academic support services available on campus to help him in "navigating the coursework and managing his time at his new institution." She also pointed out that if in earlier meetings Luis indicated strong religious beliefs and perhaps an interest in connecting with similar others on campus, Dixon could help connect him with appropriate religiously affiliated campus organizations. Another respondent "normalized" Luis's experience with Weston's exam and his subsequent confidence in doing better next time, asking, "What . . . student doesn't bomb their first assignment in their first semester classes with the belief that they can do better on the next one?" He also suggested referring Luis to the many resources on campus that could help him succeed academically. This respondent further proposed connecting Luis with a "Latino/Latina staff member or ally," suggesting that "Luis would benefit from a mentor rather than a counselor or both especially if the counseling center has someone on staff that is Latino or Latina or is well qualified in counseling Latina/Latino students."

Initiating follow-up conversations with Weston and the students who expressed concern about or fear of Luis's behavior was a priority for three respondents. One recognized that if Luis was not determined to be a threat and therefore not removed from campus or Weston's class, Weston might be disappointed in the university's response, noting that faculty members are often unaware of students' rights. In this case, she acknowledged the faculty member's concerns and she would help "find strategies to lower anxiety to think of rational solutions." Also, this respondent mentioned the importance of including Weston in the process, perhaps inviting him to the threat assessment team meeting to "discuss the case and propose interventions." Similarly, another respondent mentioned the possibility of receiving "push back from Professor Weston" regarding a decision to not remove Luis, and the importance of being "transparent about how an effective student development approach to this issue can be useful." In addressing the specific issue of Luis displaying his Bible during class and the religious comments on his Facebook page, one respondent stated, "Dr. Dixon has an obligation to Professor Weston and the women in Luis's class who are concerned by this to examine and share information on a student's religious freedom."

Allowing Paulina and the other concerned students to express their feelings was also important to some respondents. If Luis remained in Weston's class with the other students, one contributor prioritized inviting the students in the class to "speak with [the contributor] if they want to express their concerns." Similarly, another respondent stated, "It is crucial that follow-up occur in making sure these students have been given resources to help them through the situation," noting it was possible they could benefit from "counseling services or other forms of victim advocacy programs." Another respondent mentioned that a meeting between Dixon and Paulina might provide "an opportunity to explore her feelings and develop a better understanding of her experience at the same time."

One respondent identified the following strategy as a way to move forward:

> [Bring] all parties together for a discussion. The ultimate goal would be to have Luis remain in the class while creating a new classroom environment where everyone felt safe and valued, including Luis. This cannot happen unless Professor Weston, the class members, and Luis buy into how each of them can help in creating a shared environment where respect of self and others is practiced.

He acknowledged this process could "take some time, more than one discussion, and ruffle some feathers" but stressed the importance of situations like this being addressed, discussed, and acted upon.

Other respondents mentioned the need to explore options other than keeping Luis in Weston's class for the remainder of the semester. For example, one contributor stated that "if the faculty member was adamant about

Luis not attending class, I would consult with the Assistant Dean to see if there is another section of the course that Luis might attend." Another explored this option too, while also considering factors such as whether Luis could be forced to withdraw from the class given the presence or absence of policy violations; whether there were financial aid, academic progress, or other academic implications; and whether some kind of independent study option would be agreeable to all parties. Significantly, this respondent considered the likelihood of Luis's succeeding if he was allowed to stay in Weston's class. That is, could Luis thrive in the class, given that

> several individuals are telling him he doesn't belong (including the person in the most powerful position in the class, the professor). Can he complete the work required of the class if he is being made to feel less than the other members of the class? Can he complete the group work required of the class if students refuse to work with him?

Finally, in terms of responses to this case, one contributor said it was important to "employ an evaluation process to review how the situation was approached and resolved," particularly related to the threat assessment team. Another suggested examining the membership of that group, ensuring it included "students, faculty, and staff from a wide variety of social identity backgrounds." He further suggested,

> The group should also include representatives from community based mental health agencies. These agencies often serve a much more diverse clientele and can provide invaluable insights. In addition, if a student is truly experiencing psychological distress, they will often end up being served by these agencies as most campuses are not equipped to do so.

Moreover, this respondent addressed the importance of having a clear understanding of the role of the threat assessment team in the scenario. For example, he suggested the team "make recommendations on how best to address situations and that these recommendations will be followed unless there is a compelling reason not to." Finally, he discussed the importance of gaining support for this approach from upper-level administrators, particularly the vice president for student affairs.

Another respondent also reflected on the membership of and the process used by the threat assessment team. In particular, she suggested examining the membership of the team and determining if there was sufficient diversity to challenge a prevailing bias that may exist if there was potential majority-group status among the members. In other words, were cultural issues or differences considered in their discussions and recommendations?

As with the first case, many of the student affairs professionals' responses and action steps were similar in many ways, yet there were some differences in their responses and the ways they arrived at their proposed solutions. These professionals, like the ones responding to the first case, were asked to consider the issues, stakeholders, and potential advantages and pitfalls of each proposed response, as well as their own salient identities, position levels, and the institutional context that may have influenced their thinking and decision making. Again, the purpose of exploring these contextual and identity factors in this chapter is to provide examples of how student affairs professionals thoughtfully work through difficult and complex situations, consciously taking into account how issues of power, privilege, and oppression influence outcomes.

Institutional Context, Salient Identities, Positional Power, and Emotions

As mentioned previously, respondents to this case included a midlevel professional who works at a large public university (Leticia), a senior-level professional who works at a comprehensive public college (Gary), another midlevel professional who works at an Ivy League institution (Dan), and one entry-level professional who works at an elite private institution (Eloise). The professionals who contributed responses to this case are also diverse in terms of their social identities, positions on campus, and the types and cultures of the campuses where they work. Differences in their responses and the development of their responses based on these characteristics are explored next. Each professional's reflections elaborate on individual perspectives pertaining to possible solutions to this complex case.

Leticia. Leticia, who identified as Hispanic, said being a Hispanic woman is a salient identity in this case, and she suggested that being Hispanic

> *may* give me an advantage when speaking with the student and the family member if they feel a cultural connection. However, I do not assume that this is automatically the case. If English is not the primary language of the family member, my bilingual abilities can come in handy.

While she recognized that she and Luis share a common ethnicity, she was careful to point out that this may or may not be relevant in this case, suggesting that sharing an ethnicity does not necessarily imply sharing a cultural connection. Her statements suggest other mitigating factors such as the degree to which one identifies with Hispanic or Hispanic American culture (which may be related to generational status) and country of origin, as well as other salient identities (e.g., the interplay of ethnicity and gender) that influence the potential cultural connection between two people of the same ethnicity. She said she and her supervisor, a White male, often meet with students together, and given their diversity in terms of ethnicity, gender, and past experiences, one of them is frequently able to make a connection with the student or family member. Leticia also mentioned that being an alumna of the institution "goes a long way with some of our students and family members." This is a poignant observation; this aspect of her identity is salient because her institutional context is steeped in tradition. Leticia's description of her institutional context as conservative and consisting of a largely Christian student body may have also influenced the fact that addressing the religious factors in the case (i.e., Luis having a Bible on his desk in Weston's class and religious statements on his Facebook page) was not factored into her suggested response. As she put it, at her university, "It is not unusual for someone to have a Bible sitting on their desk or have a T-shirt with scripture written on it."

Leticia attributed significant (perceived) power to Weston in this case. For instance, she suggested that if the director of counseling does not see Luis as a threat to himself or others, Luis should be able to stay in Weston's class. However, she also said, "If the faculty member was adamant about Luis not attending class, I would consult with the Assistant Dean to see if there is another section of the course that Luis might attend." Her approach demonstrates the perception of the faculty member's power in this case. It is possible that social identity and contextual factors influenced her attributing significant power to Weston, who is described as a White, male, tenured full professor who has been teaching at the university for over 20 years, juxtaposed with her identities as a relatively younger, Hispanic, female midlevel student affairs professional.

Leticia also attributed a great deal of power to Dixon and the threat assessment team in that they have the ability to gather information from police agencies, previous institutions Luis attended, campus offices such as counseling and advising, and others. The members of the threat assessment team also have the ability to make the ultimate decision: whether Luis is welcome to remain a student at the university. In contrast, Luis was identified as having minimal power in this case. He is given little influence over the outcome, even though it may affect him the most. At the same time, he may also feel that he is "being targeted because of his race and/or religious beliefs," perhaps illustrating a relationship between power (or a lack thereof) and oppression.

Finally, Leticia—although she does not say it directly—attributed significant power to information and expertise. This is evident in her strategy to gather as much information as possible from police reports, previous institutions, academic records, and so on before making any decision on the case. Power attributed to information and expertise is especially evident in statements she made, such as, "Decisions are based on facts and tangible behaviors, . . . not suppositions and stereotypes." The power in expertise is demonstrated through empowering members of the threat assessment team—namely, the director of the counseling center, director of disability services, and director of the health center—to provide their expert opinions and diagnoses. Similarly, significant weight was placed on the opinion of the counseling center director in determining whether Luis is a threat to himself or others.

Deference of power to others may be related to this respondent's most salient identity in this case, that of a student affairs professional. She "subscribe[s] to the philosophy of assisting in the development of students" and she embraced a team approach in doing so. This focus on helping "the individual get help so that they can thrive in our environment" is evident in her proposed response to meet with Luis "immediately . . . out of concern for his well being."

Gary. The second respondent described himself as "White, male, father of a college student, administrator, leader, consultant, ally, first-generation college attendee, [and] faculty member" and stated that all of these are salient for him in everything he does, including his consideration of this case. In exploring how his identities intersected in responding to the situation, this respondent wrote, "My ability to show empathy for Professor Weston would come from our roles as faculty and possibly White males." His empathy is evident in his understanding of Weston's anxiety as leader of the classroom and his acknowledging that the professor's feeling of lack of control could be related to the social expectation that he, particularly as a White male, should be in control and maintain an authoritarian role in relationship to his students. He has the knowledge they seek.

Gary took his perceived shared similarities of social identities with Weston into account when examining the power (or lack thereof) of the stakeholders in the case. For example, he described Weston as "the most powerful and least powerful individual in this scenario," explaining that the U.S. higher education system provides faculty with complete control (with few limitations) over their classrooms but very little control outside their classrooms.

Gary also acknowledged the difficulty that faculty members may face, particularly those who have been teaching for many years, in effectively teaching students who are different from those previously in college classrooms, in terms of racial diversity and generational differences. The institutional context, then, particularly the historic and current diversity of the student body, becomes important in this case. Taking all these factors into account, Gary said he would make a point of listening to the stakeholders' needs, including Weston's. He would seek to clarify the professor's concerns and was aware of the need to make sure Weston knows they are being taken seriously. For example, this is one of the intended outcomes of suggesting that Dixon or a member of his team observe Luis in Weston's class; that is, to signal to the professor that his concerns are being considered.

Gary also reported that he can relate to Luis and his experience as a first-generation college student as well as a Latino. Although the respondent himself is not Latino, his wife and children are Latinas, and he has "extensive personal and professional experience with the Hispanic culture." This insider/outsider perspective the respondent has relative to Latinos may have informed his suggestion that Dixon identify a Latina/Latino mentor for Luis. That is, he may have recognized that having significant experience working with others of a different ethnicity contributes to effectively working with others and brings value to those relationships, but that there are also limitations and in some cases sharing the same culture is important. In considering how potential responses to this situation may influence stakeholders' privileges or feelings of oppression, Gary said,

> Luis appears to have no real idea that he may be being oppressed in this situation. He may have become so accustomed to his oppression that he has accepted it as a part of this stage in his racial/ethnic identity development.

Moreover, Gary recognized that as a first-generation student, Luis may not have a good understanding of the "defined roles" students are expected to play in the "didactic authoritarian structures" that exist in most college classrooms. His family may not be able to contribute that information to the capital Luis brings with him to college, and as a Latino, he may not connect easily or at all with other students to learn the norms and "predominant cultural context of the norms." Thus, Luis is left to figure out what is expected of him, often through trial and error.

Gary's identity as an administrator, and what he sees as the appropriate role of administrators, also influenced his thinking about this case and his response. For example, it is clear that he values student development theory as an information source and as one basis for making decisions. He mentioned that "student development theory tells us that there will be significant differences in how students of different ages learn and interact," as one factor that may potentially contribute to the problems Luis and his classmates—some of different ages—have interacting. He also made a distinction between "administrating" and "intervening," placing greater value on the latter, which involves "good old-fashioned hands-on work." For example, one suggestion Gary made is for Dixon or another team member to observe Luis in Weston's class and also to speak with him after class. He also mentioned that suspending a student for missing a meeting with an administrator—a decision he strongly disagreed with—is an example of "administrating." Gary said the skills and approaches professionals use to intervene on behalf of students are essential but are too often forgotten when they move up the career ladder.

Gary's observation was also likely influenced by his position as a senior-level administrator. As such, he recognizes that his positional power gives him the advantage of easily accessing all relevant information about the case and to ultimately determine or initiate the action that he deems necessary. He said,

> But I also have the ability through this power to enlist in a group of consultants who may have awareness I lack that can inform the process to be better and much more inclusive. In this way, I can use the positional power to help me not abuse the positional power.

The choice to use positional power is evident in the process he set up for the threat assessment team: As standard procedure, the recommendations of the team (comprising diverse experts) will be followed except in rare cases when there is a compelling reason not to do so. Reserving the option to diverge from the team's recommendation in special circumstances, and to determine what constitutes a compelling reason, is also a manifestation of Gary's positional power.

Finally, Gary considered emotions evoked by this case as well as the institutional and national contexts that influence it. Tragic incidents such as those at Virginia Tech and Northern Illinois University contribute to the fear and anxiety stakeholders feel in situations like the one in this case. Fear, the respondent said, "is never a good place from which to problem solve." He went on,

> Those of us who are entrusted with safety and security of the campus community want to do everything possible to make certain that events like [those at Virginia Tech and Northern Illinois University] do not happen on our campus. However, it is important that we are able to understand this fear and anxiety from a context of care rather than protectionism. We cannot create communities of care unless we as administrators can demonstrate that care in our behaviors and decisions.

The context of the case on a more local level, the institutional context, influenced the issues in the case as well. For example, Gary acknowledged that "at an institution where the faculty is unionized, faculty in the situation presented by Professor Weston may enlist their union representative to assist in the resolution thus creating an additional overt stakeholder." He also alluded to the potential impact of the nature of relationships between faculty and student affairs staff. For instance, Gary mentioned that Dixon may have limited interaction with faculty on his campus, and "subsequently, he may see Professor Weston's demands as a threat to his authority over student behavior." Relationships between faculty and administrators may play out differently on a campus that has a culture of mutual respect and frequent interaction between faculty and student affairs administrators.

Dan. This respondent, who described himself as a White man, identified this student affairs–academic affairs divide as an important contextual element to consider in this case as well. As someone who has held positions in academic and student affairs on a variety of campus types, he stated, "Whether we like it or not, this divide does exist." He mentioned that he has been "trained to make an effort to straddle the divide" between the two units and that this creates an interesting dynamic in this case, "one in which students affairs practitioners and faculty must work together to create a safe, healthy, developmental, productive learning environment." Dan's experience and position may have informed his proposed responses. For instance, one of his suggestions was that all parties with a legitimate stake in the outcome of this case (including Weston, Luis, and class members) should come together for discussion and cocreate mutually agreed-upon solutions. Further, Dan acknowledged that Dixon will need to carefully navigate a political element: Weston's position as a tenured, full professor with over 20 years of experience at the university—characteristics that give him significant power. Dan predicted that Weston may challenge the approach he suggested for Dixon but saw it as an opportunity to inform Weston of how a student development approach can meet the needs of all involved.

Dan also mentioned the need for colleges and universities to attend to the increasing demands for safe environments, given the context of campus tragedies involving shootings that have attracted significant attention. The degree to which professors, classmates, and other campus community members feel safe is an important factor to consider when weighing the advantages and disadvantages of potential responses. This respondent's suggestion to bring all stakeholders together acknowledges his commitment to creating a safe environment for students, faculty, and staff on his campus. However, Dan also considered the context of Luis as a Latino at what is most likely a PWI. The degree to which Luis feels safe and welcomed at his institution matters in this case and should be considered. The in-depth discussion Dan suggested between Dixon and Luis would explore this issue.

Dan's social identities likely influenced his responses as well, although perhaps in subtler ways than for the previous respondent. For example, Dan referred overtly to race/ethnicity only once in his response when discussing the importance of attending to Luis's feelings of safety as a Latino at a PWI. There are several potential explanations for his decision to discuss race/ethnicity minimally, ranging from the view that it was not an important factor in the resolution of this particular situation to the possibility that as a White person Dan may feel some discomfort in overtly addressing race when the issue was not presented specifically as a racial issue. It is also plausible that Dan's minimization of race in his response reflected his privilege associated with not having to view the world through a racial lens as a White person.

Whatever the explanation, it is clear that being a "student advocate, student affairs practitioner, an engaged campus community member, and an agent of change" were more salient identities for him in this case.

For example, Dan's identification as a student affairs professional was evident when he pointed out "teachable moments" in the case, such as an in-depth conversation with Luis about standard expectations for student behavior and a discussion with Paulina to "explore her feelings and develop a better understanding of her experiences." Dan described these teachable moments as opportunities for student affairs professionals to use their student development expertise to help students through difficult situations. Moreover, his suggestion for Dixon to bring all parties together implies he places a high value on collaborative processes that respect the perspectives and opinions of colleagues, including students and faculty. The goal of this discussion would be "to have Luis remain in the class while creating a new classroom environment where everyone felt safe and valued, including Luis." This is evidence of his advocating for students—Luis and his classmates— and of his desire to create positive change.

Eloise. The fourth contributor to this case is a White heterosexual woman who described herself as a social justice advocate who does not affiliate with a particular religion or religious community. Each of these identities likely influenced her response to the case. For example, she acknowledged there may be some misunderstandings based on cultural differences between Luis and Weston and the White students in the class, noting that "often, standards for behavior are set by the dominant group to dictate what is considered disorderly or a threat." It is significant, though, as a White person she did not presume to know or describe how Luis's behavior may or may not be different from the dominant culture in the class nor how it may or may not be consistent with his Latino culture. Rather, she simply raised the possibility that culture could be one explanation, and she encouraged direct conversations with Luis to explore the issue further. She explained, "As a White person, I don't rely on knowledge about students of color and attribute that knowledge to every situation and every student of color." Instead, she acknowledged cultural differences as a possibility but emphasized the importance of learning about the particular person's unique experiences (in this case, Luis's). Similarly, Eloise mentioned it is important for her not to speak for students of color but instead to "advocate for students in a way that provides them the opportunity to have their own voices heard."

As someone who has a good deal of experience working with groups of students who are marginalized in any number of ways, Eloise said it has become important to her to look at situations from dominant and oppressed perspectives. One example is her suggestion that the role of religion (or religious freedom/tolerance and/or perceptions of religion) in this case—as it relates to the Bible on Luis's desk and religious statements on his Facebook profile—be explored and addressed. She discussed Dixon's obligation to share information about religious freedom with Weston and the rest of the class and his obligation to ensure Luis's right to practice and display his religion as he sees fit within the bounds of institutional policies. Eloise also raised the possibility of Luis's perceived isolating behavior being related to his feeling unwelcome in the classroom. She said in her work some students who hold strong religious views have mentioned to her that they sometimes feel uninvited to share their real (unpopular) perspectives on some issues in class, and that has had a negative impact on their classroom experience. In responding to this case, Eloise suggested exploring that possibility with Luis. Further, she suggested introducing Luis to religiously affiliated organizations on campus, stating that if religion is indeed important to him, such an organization could help him form a stronger connection with the campus.

Financial considerations were also apparent throughout this contributor's response and were influenced by her own financial situation in college. For example, Eloise raised the possibility that Luis does not have access to a personal computer, so it could be that he did not receive an e-mail message from Dixon regarding his requirement to meet. As someone who did not have her own computer in college, Eloise said she relied on computer labs with limited hours to check e-mail, a limitation that many of her peers did not have. Additionally, Eloise raised the importance of considering financial implications of Luis's remaining in or withdrawing from Weston's course for the remainder of the semester.

Like the previous respondents, Eloise also considered the significance of institutional context in her examination of the case. For example, she said it is "possible that Luis's behavior was acceptable at his last institution and was never questioned." Since he was not made aware of the concerns raised by his classmates, professor, and others, and given that this was his first semester at the institution, he simply had no way of knowing he was behaving outside accepted norms. Eloise also mentioned that a heteronormative assumption is at play in this case, which may be indicative of either the institution's culture or society in general. Specifically, the assumption is that Luis's behavior stems from a romantic or sexual interest in the women he is "inappropriately" staring at. "Through in-depth conversations with Luis, one could extrapolate more information from him on why he is exhibiting this off-putting behavior and why it is specifically targeted toward the women in his class."

In both of these situations, the respondent implied a lack of power on the part of Luis, first, in that he lacks information about the accepted norms and that his behavior is scaring others, and second, in that he has not been given the opportunity to discuss his perspective. Similarly, she considered that in not responding to Dixon's request for a meeting, Luis was not made aware of the urgency or he "may be intimidated by the power dynamics that exist between him, the university office, and Dr. Dixon."

As in the first case, each respondent viewed this second case from slightly or vastly different perspectives, perhaps based on their social identities, institutional contexts, and position levels. Many elements of their suggested responses are similar, including the gathering of additional specific information about Luis's behaviors, the importance of intervening with him early and maintaining open communication with other stakeholders, consulting with the threat assessment team and other experts in a manner consistent with previously developed guidelines, and focusing on creating a safe and caring campus community. Although their solutions were similar, the paths to reaching them often differed among respondents; they attributed a distinct range of power to the stakeholders; and their specific suggestions, such as the resources to refer Luis to, varied.

The goal of the chapter is not to present a single most appropriate response; rather, it is to illustrate the multitude of responses and perspectives to consider in enacting positive multicultural change on campus. We believe the differing analyses of these two cases, the discussion of how the respondents' identities influence their perspectives, and the illustration of institutional contexts addressed this goal.

NOW WHAT? CONTINUING THE DIALOGUE

The cases in this chapter are not situated in a vacuum. As noted, they are based on real experiences of students on college campuses. Several respondents poignantly posed the critical question, "What was the climate on

campus prior to this event that sparked these incidents?" The chapter opened
with the premise that there is not one right way to make our campuses
engaging and welcoming for all students. Both cases are rife with examples
in which Toussaint, Eric, Luis, and Paulina (and perhaps others) felt
wronged or mistreated by campus personnel, or respondents felt students
were mistreated even if the students did not seem to express this themselves.
Often the ways the students felt wronged were related to their social identities, such as race, class, religion, gender, or sexual orientation. The perceptions of the students and administrators in the cases, and the perceptions of
the student affairs professionals who responded to the cases, were influenced
by their social identities, institutional contexts, and levels of perceived and
actualized power. Although respondents suggested similar solutions for both
cases, they shared unique perspectives and approaches, and in some cases
proposed unique solutions as well.

As the authors, we intentionally opted to provide plausible solutions in
response to the cases before discussing the intersections of salient identities,
institutional context, power, and emotions informing the decision making for
each respondent. We made this choice because frequently students and stakeholders on campus are not exposed to the ways student affairs administrators
situate themselves based on their salient social identities and other contextual
factors when decisions are made. Only after we presented the collective
responses did we explore the intersecting influences of self-awareness, values,
identities, and contexts for each individual contributor. Whether you as a
reader agree or disagree with the solutions offered by these respondents, we
invite you to recognize the ways they grappled with the difficult issues in both
cases and how their positionality influenced their ideas. We hope you will see
how challenging the status quo to create welcoming environments for students
to learn and thrive starts with seeing yourself as a part of the system. Several
respondents aptly included questions such as, "Am I missing something?" and
"What is it about my social identity(ies) that inhibits me from seeing particular
elements in each case?" We hope this encourages and helps you to work intentionally and purposefully from your own perspective, asking these questions of
yourself while acknowledging that all of our perspectives are limited. We also
asked these questions of ourselves in the process of writing this chapter.

We wrestled with the complexities of not only writing the chapter but of
considering how our unique identities shaped the story we chose to tell and

how the voices of respondents were represented. We are both White, mid-level student affairs professionals currently situated at large public research institutions; one of us is a full-time professional, and the other is a full-time doctoral student and part-time graduate assistant. We developed a collegial relationship not only as members of the College Student Educators International Task Force that initiated this book, but also as members of the National Orientation Directors Association. We questioned each other as we selected excerpts from contributors' responses and decided how to weave them into this chapter, recognizing the significant power we had in making these determinations. We also questioned one another about the suppositions and conclusions we made about how the contributors' identities may have influenced their responses, recognizing that our own identities were likely influencing our interpretations. Thus, the process of writing this chapter with one another and with the respondents in some ways mimicked the process we hope readers will practice with their students and colleagues after reading the book. In addition to posing these sometimes difficult and uncomfortable questions to each other, we incorporated our own form of member checking by involving respondents at multiple points in the process.

We hope this chapter helps student affairs professionals engage in this kind of dialogue about how social identities, power, emotions, and institutional context influence decision making in everyday practice. Imagine how our campuses might be more inclusive if we routinely asked ourselves and colleagues questions such as, Do our current systems, policies, and practices (such as those relating to student conduct and those governing student activities events) allow room for the voices of the students and stakeholders to emerge? and, How does who I am (as a person and as a professional) influence my thinking about this situation, and what are other perspectives that I might not be seeing? While this chapter elucidates the significant complexity involved in creating and advocating for multicultural change on campus, we hope it encourages and empowers readers of all position levels and of all identities to engage in the process. Wading through the complexities of multicultural work and pressing forward despite uncertainty and ambiguity is essential, because developing multiculturally competent professionals and creating truly inclusive campus environments is an ongoing process.

REFERENCE

Kivel, P. (2007). Social service or social change? In INCITE! Women of Color Against Violence (Eds.), *The revolution will not be funded: Beyond the non-profit industrial complex* (pp. 129–149). Cambridge, MA: South End Press.

APPENDIX

Instructions Provided to Respondents

After reading through the case scenario, we ask that you consider and respond to each of the following statements. The bulleted questions are intended to provoke thought and guide your responses, but please do not feel obligated to respond to every one, and please do not feel limited to respond only to those questions.

1. Identify the issues raised in the scenario that should be considered.
   * What are the problems/challenges/issues in this case?
2. Identify the stakeholders.
   * Who are the people (including students, student groups, faculty, and staff) who may be affected by the case?
   * What (or how much) power does each stakeholder have in this case? Why do they have this power (or lack of power)? What kind of power do they possess?
   * How might potential responses contribute to or challenge stakeholders' privileges and/or feelings of oppression?
   * How will you consider the needs of the stakeholders in this case?
3. Explore yourself and your role.
   * What are your salient identities in this situation?
   * How do your identities interact in this situation?
   * How do your own power, oppression, and privilege shape the way you perceive and potentially respond to this scenario?
   * How does your positional power (i.e., role on campus) shape the way you consider aspects of this case?
   * What emotions are evoked for you as you consider this case? How might those emotions influence your potential responses?
4. Consider the context.
   * How does the institutional context shape the way you see this case and/or influence your potential responses?
   * How does the current national context (i.e., student affairs, higher education, national news, etc.) shape the way you see this case and/or influence your potential responses?

185

5. Decide on a response.
    + How would you respond to this case and why?
    + How might you react to/act toward each of the stakeholders in this scenario?
    + How would your response to this case make a positive difference on campus?
    + How do you walk the talk in this scenario? In other words, how does your response demonstrate a commitment to enacting the core values of inclusion in student affairs?
    + What follow-up action would you recommend? How do stakeholders in this scenario keep learning and keep discussing even after the case is resolved?

7

Integrating Student Affairs Values With the Elements of Inclusion

Jan Arminio, Vasti Torres, and Raechele Pope

A
FTER A NEW FACULTY ORIENTATION SESSION with the dean of students, Louise (a White woman) asked the dean about the avail-ability of parking on campus. The dean (a White man) said parking problems were exaggerated; there were always parking spaces available on campus. Taking him at his word, several days later Louise was driving around campus looking for open spaces. She was becoming concerned that she would be late for her own class when she spotted a space reserved for the dean of students. She marveled that the dean, who had a reserved parking space, had comfortably described the experience for those without a reserved parking space. It seemed to Louise that his overly simple response was all wrong, that a more complex and comprehensive response would have given her a more accurate sense of the situation. She wondered what other experiences of campus community members he might be misinterpreting.

Though parking is more trivial than other situations explored in this book, this scenario serves as an example of what can happen when educators think they know about the lived experience of others; are in a position to speak on behalf of others' experiences; and do so through solely their own identities, experiences, and lens of privilege. We hope this book serves as a utilitarian guide for a process that promotes the creation of a truly inclusive campus where missteps like the parking situation would be less likely to occur. Our goal was that by threading together the elements of the process

187

toward creating inclusive campuses described in these chapters, student affairs professionals would be encouraged to take reflective action, to involve themselves in synergistic dialogue that is cognizant of self-in-relationship with others, and to consider institutional and historical contexts. These process elements (the topics in each chapter) emphasize the need to increase awareness of self and self-in-relationship, including the histories that identities embody. The case studies in Chapter 6 illustrate there is no one right way to initiate change. By including multiple responses to the situations in the cases, the authors demonstrated there is no one magical response or silver bullet. We believe these elements serve as a series of steps creating a blueprint for organizational culture change. Furthermore, we believe discussing these process elements brings student affairs educators in closer alignment with the reenvisioned roots of our profession. To refresh readers' memories we want to connect these elements of inclusion with the values essential to the root of student affairs. The process elements for creating inclusive campuses are

- seeking self-awareness;
- reconciling the tension between self and the other in relationships;
- considering history;
- considering institutional context; and
- initiating dialogue as a precursor to action steps.

These elements, combined, help practitioners understand their own and the institution's role that must be developed to create space for difficult dialogues. This book was not written with a recipe in mind; rather it was written to explore these issues in the context of the complexity of life. Creating an inclusive community is not easy work and cannot be accomplished quickly. Time, reminders, and continual attention are required to truly achieve an inclusive community.

STUDENT AFFAIRS VALUES THAT
GROUND THESE ELEMENTS

Considered by most as the text that gave birth to the current concept of student affairs, the 1937 Student Personnel Point of View (SPPOV) statement said educators had the "obligation to consider the student as a whole"

(American Council on Education, 1937/1994a, p. 68). Development should be well rounded and include intellectual, emotional, physical, social, vocational, moral, economic, and aesthetic dimensions. The 1949 SPPOV statement acknowledged and expanded upon consideration of the whole student and added concern for individual differences in "backgrounds, abilities, interests, and goals" (American Council on Education, 1949/1994b, p. 110). Certainly the whole person and individual differences include various social identities, those recognized today and those yet to be illuminated in the future. Educators now acknowledge that considering students' development holistically and an individual's uniquenesses are best educational practices. We too must consider ourselves as whole and unique beings including the social identities we bring with us.

"The realization of this objective—the full maturation of each student—cannot be attained without interest in and integrated efforts toward the development of each and every facet" of a student (American Council on Education, 1949/1994b, p. 109). One way to accomplish that is by "encouraging the development of a diversified social program" (p. 113). Our book advocates for more intentional and structured encouraging. Even in 1949 the creators of the SPPOV statement implored practitioners to "foster a program of recreational and discussional activities that is diversified" (p. 114). The American College Personnel Association (ACPA, 1996) reiterated this point, stating that our role is to "create conditions that motivate and inspire students to devote time and energy to educationally-purposeful activities" (p. 118). All the chapters in this book remind educators that what these conditions are and how they are implemented are influenced by the experiences of oppression, positions of power, and social identities of educators. Perhaps what we propose in this book is not new.

In 1985 Harry Cannon (as cited in Dalton, 2003) wrote that student affairs staff and traditionally the dean of students serve as the conscience of the campus. As our campus's conscience, must make it their student affairs educators duty to advocate for inclusion beyond structural diversity and diversity as a problem, and instead take advantage of the benefits of diversity to create pluralistic communities. One means to accomplish this is through enacting structured and intentionally difficult dialogues as illustrated by Sherry Watt in Chapter 5. These dialogues are similar to those that Fried (2003) insisted are necessary for ethical communities. The 1949 SSPOV statement required that educators teach students how to "create desirable

social changes" (American Council on Education, 1949/1994b, p. 110).
What better pedagogy than that of firsthand experience?

John Dewey (1938/1997) advocated for the intentional creation of experiences in education that spur students' growth. According to Dewey, it is
the role of educators

> to arrange for the kind of experiences which . . . live on in further experience.
> Hence the central problem of an education based upon experience is to select
> the kind of present experiences that live fruitfully and creatively in subsequent
> experiences. (pp. 27–28)

For what purpose are these experiences? According to Dewey, the purpose is
"the active participle, *growing*" (emphasis in original; p. 28). This is consistent with the notion of seamless learning as noted in the Student Learning
Imperative (ACPA, 1996):

> Student affairs professionals attempt to make "seamless" what are often per-
> ceived by students to be disjointed, unconnected experiences by bridging
> organizational boundaries and forging collaborative partnerships with faculty
> and others to enhance student learning. (p. 120)

The case studies in Chapter 6 in this book illustrate numerous examples
of how practices before and after difficult situations serve as fruitful experiences that encourage growth for subsequent experiences.

Young and Elfink (1991) identified eight important values that guide
student affairs work: altruism, equality, aesthetics, freedom, human dignity,
justice, truth, and community. Young (1996) also proposed equality and
justice as two "prominent" values (p. 94). How can educators purport to
enact these values when so many of our students continue to feel marginalized, and the achievement gap continues to grow?

Wolfe (1999) wrote that free expression of ideas encourages humility, for
it discourages anyone from believing his or her ideas are so superior they
should not be challenged. Chapters 2 and 6 remind educators that power
over others reduces the opportunity for such free-flowing expression. We
believe it is our ethical obligation to identify the power, privilege, and
oppression on our campuses.

USING ADDITIONAL RESOURCES

The chapters in this book contain numerous references for additional reading and reflecting. This book should not be seen as the sole resource for creating inclusion. To understand self and others, additional reading is essential. It is our hope readers will view the references in this book as resources to enhance their own understanding as well as knowledge of those around them. All of us must take on the responsibility of educating ourselves and others—this should not be seen as a once-a-year activity; instead it has to be an ongoing task throughout our divisions and departments. In addition to the resources in the references, we offer additional ones here. Books that could prompt additional reflection and conversations particular to higher education and student affairs include Borrego and Manning's (2007) *Where I Am From* and Nash, Bradley, and Chickering's (2008) *How to Talk About Hot Topics on Campus*. Films we would recommend include *No Dumb Questions* (Regan, 2001), *African American Lives I* and *II* (2006, 2008), and *What's Race Got to Do With It?* (Chen, 2008). Historical documentaries and websites provide alternative interpretations for beliefs held by many. Blackside's (2009) *Eyes on the Prize*, *The Shadow of Hate* (Guggenheim, 1995), *Ethnic Notions* (Riggs, 1987), and http://www.slavevoyages.org would certainly be examples. *Barnga* (Thiagarajan, 1990) is an activity that simulates how environments become exclusive. There are many others, but the point is that by approaching the issue of inclusion through multiple means (films, activities, dialogues, and reading) student affairs professionals offer an extended representation of ideas across a spectrum of learning styles.

FINAL WORDS

The process elements described in this book promote a means for deep engagement with difficult issues: What are our own behaviors, our own conversations modeling for students? What kind of environment are our dialogues, actions, and competencies creating for all students? These questions should be at the forefront of diversity efforts.

So, are we there yet? No, but the elements discussed in this book offer a process of bringing human dignity, equality, and community to our campuses through our multicultural competencies. The road trip toward inclusion is one that will continue for the rest of our lives. A better question to ponder is: In what ways have I prompted a dialogue that promoted human dignity, equality, and community that serves to move us toward our destiny of inclusive campuses?

REFERENCES

African American lives I [DVD]. (2006). Kunhardt Productions. Available from http://www.shoppbs.org/search/index.jsp?kwCatId=&kw=african%20american%20lives&origkw=African+American+Lives&sr=1

African American lives II [DVD]. (2008). Kunhardt Productions. Available from http://www.shoppbs.org/search/index.jsp?kwCatId=&kw=african%20american%20lives&origkw=African+American+Lives&sr=1

American College Personnel Association. (1996). The student learning imperative. *Journal of College Student Development, 37*(2), 118–122.

American College Personnel Association (1996). The student learning imperative: Implications for student affairs. *Journal of College Student Development, 37*(2) 118–122.

American Council on Education. (1994a). The student personnel point of view. In A. L. Rentz (Ed.), *Student affairs: A profession's heritage* (2nd ed., pp. 66–77). Lanham, MD: University Press of America. (Original work published 1937)

American Council on Education (1994b). The student personnel point of view. In A. L. Rentz (Ed.), *Student affairs: A profession's heritage* (2nd ed., pp. 108–123). Lanham, MD: University Press of America. (Original work published 1949)

Blackside. (Producer). (2009). *Eyes on the prize* [DVD]. Available from http://www .shoppbs.org / product / index.jsp ? productId=3999340 & cp= & sr=1 & kw=eyes+ on+the+prize&origkw=eyes+on+the+prize&parentPage=search

Borrego, S. E., & Manning, K. (2007). *Where I am from: Student affairs practice from the whole of students' lives.* Washington DC: NASPA.

Chen, J. (Producer). (2008). *What's race got to do with it?* [DVD]. Available from http://newsreel.org/nav/title.asp?tc=CN0188

Dalton, J. C. (2003). Managing human resources. In S. R. Komives & D. B. Woodard, Jr. (Eds.), *Student services: A handbook for the profession* (4th ed., pp. 397–419). San Francisco, CA: Jossey-Bass.

Dewey, J. (1997). *Experience and education.* New York, NY: Touchstone. (Original work published 1938)

Fried, J. (2003). Ethical standards and principles. In S. R. Komives & D. B. Woodard, Jr. (Eds.), *Student services: A handbook for the profession* (4th ed., pp. 107–127). San Francisco, CA: Jossey-Bass.

Guggenheim C. (Director). (1995). *The shadow of hate* [DVD]. Available from http://www.gpifilms.com/orders.html

Nash, R. J., Bradley, D. L., and Chickering, A. W. (2008). *How to talk about hot topics on campus.* San Francisco, CA: Jossey-Bass.

Regan, M. (Writer/producer). (2001). *No dumb questions* [DVD]. Available from http://www.newday.com/films_title.html?letter=N

Riggs, M. (Producer). (1987). *Ethnic notions* [DVD]. Available from http://news reel.org/video/ETHNIC-NOTIONS

Thiagarajan, S. (1990). *Barnga: A simulation game on cultural clashes.* (1990). Yarmouth, ME: Intercultural Press.

Wolfe, A. (1999, December 3). The Hillsdale tragedy holds lessons for colleges everywhere. *The Chronicle of Higher Education*, A72. Retrieved from http://chronicle.com/article/The-Hillsdale-Tragedy-Holds/25498/A72

Young, R. B. (1996). Guiding values and philosophy. In S. R. Komives & D. B. Woodard, Jr. (Eds.), *Student services: A handbook for the profession* (3rd ed., pp. 83–105). San Francisco, CA: Jossey-Bass.

Young, R. B., & Elfink, R. B. (1991). Essential values of student affairs work. *Journal of College Student Development*, *32*(1), 47–55.

Contributors

Jan Arminio received her doctorate in the College Student Personnel Program at the University of Maryland, College Park, after serving as a student affairs professional for 13 years. In 1996 she began teaching in a graduate student affairs program at Shippensburg University, where she is professor and department chair. Arminio's scholarship focuses on multicultural issues as well as qualitative research, assessment, and campus programs and leadership. She is the 2008 recipient of the Founders Award for outstanding service to NACA and the 2011 recipient of the Robert Shaffer Award for excellence in graduate teaching. She currently chairs the Senior Scholars of College Student Educators International.

Ellen M. Broido is associate professor of higher education and student affairs at Bowling Green State University, where she has worked since 2001. She received her doctorate from Pennsylvania State University in counselor education. Broido's research focuses on the experiences of underrepresented or marginalized groups in higher education, disability issues in higher education, the development and effects of undergraduate students' social identities on their collegiate experiences, the effects of the environment on students from targeted social groups, and social justice issues on college campuses.

Lucy A. LePeau is a doctoral candidate in college student personnel in the Department of Counseling, Higher Education, and Special Education at the University of Maryland, College Park. Her dissertation study is on investing academic affairs and student affairs partnerships concerning diversity initiatives, a grounded theory. Lucy earned an MS from Indiana University, Bloomington, in higher education and student affairs and a BA in psychology from Marquette University.

John A. Mueller is professor in the Department of Student Affairs in Higher Education at Indiana University of Pennsylvania. He has worked in higher education for over 25 years, with professional and teaching experience at five institutions. His publications, presentations, and service activities have focused primarily on issues of diversity, multiculturalism, and inclusion. Mueller is an active member in the American College Personnel Association and is the recipient of several awards from the association including Annuit Coeptis, Emerging Scholar, and Diamond Honoree.

ANNA M. ORTIZ is professor of educational leadership and student development in higher education at the University of California at Long Beach. She received her doctorate from the University of California at Los Angeles and has been a student development educator as a professor and professional in the field for over 20 years. In addition to teaching, she is a coordinator for the counseling program and director of the independent doctoral program at the University of California at Long Beach. Her research emphasizes ethnic identity development, multicultural education, and professional issues in student affairs. She is an active member of NASPA, American College Personnel Association, Association for the Study of Higher Education, and American Educational Research Association.

LORI D. PATTON is associate professor and program chair of higher education in the Morgridge College of Education at the University of Denver. She received her doctorate in higher education administration at Indiana University. Much of her research targets issues regarding the access, equity, and evidence of racial injustice of higher education with focuses on African Americans in higher education and the role of culture centers in predominantly White institutions. She is active in numerous professional organizations and is the recipient of the Emerging Scholar and Annuit Coeptis awards from the American College Personnel Association.

RAECHELE L. POPE is associate professor of higher education and student affairs administration in the Department of Educational Leadership and Policy at the University at Buffalo, State University of New York. She received her doctorate from the University of Massachusetts at Amherst. Her research focuses on multicultural organizational development in higher education, multicultural competence of student affairs administrators, and the psychosocial development of college students of color. She serves on the editorial review board of *Journal of College Student and Development*. She received the

Emerging Scholar Award and the award for Outstanding Contribution for Multicultural Education from the American College Personnel Association, which inducted her in 2010 as a Diamond Honoree.

VASTI TORRES is professor of educational leadership and policy studies and director of the Center for Postsecondary Research in the School of Education at Indiana University. Prior to joining the faculty, she had 15 years of experience in administrative positions, most recently serving as associate vice provost and dean for enrollment and student services at Portland State University. She has been the principal investigator for several grants including a multi-year grant investigating the choice to stay in college for Latino students as well as a multiyear grant to study the experiences of working college students. She has worked on several community college initiatives including Achieving the Dream, Rural Community College Initiative, and Building Engagement and Attainment for Minority Students. She is associate editor of *Journal of College Student Development*. She is active in several higher education and student affairs associations, and in 2007–2008 she became the first Latina president of the American College Personnel Association. Between 2008 and 2010 she served as cochair of the Future of Student Affairs Task Force. She has been named as a Diamond Honoree, Senior Scholar, and Wise Woman by the American College Personnel Association; received the Contribution to Literature and Knowledge Award from NASPA; and named Program Associate for the National Center for Policy in Higher Education. In the fall of 2011 she served as a Fulbright Specialist in South Africa. Torres is a graduate of Stetson University and holds a PhD in counseling and student affairs administration from the University of Georgia.

SHERRY K. WATT is associate professor in the Higher Education and Student Affairs Program at the University of Iowa. Her research examines privileged identities through the lenses of studying participant reactions to difficult dialogues on race, sexual orientation, and disability. She has 15 years of experience researching and facilitating dialogues on social issues. Watt applies her expertise in designing and leading educational experiences that involve strategies to engage participants in dialogue that is meaningful, passionate, and self-awakening.

MATTHEW J. WEIGAND is director of New Student Programs at the University at Buffalo, where he oversees orientation programs, first-year seminars, and parent and family programs. He has presented and published on such topics as first-year student success, multicultural competence and diversity, and transfer student services. He is actively involved with professional associations, serving on the directorate board for the American College Personnel Association's Commission for Admissions, Orientation, and First Year Experience, and is a past member of the National Orientation Directors Association board of directors. He received his bachelor's, master's, and doctoral degrees from the University at Buffalo, where he currently serves as an adjunct assistant professor in the Department of Educational Leadership and Policy.

Index